Contents

Preface	**vii**
Acknowledgements	**ix**
UNIT 1 — THE BUSINESS WORKING ENVIRONMENT	
Introduction	**1**
Chapter 1 — Business Organisations and Functions	**3**
Types of Organisation	3
Legal Forms of Business	4
Organising the Business	10
Business Functions	11
Short Questions	18
Chapter 2 — Office Functions, Design and Equipment	**19**
The Office and its Functions	19
General Sources of Reference	20
Office Design	23
Office Equipment	25
Short Questions	31
Chapter 3 — Financial Institutions	**32**
The Euro	32
The Irish Banks	33
The Current Account	34
Bank Cards	39
Lodgements	41
Withdrawals	42
Electronic Funds Transfer (EFT)	43
Foreign Exchange	44
Internet and Telephone Banking	45
Credit Unions	46
Short Questions	47
Chapter 4 — Legislation in the Workplace	**48**
Employment Legislation	48
Employee Welfare Legislation	54
Data Protection Legislation	58
Short Questions	59
Summary	**60**
Assignments	**62**

UNIT 2 — OFFICE DUTIES

Introduction **65**

Chapter 5 — Receptionist Duties **67**

Maintaining the Reception Area 67
Receiving Visitors 68
Dealing with Complaints 70
The Switchboard and Features 70
Operating the Switchboard 73
Voicemail Answering Facility 75
Telephone Charges 77
Making National and International Calls 80
Short Questions 82

Chapter 6 — Administration and Accounting Duties **84**

Planning and Organising Work 85
Arranging Appointments 87
Arranging Travel 88
Preparing for Meetings and Conferences 91
Accounting Activities 93
Wages and Salaries 94
Short Questions 100

Chapter 7 — Business Transactions **102**

Stages of a Business Transaction 102
Procedure for Dealing with Incoming Orders (Supplier) 108
Procedure for Dealing with Incoming Goods (Purchaser) 110
Statement of Accounts 115
Overview of Stages in Business Transactions 117
Stock Control 118
Short Questions 121

Chapter 8 — Meetings **123**

Types of Formal Meeting 123
Convening Company Meetings 124
Documentation for Meetings 125
Duties of the Chairman and Secretary 128
Short Questions 129

Summary **129**

Assignments **130**

UNIT 3 — COMPUTERS AND NETWORKS

Introduction   **139**

Chapter 9 — Computer Basics and Peripheral Devices   **141**
Computer Systems   141
Components of a Computer System   142
Storage Media   144
Printers   147
Scanners   149
Guide to Buying a Computer   150
Short Questions   154

Chapter 10 — Computer Applications   **155**
Word Processing   156
Spreadsheets   160
Databases   163
Desktop Publishing   164
Computer Viruses   166
Short Questions   167

Chapter 11 — Networks and the Internet   **169**
Types of Network   169
The Internet   171
The World Wide Web (WWW)   173
Understanding Web Addresses   175
Searching the Web   176
Intranet and Extranet   177
Short Questions   178

Chapter 12 — Information Systems   **179**
Operational Support Systems   180
Management Support Systems   181
Designing an Information System   183
Short Questions   184

Summary   **184**

Assignments   **185**

UNIT 4 — POSTAL, ELECTRONIC AND MOBILE COMMUNICATION

Introduction   **189**

Chapter 13 — Post and Postal Services   **191**
Postal Equipment   191
Dealing with Incoming Post   195
Dealing with Outgoing Post   196
Delivery Services Provided by An Post   197

Other Postal Services Provided by An Post   200
Marketing Services Provided by An Post   201
Non-postal Services Provided by An Post   203
Short Questions   203

Chapter 14 — Electronic and Mobile Communication   **205**
The Fax Machine and Features   205
Compiling, Sending and Receiving Fax Messages   207
Electronic Mail (Email)   208
Creating and Sending Email   209
Receiving and Managing Email   210
Email Fraud   214
Mobile Communication   216
Mobile Network in Ireland   218
Short Questions   219

Summary   **220**

Assignments   **221**

UNIT 5 — STORING AND RETRIEVING INFORMATION

Introduction   **223**

Chapter 15 — Manual Filing System   **225**
Elements of a Manual Filing System   225
Categorising and Sorting Information   227
Rules for Alphabetical Filing   233
Filing Equipment   236
Filing Procedure   239
Cross-referencing and Indexing   239
Short Questions   244

Chapter 16 — Electronic Document Management (EDM)   **246**
Microform Filing System   246
Electronic Document Management System   248
Short Questions   251

Summary   **252**

Assignments   **252**

Appendix — Blank Documents for Business Transactions   **255**

Preface

The objective of *Modern Office Technology and Administration* is to explain in detail the business environment, the workings of an office, the functions and impact of new technology on the office and the services available to a business from the banks, the post office and the telecommunication sector.

A fourth edition of this book was necessary to take account of the changes in the working environment, particularly in the area of employment law and significant advances made in electronic and mobile communication.

The text is written from both a practical and an educational point of view. It explains the activities of an office and how technology has helped to improve efficiency levels within the office. Essential administration and reception skills are covered comprehensively in a step-by-step approach that includes planning and organising work, operating the switchboard, dealing with correspondence, filing, calculating wages, banking and processing business transactions. The function and impact of technologies on the office are explored and presented in a style suitable for the beginner and yet comprehensive enough to enable the student to make informed decisions about purchasing and using technology.

The book is divided into five units to facilitate the presentation of related topics. Each unit deals with a particular aspect of the office environment and consists of between two and four chapters, as outlined in the Table of Contents.

All units have a common structure designed to facilitate comprehension, self-study and retention. Each unit begins with an introduction – a brief summary of the major topics covered. The introduction acts as a preview to the chapters and illustrates how the chapters are related to each other.

Each unit concludes with a summary – a concise review of each chapter. Short Questions at the end of each chapter are in line with FETAC examination requirements. Assignments are given at the end of each unit. Some assignments are based on individual chapters and others require an integrated approach. These assignments are designed to guide the student toward further research on the topic and can be used as either individual or group projects, at home or during class time.

Modern Office Technology and Administration was written to meet the requirements of the FETAC Level 5 Information and Administration syllabus (B2D144). It is also a suitable supplementary text for the HETAC syllabus – National Certificate in Office Information Systems, and the City and Guilds IT and Business Administration and Office Procedures course. Furthermore, it can be used as a text for any 'back-to-work' course.

We wish to thank our families and colleagues for their support in this fourth update, particularly our partners John Hegarty and John Creedon, both of whom took on childminding and entertainment roles to make this fourth edition possible. Since the last update, technology has moved on and so have our lives.

For Joan, Niamh and Siobhán are now 10 years and 8 years, respectively. A big thank you goes to both Niamh and Siobhán for their contributions to the book, which was entertaining themselves by turning the house upside-down.

For Siobhán, Eve, 8 years, and Eoin, 5 years, and baby Rachel, now 3 years, are very busy little people but still allowed Siobhán to complete this fourth edition.

We also extend special thanks to our colleagues at Senior College, Dún Laoghaire, and the Institute of Technology, Tralee, for their continued support and to Marion O'Brien of Gill and Macmillan for her continued support and understanding in the completion of this fourth edition.

Acknowledgements

For permission to reproduce material, grateful acknowledgement is made to the following:

- 2008–2009 SECAP
- 2009 Research in Motion
- Alamy
- Apple Computers
- Bank of Ireland
- Bisley
- Cable & Wireless
- Canon (UK) Ltd
- Dell
- Dymo
- Eircom
- Epson America, Inc.
- Flowline Mailing Systems Ltd
- FP Mailing
- Getty
- Imagefile
- Intel
- M. J. Flood (Ireland) Ltd
- Neopost 2009 Incorporated
- O'Sullivan Graphics
- An Post
- Scanna MSC Ltd
- Sygma Wireless Communications Ltd (Motorola Distributors)
- Toshiba
- Viking Direct
- Zefa Pictures

Unit 1 — The Business Working Environment

Introduction

Unit 1 provides an overview of the business working environment, focusing on how businesses are legally formed and organised, the functions of the office, financial services available to businesses and legislation in the workplace.

Unit 1 is divided into four chapters:

Chapter 1 — *Business Organisations and Functions*

Deals with the business as an organisation and the legal requirements of setting up a business, and examines the main functions of a business, ie, marketing, finance, production and human resources:

◆ Types of Organisation
◆ Legal Forms of Business
◆ Organising the Business
◆ Business Functions

Chapter 2 — *Office Functions, Design and Equipment*

Examines the primary functions of the office in relation to receiving, storing, processing and distributing information. Office design and typical office equipment are discussed.

◆ The Office and its Functions
◆ General Sources of Reference
◆ Office Design
◆ Office Equipment

Chapter 3 — *Financial Institutions*

Reviews banking for business and the major technological advances made in routine banking activities such as telephone and Internet banking.

- The Euro
- The Irish Banks
- The Current Account
- Bank Cards
- Lodgements
- Withdrawals
- Electronic Funds Transfer (EFT)
- Foreign Exchange
- Internet and Telephone Banking
- Credit Unions

Chapter 4 — Legislation in the Workplace

Provides a review of legislation that affects the workplace, such as laws governing terms and conditions of employment, health, safety and welfare at work and the protection of personal information stored manually or electronically.

- Employment Legislation
- Employee Welfare Legislation
- Data Protection Legislation

Chapter 1 — Business Organisations and Functions

To understand the role of the office within the context of an organisation, it is necessary to examine the types of organisation that exist. An organisation exists where people and other resources such as equipment and finance combine to achieve some objective. Objectives will differ according to the type of organisation. For example, the objective of a voluntary organisation may be to provide a social service to the community, while the main objective of a private enterprise, ie, a **business**, is to make a profit.

Types of Organisation

Three main types of organisation exist in Ireland.

Voluntary Organisations

Voluntary organisations are non-profit-making and depend on State funding and/or voluntary contributions to survive. This type of organisation is run largely by volunteers and the main objective is to provide aid, support or some social service to the community. Examples of voluntary organisations are charities, (eg, Goal and Concern) and non-profit-making sporting societies (eg, local GAA and rugby clubs). Registered charities are exempt from paying tax on donations received.

Public-Sector Organisations

The main objective of public-sector organisations such as the Health Boards is to provide cost-effective services to the community, rather than to make a profit. While the general public is charged for the use of the services, these organisations are subsidised heavily by the Government. They are managed by civil servants and are accountable to the Government.

Private-Sector Organisations

Private-sector organisations are privately owned business enterprises. A business is an organisation that is set up to produce or distribute a product or service. The primary objective of a business must be to make a profit. Without profits or some spending power, a business will not survive in a competitive market.

Business objectives will vary depending on circumstances. For example, in the first year of trading the main objective may be to *break even*, (ie, to cover expenses, not make a profit or a loss). If the business is successful, increasing market share or developing new products may become important objectives.

Legal Forms of Business

When setting up a business in Ireland, it is important to comply with all the relevant documentation so that the business can legally commence trading. For example, a company must have a Certificate of Trading before trading can begin.

All businesses must register with the Register of Business Names, and register with the Revenue Commissioners to pay tax on profits and to collect taxes from employees, eg, PAYE and PRSI. Sole traders and partnerships pay income tax on profits, while companies and co-operatives pay corporation tax on profits.

A business must also register for VAT with the Revenue Commissioners if the turnover of the business exceeds €75,000 on the supply of goods and €37,500 on the supply of services.

Business enterprises in Ireland tend to operate as one of the following:
1. Sole Traders
2. Partnerships
3. Limited Companies
   a) Public Limited Company (PLC)
   b) Private Limited Company (Ltd)
4. Co-operatives
5. Franchises

Sole Traders

Sole trader is a term used to describe a business wholly owned by one person. The owner takes responsibility for all the activities of the business, such as selling, purchasing, marketing, hiring staff and preparing the accounts. Typical examples are small retail outlets and local grocery shops.

Features of a sole trader

- Sole owner of the business, with control over all business functions.
- Generally small in nature, with a small number of staff employed.
- Has *unlimited liability*. This means that while the owner controls all aspects of the business and reaps all the profits, s/he is also personally liable for any debts that the business may incur. Therefore if the business fails, the sole trader may sacrifice personal assets to pay creditors.

◆ The sole trader pays income tax on profits to the Revenue Commissioners and can offset business losses against other personal income.

◆ The business ceases to exist on the death of the sole trader, ie, the new owner must register the business with the Register of Business Names and with the Revenue Commissioners.

Partnerships

A *general partnership* exists where two or more people (usually to a maximum of 20) come together and contribute finance and/or expertise to a business. Accountants, solicitors and doctors commonly practise under the partnership structure.

Features of general partnerships

◆ When forming a partnership, it is usual to draw up a Deed of Partnership. This is an agreement between the partners that specifies the duties and responsibilities of each partner. As the partners may contribute to the business to varying extents, the Deed of Partnership also specifies the extent of liability of each partner and how profits and losses are to be distributed.

◆ If a partnership agreement is not drawn up, then each partner is jointly liable for the debts of the partnership, ie, each partner has unlimited liability.

◆ It may be easier to access credit facilities when more than one person is responsible for repayments.

◆ Partners, like sole traders, are charged income tax on profits and can offset business losses against personal income.

◆ A new partnership must be formed on the death or resignation of a partner.

A *limited partnership* may be set up in which the partners' liability is limited to the debts of the partnership. However, a limited partnership must have at least one partner with unlimited liability and must register with the Companies Registration Office (CRO).

Companies

Companies are one of the most common forms of business in Ireland. The owners of the company are the shareholders who purchase shares in the company and receive dividends on their shares if the company is profitable. The shareholders elect a Board of Directors and/or a Managing Director to manage the company on their behalf.

A company has a legal status (ie, separate entity) distinct from its owners. This means that the company, rather than the individual shareholders, can sue and be sued for any wrongdoings in the normal course of business.

A company can be formed as a public or private company with either limited or unlimited liability. *Limited liability* means that the liability of the shareholders is limited to either the amount that remains unpaid on the shares they have invested in the company or to the amount guaranteed by the shareholder when forming the company. Clubs, societies and charities are generally formed as companies limited by guarantee where the business is not seeking to raise funds from its shareholders. *Unlimited liability* means that the shareholders are personally liable for the debts of the company.

Public Limited Company (PLC)

A public limited company (PLC) is formed with a minimum of seven members, and with no upper limit. PLCs are companies that are quoted on the stock exchange. This means that the company can raise finance by selling shares to the general public. Examples of Irish PLCs include the commercial banks, Kerry Group PLC and CRH (Cement Roadstone Holdings) PLC.

Private Limited Company (Ltd)

A private limited company (Ltd) is formed with a minimum of one member and with an upper limit of 99 members. A private limited company is similar in legal standing to a PLC; however, private companies are not quoted on the stock exchange and there are strict regulations regarding the buying and selling of the company's shares.

A *single-member company* (ie, where one member owns all the shares) must have at least two directors and a secretary (who can be one of the directors).

Forming a Company

When forming a company, the following documentation must be submitted to the CRO with an appropriate fee:
1. *Memorandum of Association:* a document detailing the nature of the business, the names of the directors, company secretary and shareholders involved in the business, the liability status of the company (limited by shares or by guarantee or unlimited) and the amount of share capital the company will hold.
2. *Articles of Association:* a document detailing the internal regulations of the company, eg, how shares are transferred, how meetings are convened, how directors are elected, etc.
3. *Form A1*: a form which requires details of
    a. the name and registered address of the business
    b. the name and address of the Company Secretary

    c. the name, address, occupation and nationality of each director

    d. other directorships held by the directors

    e. a statement of the amount of authorised share capital and the money received from shares to date. (The minimum amount of authorised share capital a public limited company must hold is €38,092.14 and must have 25% of this paid up before a Certificate of Trading can be obtained.)

Form A1 is signed by the Company Secretary, Directors or a solicitor declaring that the Companies Acts requirements have been complied with.

When all the documents are submitted and approved, the CRO will issue a Certificate of Trading to the company and will publish notification of the formation of the company in the CRO on-line gazette publication. The company can then begin trading.

Features of a company

◆ The company is legally recognised as a separate entity from the owners.

◆ The company is managed by a Managing Director and Board of Directors elected by the shareholders.

◆ Detailed documentation is required to set up a company.

◆ The company must register its business name with the Registrar of Business Names, and must register for taxes with the Revenue Commissioners.

◆ A company is charged corporation tax on profits, unlike partnerships or sole traders.

◆ In a limited company, the liability of the shareholders is limited to the amount owing on unpaid shares or the amount owing as per the guarantee agreement.

◆ In an unlimited company, the shareholders are personally liable for the debts of the company.

◆ Both public and private companies must file audited financial accounts (Profits & Loss Accounts, Balance Sheets, Auditors' Reports and Directors' Reports) with the CRO. These accounts must be available for shareholders, auditors, creditors and potential investors. However, the accounts of a private company are not as detailed as the PLC accounts.

Co-operatives (Co-ops)

A co-op is formed with seven or more members with an ethos of fairness, democracy and mutual benefit to all members. A co-op is based on the principle that by pooling resources and working together, better trading terms can be obtained. It is easier to raise finance and the risk to members of exposure to the business debts is reduced.

Upon registering with the Registry of Friendly Societies, the co-op becomes incorporated, ie, it is a legal entity separate from the members and can make business contracts, sue and be sued in the name of the co-op. The liability of the members is limited to the shares they have applied for in the co-op. By law, there is a limit on the amount an individual member can contribute to a co-op (eg €126,973 is the limit a member can invest in an agricultural or fishing co-op). Co-ops are taxed similarly to companies, but with minor exceptions. Audited accounts must be submitted annually to the Registrar of Friendly Societies.

Businesses that are formed under the co-op model include Credit Unions and housing and community projects, but the main co-ops in Ireland are based in the agricultural or rural sector. Co-ops are affiliated to ICOS (Irish Co-operative Organisation Society – www.icos.ie) which is the umbrella group that represents and supports co-operatives in Ireland.

Features of a co-op

- A co-op consists of seven or more members.
- A co-op must register with the Registrar of Friendly Societies to avail of a separate legal identity and limited liability for its members.
- Members invest in the co-op by purchasing shares and appoint managers to run the business on their behalf.
- Members have an equal vote regardless of the amount of shares held.
- Shares are not directly transferable between members.
- Co-ops are charged corporation tax on profits.

Franchise

A franchise is a business model whereby an established business, the *franchisor*, licenses or 'franchises' their product/service to another person, known as the *franchisee*, to set up the same business in a different location. Franchises are common in the following business sectors: grocery (ie, Spar), fast food (ie, McDonalds), dry cleaning (ie, Chem Dry), etc. Because the franchisee is investing in a proven, successful business, there is less risk that his/her business will fail.

Features of a franchise

- A franchise contract/agreement outlines the responsibilities of both the franchisor and franchisee. This agreement is legally binding.
- The franchisee pays an initial capital investment and on-going royalties based on turnover or profit depending on the contract to the franchisor. In return the franchisor will:
  — assist the franchisee to locate a suitable property for the business
  — train and support the franchisee and his/her staff

— supply goods and/or services

— be responsible for certain advertising, marketing and promotional activities

— provide support functions such as bulk buying, accounting and management services

— improve, enhance and develop the business

♦ The franchisee operates the business as an owner rather than as an employee.

♦ The franchisee must adhere to the agreed business standards and practices; otherwise, the licence to operate the business will be revoked.

♦ Taxes and liabilities are dependent on the legal form of the business, ie, sole trader, partnership, company, etc.

Comparisons of Business Forms					
Business Form	No. of Owners	Owned By	Managed by	Liability	Tax
Sole trader	1	Owner	Owner	Unlimited	Income
Partnership	2–20	Partners	Senior Partners	Unlimited	Income
Private (Ltd)	1–99	Shareholders	Directors	Limited	Corporation
Public (PLC)	7+	Shareholders	Directors	Limited	Corporation
Co-operative	7+	Members	Manager	Limited	Corporation
Franchise	1+	Franchise (under licence)	Franchisee	Depends on form of business	Depends on form of business

The decision to form a business as a sole trader, partnership, company, co-operative or franchise depends on:

a) the number of people involved

b) the nature of the business and level of risk attached to it

c) the resources and funds necessary for the business.

Sources of Funds

A business needs a supply of funds to start or develop the business. There are various sources of finance available to businesses in Ireland, some of which include:

— *Private funds*: personal savings, assets such as properties that can be used as security against loans, loans/gifts from friends, etc.

— *Loans from Financial Institutions*: bank overdraft facilities, short-, medium- or long-term loans, mortgages for purchasing business premises, capital equipment loans, etc.

— *Shares*: public limited companies may be able to issue more share capital on the open stock exchange to obtain funds to finance large projects such as an acquisition of new businesses, etc.

— *Venture Capital:* A young developing business is often high risk and may have difficulty raising finance from the mainstream financial institutions. Individuals or private investment companies known as 'venture capitalists' specialise in investing funds and expertise into a growing business in return for an ownership stake in that business. Finance is provided for a set period of time with an option for the business to buy back their shares at an agreed (higher) price, or the objective may be to sell the business and realise large profits for the venture capitalists and the other business owners.

— *Government Grants:* Financial support is available from a variety of government agencies to help businesses in the start up and growth phase. Grants for feasibility studies, training, research and development, purchasing of capital equipment, marketing the products/services, etc., can all be obtained through agencies such as Enterprise Ireland (www.enterprise-ireland.com).

Organising the Business

When the business is formed, the resources must be organised so that the objectives can be achieved, which is to say that the business is structured so that work can take place effectively. Once the structure is in place, rules and procedures for carrying out tasks can be developed and responsibility for the performance of these tasks can be allocated to individuals or teams within the business. The formal structure of a business can be depicted by an organisation chart.

Organisation Chart

An organisation chart is a diagram outlining the work relationships between people and tasks. It shows:

a) formal lines of communication, ie, who reports to whom
b) the framework of the business, ie, departments
c) levels of management (or the 'chain of command').

The organisation chart does not show:

a) the duties associated with the positions shown on the chart
b) informal relationships between staff.

The diagram below depicts a simple organisation chart for a company, showing six levels of management in a hierarchical structure, ie, the general workers report to the supervisor, the supervisor reports to the department manager, etc.

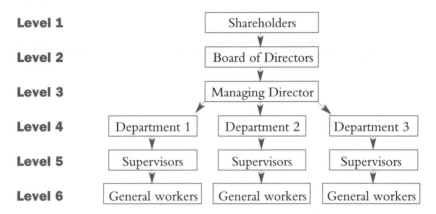

Level 1	Shareholders
Level 2	Board of Directors
Level 3	Managing Director

Level 4	Department 1	Department 2	Department 3
Level 5	Supervisors	Supervisors	Supervisors
Level 6	General workers	General workers	General workers

Business Functions

In a small business, all the business activities may be carried out by one person or a small number of people. For example, a sole trader will order supplies, market and sell the goods or services, negotiate finance with the banks, keep accounts, recruit and train staff.

As a business grows, both in physical size and complexity, it may be necessary to divide business activities into departments according to their function, such as:

◆ Production
◆ Marketing
◆ Finance
◆ Human Resources
◆ Administration.

These functions may be further divided as shown in the chart overleaf:

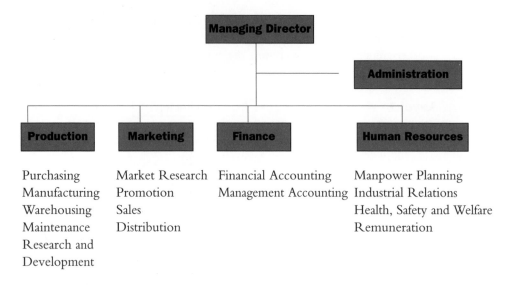

Production	**Marketing**	**Finance**	**Human Resources**
Purchasing	Market Research	Financial Accounting	Manpower Planning
Manufacturing	Promotion	Management Accounting	Industrial Relations
Warehousing	Sales		Health, Safety and Welfare
Maintenance	Distribution		Remuneration
Research and Development			

Production Activities

The Production Department is concerned with the complete manufacturing process, which includes: purchasing raw materials; scheduling work orders; quality control; maintaining the premises, machinery and equipment, warehousing; developing new products and improved procedures for carrying out the production process.

Purchasing

A Purchasing Officer may be appointed within the Production Department to negotiate with suppliers to obtain the best available terms on prices, discounts, credit terms, and delivery. S/he ensures the quality of the materials purchased, establishes a system for ordering and is responsible for stock control.

Manufacturing

The Production Manager must ensure that the production process is operating at an optimum level. This involves devising a schedule to minimise disruptions to the production process and liaising with the Purchasing Manager to ensure that raw materials are available.

The planning and scheduling process generally uses computer software such as MRP (Materials Requirements Planning), which facilitates materials planning and machinery scheduling, and CAM (Computer-Aided Manufacture), which controls the production process.

At all times, the quality of input (eg, raw materials) to the production process and the resulting output (eg, finished goods) must be monitored.

Warehousing

The stock-control manager must ensure that correct procedures are in place for storing both raw materials and finished goods. The costs of warehousing can be quite significant; among the costs involved are: security, insurance (on premises and contents), lighting, heating, rent of premises, fit-out for orderly rotation of goods, and costs of replacing obsolete products if storage is not organised properly.

Many businesses try to reduce the amount of stock in storage by using computerised ordering systems which ensure that raw materials are ordered on a 'just-in-time' basis as required by the production process.

Maintenance

The maintenance team ensures that machinery and equipment are regularly maintained to avoid breakdowns in the production process. Breakdowns are a serious cost to the business in terms of production time lost in fulfilling orders and paying employees for non-productive work. Equipment should be checked regularly and a reporting procedure should be implemented to report faulty equipment, in accordance with Health and Safety legislation.

Research and development (R&D)

The R&D team is responsible for researching, designing, testing prototypes (models) of new products and devising new procedures to carry out production more efficiently. Computer software such as CAD (Computer-Aided Design) can aid the R&D team in designing new products.

Marketing Activities

The function of the Marketing Department is to satisfy consumer needs by selling a quality product at a price that returns a profit to the business. This is achieved by identifying:

1. what the *product* is
2. what *price* to sell the product at
3. where to *place* the product (ie in what market)
4. how to *promote* the product.

The above activities are often expressed in marketing terms as obtaining the correct *marketing mix*. The marketing mix refers to all aspects of the *four Ps* (Product, Price, Place and Promotion). To obtain the correct marketing mix, the Marketing Department must engage in market research to identify what the consumer requires.

Market research

Market research is a process of gathering and analysing information to identify who the customer is, what products or services are required by the customer and how best the Marketing Department can meet the requirements of the customer.

Promotion

Promotion involves bringing the products/services to the attention of the customer. A promotion campaign can consist of:

(i) *advertising:* aimed at a wide audience through the media (ie, television, radio, papers, journals, magazines and the Internet);

(ii) *sales promotions:* such as samples, in-store demonstrations, price cuts and competition offers. This form of promotion is best suited to retail products such as food items, cosmetics and general household items;

(iii) *publicity:* concerned with obtaining good press reports from the media. A business may gain publicity by supporting local or national events, eg, donating money to charity or sponsoring sporting events;

(iv) *personal selling:* suitable for selling products/services that require detailed demonstration or explanation on a one-to-one basis (eg, software or financial products).

Sales

The marketing team must sell products. Apart from the product itself, the level and quality of service offered to a customer can often be a distinct selling advantage.

The sales team regularly supplies invaluable information directly from the customer to the marketing research team to maximise competitive advantage.

Distribution

A large business will have a separate distribution department responsible for getting the product to the final destination. In a small business the Marketing Department is responsible for deciding what *channel of distribution* is most suitable to get the product to the market. Once the channel of distribution is decided upon, the marketing team can organise warehousing and coordinate transport for effective delivery to the market.

The three main channels of distribution are:

Manufacturer ⟶ Consumer
Typical businesses that use this channel produce customised products, eg, specially commissioned furniture, paintings, etc.

Manufacturer ⟶ Retailer ⟶ Consumer
Typical businesses that use this channel are producers of perishable items, or where the manufacturer needs an agent or broker to distribute goods in wide geographical locations on their behalf. For example, car manufacturers will sell to an agent (garages) for sale to the customer.

Manufacturer ————► Wholesaler ————► Retailer ————► Consumer
Typical businesses that use this channel are manufacturers of large volume, non-perishable consumer goods such as detergents and household items.

Financial Activities

The Finance Department is responsible for planning and controlling the finances of the business and prepares the final accounts, eg, Trading, Profit and Loss and Balance Sheet, at the end of each trading period – usually yearly. The final accounts are necessary for the Revenue Commissioners for tax purposes and other interested parties, such as shareholders, suppliers, creditors and potential investors. Financial systems (eg, accounts receivable and accounts payable, etc.) are implemented so that an accurate statement of the trading position of the business can be established.

Financial Accounting

The Financial Accountant is responsible for recording accounting activities. S/he prepares the yearly final accounts, and throughout the trading year will produce monthly or quarterly reports (interim reports) stating the current trading situation. This information is used by management for decision-making purposes. For example, if the first quarterly report shows that sales are falling in a particular foreign market, management may decide to invest more in advertising, employ a local agent to distribute the product or discontinue the product.

Management Accounting

The Management Accountant is responsible for analysing and controlling business costs and preparing overall budgets for the business. Budgets are plans of how money should be allocated in the future. Usually budgets are based on historical information, such as what the costs of production were last year, and what the cost is likely to be this year, given inflation, wage increases, material increases, etc. The individual departments are then required to operate within the allocated budget.

Human Resources Activities

The Human Resource Department (HR) is not linked directly to the manufacturing of products. It provides a service to all the departments within the business by developing overall employment policies such as manpower planning, industrial relations, employee health, safety and welfare, and remuneration policies.

Manpower planning

Manpower planning is an ongoing process to ensure that the business has employees who are skilled to perform the tasks necessary for the survival of the business. The planning process involves:

(i) *manpower audit:* an audit to assess the current skill levels of employees and to identify requirements for the future

(ii) *job evaluations:* an evaluation of a job is carried out to assess the level of skill and ability necessary for the job. Job evaluations are necessary to devise job descriptions and pay structures.

(iii) *recruitment, selection and training:* a combination of selection processes such as psychometric tests, aptitude tests and interviews may be used when recruiting staff. When staff has been selected, an *induction course* should be arranged so that new employees can become familiar with the business policies, their duties and responsibilities. Initial and ongoing training should be provided for staff to develop and maintain skill levels.

(iv) *performance appraisal:* performance appraisal interviews should be carried out with all employees on a regular basis. The information received is used to provide extra training, support, reward staff, etc., where appropriate.

(v) *management development:* it is important that the business has a management development policy to ensure that the management structure not be weakened. Training for potential managers should include courses on time management, leadership, communication, stress management and training for specific roles.

(vi) *terminations (redundancies and retirement):* the HR Department negotiates with management and unions in the event of redundancies. The business may devise its own redundancy package, but it must adhere to the legal requirements. Conditions of retirement are detailed in the employee's contract of employment.

Industrial relations

The HR Department will facilitate at consultations between management, unions, employees and the various adjudication bodies such as the Employment Appeals Tribunal and the Labour Court.

Grievance and disciplinary procedures are usually drawn up by the HR Department in consultation with other interested parties (eg, trade union representatives and senior management) to establish guidelines for acceptable standards of behaviour at work and to provide formal channels for making complaints.

Health, safety and welfare

Every business is legally obliged to provide a safe place of work. The HR Department is instrumental in devising health and safety policies and ensuring that health and safety procedures are in place and monitored in accordance with Health and Safety legislation.

Remuneration

This involves devising reward systems so that employees are paid/rewarded in line with duties and responsibilities. Pay structures should be clearly defined and regularly reviewed. Reward systems can include share option schemes, medical insurance, assistance with child care or further education, etc.

Restructuring the Organisation

As a business grows in size and complexity it may relocate geographically and some functions may be centralised, ie, operated from head office. For example, in the organisation chart below, the Marketing Department will coordinate the marketing functions for all branches, the Transport/Distribution department will be responsible for ensuring stock is delivered to all the branches, the HR department will carry out all the personnel activities for all branches, and the Finance department will control the major financial functions such as preparing overall accounts, setting budgets and monitoring costs. The Information Technology (IT) department will be responsible for monitoring networks and information systems between the branches.

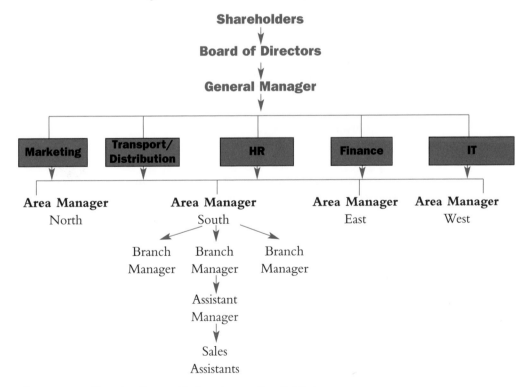

Organisation Chart by Geographic Location — Retail Chain.
Note: the shaded functions are centralised and service all the branches.

Short Questions

1. Distinguish between public-sector organisations and private-sector organisations.
2. List five legal forms of business.
3. Describe two main differences between a sole trader and a partnership.
4. Briefly describe four features of a private limited company.
5. Draw up a table to contrast a private company with a partnership, a sole trader and a co-operative. List four points.
6. State two main differences between a private limited company and a public limited company.
7. Explain the term 'limited liability'.
8. Outline the details required on Form A1 when forming a company.
9. Identify four groups of people that have an interest in viewing a public company's annual financial accounts and reports.
10. List three benefits for both a franchisor and a franchisee who enter into a franchise agreement.
11. What is a venture capitalist?
12. List features of an organisation chart.
13. Briefly describe four activities carried out by the Production Department.
14. Outline the costs involved in maintaining stock in a warehouse.
15. Briefly describe four activities carried out by the Marketing Department.
16. What do the 'four Ps', as used in marketing terminology, refer to?
17. List three main channels of distribution.
18. List four promotional activities a Marketing Department may utilise when marketing a new product.
19. What is the function of the Finance Department in a business?
20. Distinguish between the Financial Accountant and the Management Accountant.
21. Briefly describe four activities carried out by the Human Resources Department.
22. What is manpower planning? List four activities that generally form part of the planning process.

Chapter 2 — Office Functions, Design and Equipment

The Office and its Functions

The office is responsible for handling information that flows to and from the business. The location and size of the office is determined by the nature and size of the business and volume of information to be processed.

A large business may have an administration office attached to each department that will carry out work specific to that department: for example, in the Marketing department, the administration office may be responsible for preparing sales presentations, processing sales orders and calculating travel expenses for sales representatives. However, it is common practice for a large business to have a *centralised office* to deal with the activities that are common to all departments.

Some of the support services that may be centralised are shown below:

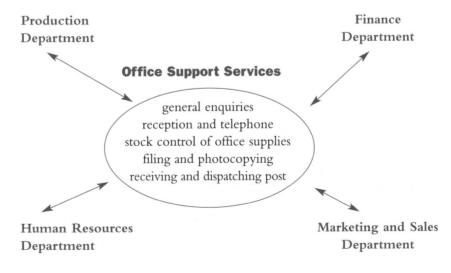

Functions of the Office

The functions of the office can be classified as follows:

Receiving and Sorting Information

Typically the office deals with information received from:
— *Customers*, ie, enquiries, quotations, orders, payments, complaints
— *Suppliers*, ie, invoices, statements, catalogues, promotional literature
— *Government bodies*, ie, Revenue Commissioners, Department of Enterprise, Trade and Employment, Central Statistics Office, Employment Welfare Agencies
— *Financial institutions*, ie, bank statements, interest rates, currency rates, stock valuations
— *The business itself*, ie, company reports, internal mail, minutes of meetings, final accounts and other internal business documents.

The information received is sorted for further processing or immediate distribution.

Processing and Communicating Information

Generally, information received requires some further processing before it can be used effectively or distributed. The office must impart the processed information to the recipient in the most effective way for clear understanding. There are four ways to communicate:
— *Orally:* eg, face-to-face meetings, telephone, videoconferencing
— *Written:* eg, letters, reports, minutes
— *Electronically:* eg, email, fax
— *Visually:* eg, bar charts, pie charts, histograms.

Storing and Protecting Information

When information is processed, it is stored for future reference using a manual filing system or an electronic document management system (EDM – see Chapter 16). Information regarding individuals that is maintained in paper format or on a computer must be maintained according to the Data Protection Acts 1988–2003. Confidential information should be safely stored to prevent unauthorised access.

General Sources of Reference

Most offices deal with a variety of general business enquiries during the working day. The office personnel should have a series of references (books and websites) to access for accurate and up-to-date information. The following section lists typical reference sources that should be available in the office.

The list is not exhaustive, as the references required will depend on the nature of the business.

Dictionary and Thesaurus

A dictionary is used to check the meaning and spelling of words. A thesaurus is used to find different words with the same meaning (synonyms), eg, 'busy' can be interchanged with 'occupied', 'engaged' or 'employed'. A spelling and thesaurus facility can also be referenced using word processing software, ie, Microsoft Word.

Accommodation References

Office personnel who prepare travel arrangements should have information on accommodation available and places of interest in the surrounding area. Up-to-date information is available from tourist offices and relevant websites such as www.failteireland.com.

Timetables

Timetables are necessary to check transportation times for employees travelling on behalf of the business. Timetables of buses and trains can be obtained from the local Bus Éireann and Iarnrod Éireann stations respectively. Iarnrod Éireann operates a 'talking timetable' facility and the telephone numbers for specific routes are listed in the telephone directory. When the number is dialled, a recorded message gives the times of departures and arrivals for that route. Travel timetables can also be viewed on relevant transportation websites such as www.buseireann.ie and www.irishrail.ie.

Road Maps

Road maps are necessary in any office where employees travel as part of the business. Maps of local areas, national and international routes may be obtained from the AA (Automobile Association) or any bookshop.

Some maps have a chart which gives details of distances in kilometres. This chart can be used to calculate travel expenses and the duration of a journey.

A more technical solution is to provide drivers with a satellite navigation device, which uses global positioning satellites to locate and direct the driver. In addition, mapping software such as Microsoft Autoroute can generate directions and give exact distances.

Internal Telephone Directory

The receptionist will maintain a list of all employees' telephone extension numbers, and an internal telephone directory for commonly used telephone numbers.

Telephone Directory and Golden Pages

The Telephone Directory lists telephone numbers and addresses in alphabetical order according to the name of the telephone account holder. National and international dialling codes are also listed.

The Golden Pages is a business directory, organised alphabetically under products and services, with a fast-find index at the back of the directory. Businesses that want more than a single-line listing can purchase advertising space to highlight their products or services.

Both the Telephone Directory and the Golden Pages are available in each of the six telephone zones and can also be referenced on-line at www.eircomphonebook.ie and at www.goldenpages.ie.

Kompass

Kompass is a national directory of businesses in Ireland. This directory gives a brief description of the organisation, types of product/service supplied and a list of executives involved in the business. Kompass can also be referenced on-line at www.kompass.ie.

Stubb's Gazette

This journal is invaluable for checking the performance and solvency of trade partners such as customers and suppliers. It publishes information on businesses that have judgments made against them, have been struck off the companies register or have been declared bankrupt. Competitors' solvency can also be analysed for business opportunities.

Postal Rates Guide

A guide to postal rates, available from the Post Office or online at www.anpost. ie, lists national and international costs of postage for letters and parcels in accordance with the weight of the item to be posted. This guide is essential in an office where a variety of outgoing post is to be franked. The user can check the guide and adjust the franking meter to reflect the correct cost of postage.

Industry Magazines

Industry magazines, journals, newsletters and reports may be left with the administrator for circulation among employees. The variety of magazines available in the office will depend on the nature and budget of the business.

Teletext

Teletext is an information system available through the television network. 'Aertel' is the teletext system supplied by RTÉ that provides general information such as news, stock market prices, travel timetables, etc. Teletext is free to view and is financed by advertising.

Office Design

Office design refers to how the office is organised in terms of the number of workstations and the equipment used in the office.

Motivation theories suggest that the physical environment of the workplace has a significant effect on employee morale and productivity. An unpleasant physical environment, such as cramped space, inadequate natural light, or extremes of temperature, can cause unnecessary stress, fatigue and strain on employees and can result in poor productivity – so-called 'sick-building syndrome'.

In many cases the Office Manager will be constrained by the amount of physical space allocated to the office and by financial constraints, which will affect the eventual design selected.

There are three common types of office design:

Open-plan Office

The open-plan office is suited to a business that handles a large volume of general (non-sensitive) information, for example, a travel agent.

In open-plan offices there are no obvious divisions or partitions between working areas. The workstations are normally organised so that the work flows from station to station in a logical manner.

Open-plan office

With an open-plan office, space is optimised and economies of scale are obtained with the shared use of electricity, heating and resources such as printers and photocopiers.

However, there is evidence to suggest that lack of privacy and the surrounding noise impairs concentration. This can lead to poor levels of productivity and low job satisfaction for the employee, which in turn may lead to higher rates of staff turnover.

An important consideration when designing an open-plan office is to ensure that pedestrian traffic routes are kept clutter-free and are clearly defined.

Landscaped Office

Landscaped offices are suited to businesses that deal with a large volume of work, but also require some privacy for group work.

This is generally the preferred style. The landscaped office can consist of semi-permanent partitions or else a modular approach can be used. A modular approach uses furniture to create work areas and can be easily rearranged. Within the landscaped office, a section of the office space can be portioned off as a 'cellular office' to facilitate meetings or briefings of a sensitive nature.

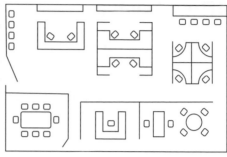

Landscaped office

The Corridor/Closed Door Style

Some offices use a corridor style, where a small number of staff is segregated into separate private offices. Usually the manager will have a private office.

This style of office design is suited to a business that handles highly sensitive inform-ation. For example, banks will

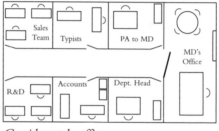

Corridor-style office

have private offices for advising customers on loans, and solicitors will have private offices where confidential issues can be discussed with the client.

Planning Office Layout

A change in office layout or a move to a new office needs to be carefully planned to avoid or reduce resistance from office staff. A work-study analysis may be carried out to determine the optimum layout. In planning the office layout, the number of staff working in the office and the office equipment must be considered before space can be allocated to each individual work area. The Office Manager should consider:

1. *Space:* What space is available for the office? How should it be utilised, ie, open-plan, closed door style, etc.? Present and future staff requirements?
2. *Work flow:* Volume of work? Frequency of the work?
3. *Privacy:* How confidential is the work? Can employees focus on their work without constant interruption from passing co-workers?
4. *Equipment:* Is shared equipment, such as a printer, fax, photocopier, etc., well located for easy access and minimum disruption?
5. *Safety legislation:* Are procedures in place for implementing and maintaining a safe and secure office?

Depending on the volume of work in the office, it may be necessary to plan for centralised equipment areas for dispatching post, filing, printing and photocopying, etc., to minimise disruptions in the main office.

Office Equipment

Typical office equipment includes computers, printers, scanners, telephones, faxes, filing equipment and shredders. These are detailed in later chapters. This chapter describes general office equipment such as photocopiers, binders, guillotines, laminators and desktop sundries as described below.

Photocopier

A photocopier is a machine that makes copies of paper documents, visual images or overhead transparencies. Photocopiers range in size from desktop to freestanding machines.

Most modern photocopiers combine extra functionality such as the ability to print, scan and fax if the photocopier is connected to the office's computer network. These machines are known as multi-functional devices (MFDs). Most offices can benefit from using a photocopier as a printer as the cost per page can be significantly cheaper that printing multiply copies using a laser printer. Typical features of a photocopier are:

◆ *Number selector:* Used to set the number of copies required.

◆ *Paper drawers:* Most photocopiers have a number of paper drawers to accommodate a variety of page sizes ranging from A6 to A3. The type of photocopiable material may include bond paper (high quality), card, photocopiable overhead transparencies, etc.

◆ *ADF (automatic document feeder):* A loading facility located generally on the lid of the photocopier, which automatically 'feeds' pages to be copied, thus eliminating the need to lift the cover of the photocopier each time a page is to be copied.

◆ *Duplex feature:* Enables copies to be made on both sides of one page from two single pages, or vice versa.

◆ *Sorting and stapling:* A facility to produce sorted copies of a multi-page document. The sorted copies can be stapled automatically.

- *Automatic grouping:* A facility that copies a series of separate pages multiple times. For example, if the operator required 20 copies each of three pages, the grouping facility would produce 20 copies of the first page as a group, 20 copies of the next page as a group, etc.
- *Zoom facility:* Documents can be increased or decreased in one-per-cent increments. For example, a small diagram on an A4 page can be increased to fill the page or the content of an A4 page can be increased to an A3 page. Likewise, a magazine article which is slightly wider than A4 can be reduced to A4.
- *Two-single-copy feature:* For example, a magazine when opened is often approximately A3 in size. This feature will automatically photocopy an A3 page onto *two separate* A4 pages. This saves the time involved in moving the magazine by hand.
- *Image Editing:* A facility that superimposes a watermark, horizontally, vertically or diagonally on the document such as, 'confidential', 'evaluation copy', etc., while copying the document.
- *Booklet Facility:* A facility that takes a multi-page document, re-orders the page sequence and prints two pages of text onto either A4 or A3 paper as required. The printed pages are automatically folded and stapled into a booklet format, resulting in either an A5 or an A4 booklet.
- *Auto exposure:* This facility analyses the page to be photocopied and selects the proper image density, ie, how dark or bright the copy should be.
- *Interrupt mode:* An interrupt temporarily stops a job in progress to allow somebody else to use the photocopier. The interrupted job resumes from where it was stopped.
- *Code facility:* Codes can be allocated to individuals or departments to monitor and control copying costs. A code is entered before using the photocopier and the number of copies made is recorded against that code.
- *Diagnostic display:* A control panel that indicates problems with the machine, ie, paper jam, no paper, etc.

Using the photocopier

1. Remove any staples from the page to prevent damage to the glass surface.
2. Align the page according to the correct paper size displayed on the glass surface screen and close the lid of the photocopier. Alternatively, use the ADF facility.
3. Select the correct settings for the machine before starting, ie:
   - the size of paper required, such as A4

   – the density of the copy, which is generally set halfway between bright and dark. However, if photocopying from dark-coloured paper, select a brighter setting
   – required functions, ie, sort, group, duplex, etc.
4. For complicated tasks, a test copy should be photocopied and checked.
5. Set the number of copies required and press the 'start' button.

When photocopying onto overhead transparencies, check that they are the photocopiable type. Write-on transparencies will melt in the machine, causing damage.

Purchasing a photocopier

Consider the following factors:
1. *Budget allocated:* This will limit the purchaser's choice of models.
2. *Costs:* The purchase price must be analysed. Is servicing and delivery included? What are the typical running costs? Is training required for operators?
3. *Requirements:* What functions are required? How often are specific functions used? Is colour required? (A high-end photocopier applies colour in one copying cycle, while the low-end models apply colour separately and are therefore slower.)
4. *Volume and frequency of use:* How much work is done? How often is the machine used?
5. *Size:* Will the machine take up too much space in the office?
6. *Noise:* Will the machine be loud and interrupt work?
7. *Durability:* Will the machine need to be maintained regularly?

Binding Equipment

Binders are used to secure individual pages together in booklet form. Typical binders on the market are spiral, velobinder and thermal.

Spiral binder

1. A spiral binder punches holes along one side of the pages. This can be done by a manually operated machine by means of a lever or by an electronic machine by pressing a button.
2. When all the pages are punched, a 'plastic comb' is inserted on the spikes of the machine and opened with the lever.
3. The punched paper is then placed into the opened plastic comb, working from the back of the document to the front.

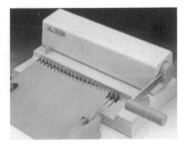

Spiral binder and combs

4. When all the pages are inserted, the plastic comb is closed with the lever and the bound booklet is removed.

Velobinder

1. A velobinder punches holes along one side of the pages, similarly to the spiral binder.
2. When all the pages are punched, they are inserted into the velobinder strips, which consist of two parts: one part has

Velobinder

prongs to hold the punched paper and the other part is a clamp that holds the pages together. A document bound with a velobinder can be easily reopened and reclosed to insert or remove pages. The booklet, however, does not open out flat as it does with spiral binding.

Thermal binder

Velobound product

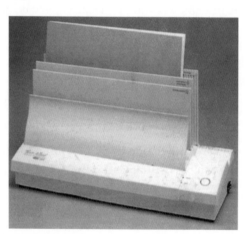

Thermal binders

Thermal-bound products

A thermal binder operates by melting the glue on the inside spine of special 'thermal covers'.

1. The pages to be bound are placed in a thermal cover.
2. The spine of the thermal cover is placed upright into the heated thermal binder.
3. The glue on the spine of the thermal cover melts, causing the pages to stick to the spine.
4. The booklet should be allowed to cool before opening.

Guillotine

A guillotine is used to cut paper, cards, etc., to the correct size evenly. It consists of a flat table area pre-printed with paper sizes, a safety guard to the right, with a blade behind to cut the paper.

Guillotine

To cut paper:
1. The blade is moved upright by a handle.
2. The pages to be cut are positioned on the paper size required, the excess going under the blade.
3. The pages are held firmly by a movable clamp which is locked into position.
4. The blade is pushed down by its handle, cutting the paper.

Laminators

A laminating machine places a transparent plastic, durable cover over paper and cards. It is used to protect documents such as ID cards, certificates, charts, photographs, etc. There are two types of laminating machine: a pouch laminator and a roll laminator.

Pouch laminator

Laminator with an assortment of pouches

A pouch laminator machine is suitable where usage is occasional, owing to the cost of the pouches. The document is placed in the correctly sized pouch and inserted into the machine. The machine uses heat to bind the plastic pouch to both sides of the document. The item to be laminated should be at least 3mm smaller than the pouch in order to give a protective border.

Roll laminator

Roll laminator machines are more expensive but are very economical for frequent long runs. The document is inserted into the machine and a roll of transparent film is used to laminate the document. The finished product may have to be trimmed at the edges.

Label Maker

A machine used to create self-adhesive labels for shelves, folders, letter trays, etc. The label maker has a small keypad and screen, with up to four lines of text and a variety of print fonts available for each label. The user can check the label on-screen before printing.

Label maker

Sundry Desktop Equipment

The following items of equipment may be placed on desks:

Letter trays: Also known as 'in' and 'out' trays for holding incoming and outgoing correspondence.

Tape dispenser: To hold and cut Sellotape.

Desk organisers: To hold sundries such as pens, pencils, rubbers, pencil parer, paper clips, Post-its (note paper), highlighters, treasury tags (string with metal at both end to hold punched documents together), etc.

Copyholder: To hold pages at eye level while entering data.

Puncher: To punch holes in paper to place into ring-binder folders.

Stapler: To hold pages together with a metal fastener (staple) more securely than with paper clips.

Calculators: To perform arithmetic calculations.

Short Questions

1. Outline three activities carried out in the office in relation to the management of information.
2. List four office activities that can be centralised.
3. List four methods of communicating information, stating when it is more suitable to use each method.
4. Where would you find the following:
   a)   a synonym for the word 'assist'
   b)   times of trains leaving Dublin for Cork after 2pm on a Tuesday
   c)   the distance by road from Athlone to Galway
   d)   a list of businesses in South Dublin that offer secretarial services?
5. What information is available in the following sources of references:
   a)   Kompass
   b)   *Stubb's Gazette*
   c)   Postal Guide
   d)   Golden Pages
   e)   Teletext
6. Distinguish between the following office designs: open-plan, landscaped and the corridor-style office.
7. Outline two advantages and two disadvantages that may be associated with an open-plan office design.
8. Outline four factors to consider when planning a change in office layout.
9. Describe a typical workstation.
10. Describe four features of a photocopier that would make the task of producing 20 copies of an eight-page document easier.
11. What is meant by MDF?
12. List four factors to be considered when deciding on a photocopier for a business.
13. Distinguish between the following types of binder: spiral binder, velobinder and thermal binder.
14. Which binder is most suitable for inserting more pages into a bound document at a later stage? Why?
15. Distinguish between a pouch laminator and a roll laminator.
16. What office equipment is used to:
    a)   cut paper to the correct size
    b)   place a transparent plastic cover over certificates, charts, etc.
    c)   make self-adhesive labels for shelves, in/out trays, etc.
    d)   hold pages at eye-level while entering data?

Chapter 3 — Financial Institutions

The Euro

When the euro came into being on 1 January 2002, there were 15 countries in the European Union (EU): Austria, Belgium, Finland, France, Germany, Ireland, Italy, Luxembourg, the Netherlands, Portugal, Spain, Greece, the United Kingdom, Denmark and Sweden.

Of these 15 countries, the United Kingdom, Denmark and Sweden opted out of joining the 'eurozone' and have not joined to date.

On 1 May 2004, ten new member states joined the EU, a precondition for adopting the euro: the Czech Republic, Estonia, Cyprus, Latvia, Lithuania, Hungary, Malta, Poland, Slovenia and Slovakia. In 2007 Bulgaria and Romania joined the EU, bringing to 27 the total number of member states.

To date, four of these countries have joined the eurozone: Slovenia in 2007, Malta and Cyprus in 2008 and Slovakia in 2009. The remaining new member states in the EU will introduce the euro as soon as they have fulfilled the necessary conditions laid down in the Maastricht Treaty of 1992, which include price stability, adequate public finances (ie, absence of excessive government debt), stable exchange rates and stable long-term interest rates.

The estimated target date for these countries to join the eurozone varies between 2010 and 2015.

Euro Notes and Coins

The symbol for the euro, '€', was inspired by the Greek letter epsilon, in reference to the cradle of European civilisation and to the first letter of the word 'Europe'. The parallel lines represent the stability of the euro.

The design of the euro notes is symbolic; windows and gateways dominate the front side of each banknote as symbols of openness and cooperation in the EU. The reverse side of the banknotes features a bridge, a metaphor for communication among the people of Europe and the rest of the world.

Euro coins carry a common European face, which represents a map of the European Union against a background of transverse lines to which are attached the stars of the European flag. The reverse side of each coin is different for each country. In Ireland, the reverse of the coin features the harp symbol and the word *Éire*, surrounded by the stars of the EU flag.

Benefits of the Eurozone

As a common currency, the euro has brought many benefits, such as:

◆ eliminating the need to change currencies when travelling within the eurozone. Travelling outside the eurozone is also easier, as the euro is an international currency and widely accepted in many places outside the eurozone, particularly in tourist destinations

◆ price transparency, ie, easier price comparison within the eurozone, leading to improved competition and lower prices for the customer

◆ a more stable trade environment within the eurozone, due to the elimination of exchange-rate fluctuations of currencies for both importers and exporters

◆ the benefit of lower interest rates in line with the European Monetary Union (EMU) recommendations, which include low inflation and improved control of government debt.

The Irish Banks

The Central Bank and Financial Services Authority of Ireland (CBFSAI) has two divisions: the Central Bank and the Irish Financial Regulatory Authority. At the time of writing, July 2009, the CBFSAI is to be replaced by a single fully integrated regulatory institution, the Central Bank of Ireland Commission. Domestic responsibilities of the Central Bank in Ireland include:

◆ provision of banknotes and coins

◆ managing investment assets on behalf of the State

◆ acting as agent and banker for the government

◆ maintaining a stable financial system

◆ ensuring safe and reliable payment systems

◆ provision of advice and guidance on Irish economic policy.

The majority of the banking requirements of business and personal customers will be catered for by a *commercial bank*. Well-known commercial banks are: Allied Irish Bank (AIB), Bank of Ireland (BOI), Ulster Bank (UB), National Irish Bank (NIB), Permanent Trustee Savings Bank (PTSB), etc.

General services offered by the commercial banks include current and deposit accounts, mortgages, loan facilities, foreign exchange, electronic funds transfer, telephone and Internet banking.

The Current Account

Current accounts are used to cater for day-to-day financial transactions, ie, lodgements, withdrawals and Laser Card transactions. Salaries are typically paid directly into a current account.

An overdraft facility can be obtained on a current account for an extra fee, ie, the bank will make extra funds available for a short period of time, usually up to one year. To open a current account, you must provide the bank with: identification, (ie, passport or driving licence), two references, proof of address (ie, recent utility bill), specimen signature(s) and a sum of money to be deposited to the new current account.

When a current account is opened, a cheque book and a bank card are issued to facilitate the payment of bills and other transactions.

The Cheque

A cheque is a written instruction to the bank to pay the sum of money that is written both in words and figures to the person named on the cheque. The use of cheques has significantly declined in recent years due to the increased usage of electronic payment methods like debit cards (ie, Laser) and credit cards.

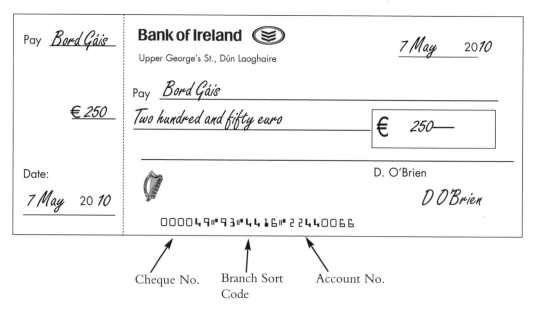

Cheque and stub

A cheque contains the following pre-printed information:
- ◆ the government stamp
- ◆ name and address of the bank, plus the bank logo, generally at the top

- the cheque number, branch sort code and the current account number, generally at the bottom
- a space for writing the value of the cheque in words and figures
- a space for dating and signing the cheque.

The cheque stub is the record of the cheque that has been written and is completed by writing:
- who the cheque was written to
- the amount of the cheque
- the date of the cheque

Parties to a cheque

There are three parties to a cheque:
a) the *drawer*: the account holder or persons authorised to sign the cheque
b) the *drawee*: the bank on which the cheque is drawn
c) the *payee*: the person named on the cheque to receive the payment.

Completing a cheque

The cheque is completed by filling in the following details:
1. – date
   – name of payee
   – amount of the cheque in words and in figures, which should be written close together to prevent alterations.
2. The cheque is signed by the drawer.
3. The drawer may cross the cheque to ensure that the cheque is lodged to a bank account.
4. The cheque stub is completed and retained by the drawer to check against his/her *bank statement*.

In practice, office personnel may fill in the cheque and obtain the signature(s) from management or whoever is authorised to sign the cheque for the business.

If the cheque is incorrectly completed, the bank will return it to the payee marked *refer to drawer*. This is sometimes referred to as a *bounced cheque* as the cheque was not honoured by the bank. The payee must return the cheque to the drawer, who may write a new cheque or initial any alterations made on the existing cheque.

Crossing a cheque

The purpose of crossing a cheque is to prevent an unauthorised person from cashing it, as a crossed cheque must be lodged to a bank account. Cheques that are not crossed are referred to as *open cheques*.

A cheque is crossed by drawing two parallel lines across the face of the cheque. Between the parallel lines, any of the following words are generally written:

a) the words '& Co' (or no words at all).

This cheque can be lodged to the payee's account or the payee can transfer the cheque to another person by *endorsing* it. The payee endorses the cheque by signing his/her name on the reverse of the cheque. An endorsed cheque must be lodged.

b) the words 'not negotiable' or 'a/c payee only'.

This cheque must be lodged to the payee's account.

c) the bank and branch specified.

This cheque must be lodged to the payee's account in the bank and branch specified.

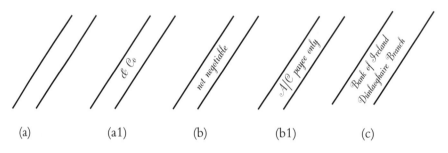

   (a)   (a1)   (b)   (b1)   (c)

Examples of crossing a cheque

Receiving a cheque for payment

When a cheque is tendered for payment:

a) request the customer's bank card and check expiry date.

b) check that the drawer's name and signature on the cheque correspond with the card.

c) check the payee's name and date on the cheque. *Post-dated cheques* (cheques written for a future date) and *stale* cheques (cheques more than 6 months old) should not be accepted.

d) check that the amount in words and the amount in figures on the cheque correspond.

e) write the bank card number and expiry date on the back of the cheque. This guarantees that the cheque will be honoured by the bank, if the amount does not exceed €130.

Bank statement

A bank statement is sent to the account holder on a monthly basis or is available on request. Nowadays, a significant majority of account holders have registered for online banking and can therefore view their bank statement at any time on their bank's website.

The bank statement shows all transactions that have occurred on the account within that period, eg, cheques presented to the bank for payment, standing orders and direct debits processed, bank charges and any other lodgements and withdrawals on the account.

Account Statement

Account Holder
PAT KELLY
Current Account

Bank of Ireland
DÚN LAOGHAIRE, CO. DUBLIN
Tel: (01) 2800273
Fax: (01) 2800810

Post to
Mr Pat Kelly
"Woodview"
Leixlip
Co. Kildare

Page   **1**   **of**   **1**

90–11–16
Branch Code

103
Statement Number

30 Apr 2010
Date of Statement

862700256
Account Number

DATE	DETAILS		PAYMENTS OUT €	PAYMENTS IN €	BALANCE €
2010					
29 Mar	Balance Forward				1120.20
2 Apr	New Ireland – Life	DD	75.90		1044.30
	Pass 2 Apr		60.00		984.30
	Pat Kelly	SO	100.00		884.30
4 Apr	AMV00102281	DD	54.10		830.20
6 Apr	PASS 06 Apr		40.00		790.20
	Banking 365 Master Card		296.60		493.60
9 Apr	Cheque 493		50.00		443.60
	Current Account Fees		10.80		432.80
10 Apr	LR Tesco Store		79.90		352.90
11 Apr	Giro Credit			1500.00	1852.90
16 Apr	Pass 16 Apr		150.00		1702.90
17 Apr	Cheque 495		120.00		1582.90
20 Apr	In Branch Cr			250.00	1832.90
22 Apr	LR Tesco Store		220.00		1612.90
23 Apr	Banking 365 Access		420.00		1192.90

Bank statement

The final figure on the statement is the *bank balance*, ie, the amount of money in the account on a particular date. However, this may not be the true balance at the time the business receives the statement. For example, there may be cheques that the business has lodged to the bank, but that have not yet been processed.

When the business receives the bank statement, the administrator should check the entries on the statement with the business records (ie, cheque stubs, lodgement and withdrawal counterfoils, Laser Card receipts, etc.) to establish the current balance. A *bank reconciliation* statement is prepared, which shows what the final balance on the account should be after adjusting for lodgements or withdrawals not shown on the bank statement.

The Journey of a cheque

The following example simplifies what happens to a cheque when it is presented for payment.

Example

Mr Hegarty has a current account in the Bank of Ireland, Limerick. He writes a cheque for €350 to Ms O'Sullivan, whose bank account is in the Allied Irish Bank, Tralee.

1   Ms O'Sullivan lodges the cheque to her bank account in the Allied Irish Bank, Tralee. (It may take up to three working days to clear a cheque drawn on another bank.)

2   AIB sends the cheque on to its clearing centre. The clearing centre sends the cheque details (ie, bank sort code, drawer's account name and number, cheque number, value of the cheque and date) electronically to the Bank of Ireland, Limerick.

3   The Bank of Ireland then debits (subtracts from) Mr Hegarty's account the value of the cheque, and the AIB bank credits (adds to) Ms O'Sullivan's account the value of the cheque.

Bank drafts

A bank draft is purchased at a bank and, like a cheque, it is an instruction to a bank to pay the amount of the draft to the payee. The bank guarantees payment on the draft. Bank drafts can be purchased in foreign currencies. Bank drafts are commonly used when:

1. A customer does not have a current account upon which to draw a cheque.
2. Once-off or non-routine payments are required (eg, examination fees).
3. A business is dealing with a new customer for the first time and requests a draft rather than risking a cheque as payment.
4. The customer wishes to send money abroad.

Bank draft application form

Bank Cards

Two main bank cards are available from all banks: a debit card (eg, Laser) and a credit card (eg, Visa, Mastercard, etc.). Both cards enable payments for goods and services to be made electronically and for money to be withdrawn from an ATM. However, their main difference is in the timing of the payment.

Bank cards are based on the *chip-and-pin* technology. A microchip containing the account details is embedded in the card, making it more difficult to duplicate. A PIN (Personal Identification Number) is issued for each card and the customer is required to enter their PIN to complete a transaction. Chip-and-pin technology ensures that the customer is the genuine cardholder. (With the previous technology of the magnetic strip, the customer just had to sign a receipt.) The cardholder should never:

◆ carry the PIN with the card
◆ reveal the PIN to another person
◆ disclose the PIN when carrying out telephone, Internet or mail-order transactions.

Debit Cards

A debit card is used to pay for goods and services electronically, directly from a current account. With debit card purchases, the customer's account is subtracted from (debited) almost immediately; therefore the customer must have the necessary funds in the account or an overdraft facility must be available. Some retailers will also facilitate a 'cash-back' withdrawal by the customer at the time of purchase. This service reduces the transaction cost involved in making cash withdrawals at ATMs.

A debit card can also be used as:

- *a cheque guarantee card*: an assurance that the bank will honour cheques drawn on the customer's account to the value of €130, provided that the bank card number and expiry date are written on the back of the cheque;
- *an ATM card*: to allow the withdrawal of cash, 24 hours per day, from an Automatic Teller Machine (ATM). The customer enters the PIN to access the account and can also order a statement or cheque book, change the PIN and top up mobile phone credit on prepaid phones. Customers can also withdraw foreign cash from ATMs abroad that display either the 'Cirrus' or the 'Maestro' symbol.

Credit Cards

A credit card is used to purchase goods and services on credit, ie, the customer is allowed a period of time (usually 30 days) before payment is required, and can also be used to withdraw cash from ATMs at home and abroad.

A customer who wishes to obtain a credit card must complete an application form and, based on the information received, the bank's credit card centre will determine a credit limit for the customer. The bank's credit card centre will issue the PIN number and credit card separately. The card should be signed at the back immediately it is received.

A statement is sent to the customer on a monthly basis, showing transaction details, balance due, any interest charged and the minimum payment required. Credit cards should be managed with care, as the interest rates charged on unpaid bills is very high. The ideal way to manage a credit card is to clear the balance every month.

Retailers who operate a credit card payment system pay a one-off set-up fee and a percentage commission on sales to the credit card company. In return, the retailer is guaranteed payment by the credit card company, which collects the payment from the customer.

When accepting a payment by debit or credit card, the retailer should:

1 Request that the customer insert the card in the 'PIN reader' to authorise the card.
2 Request that the customer enter their PIN and press enter to authorise the payment.
3 Issue the customer with a printed receipt and return the card to the customer.

Lodgements

Lodgements to the bank can be made by:
- completing a lodgement slip at the bank
- using the automatic teller machine (ATM)
- using the night-safe facility
- using the express lodgement facility in the bank.
- Internet and telephone banking.

Lodging Money Using a Lodgement Slip

Businesses that lodge money regularly will be issued with a lodgement book containing a series of lodgement slips, with the business account number and business name pre-printed on the slip. Alternatively, individual lodgement slips are obtainable at the bank. For security reasons, a business should reduce the amount of cash held on the premises by making frequent lodgements or by offering a cash-back facility to customers who pay using Laser.

When preparing money (notes, coins and cheques) for lodgement to a bank account:

1. Count all coins and place in appropriate money bags, available from the bank.
2. Sort the notes into similar denominations, facing upwards to facilitate counting. Place into bundles that are easy to count, eg, bundles of €100, and secure with an elastic band.
3. Count the number of cheques and total the value of all cheques. Note the drawer and value of each cheque for your own records.
4. Complete the lodgement slip before you go to the bank by filling in:

Lodgement stub

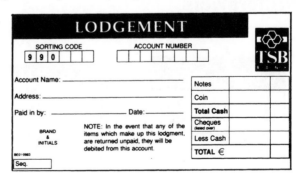
Lodgement slip

- the date of the lodgement
- the account name, bank account number and bank sort code where the money is being lodged, if you are not using a pre-printed slip
- the amount of the lodgement in notes, coins and cheques

◆ the signature of the person lodging the money

◆ the lodgement counterfoil (stub).

5. Ensure that the lodgement counterfoil is date-stamped by a bank official as your record of the lodgement.

For security reasons, when preparing cash for lodgement:

◆ Count cash in a private area, eg, a back room with the door locked.

◆ Request an escort when going to the bank with large sums of money.

◆ Vary the times and days of carrying out the lodgement.

Lodging Money Using the Night Safe

The night-safe service enables a business to lodge money after banking hours. The business is issued with a lodgement book, money pouch, security seal (which contains the customer's identity details) and a key to the night safe.

The completed lodgement slip and money are placed in the pouch. The pouch is sealed with the security seal and inserted through the night-safe slot.

The pouch is retrieved and normally opened in the presence of two bank officials the following day. The money is counted and lodged to the business account specified on the lodgement slip.

Lodging Money Using the Express Lodgement Facility

An express lodgement box is available within the bank to lodge money during banking hours. The money and completed lodgement slip are placed in a special lodgement envelope. The envelope is sealed and deposited in the Express Lodgement box.

Withdrawals

Withdrawal counterfoil

Withdrawal slip

Money can be withdrawn from bank accounts in a variety of ways:
1. by filling in a withdrawal slip at the bank
2. using the ATM machine
3. cheques
4. Electronic Funds Transfer (EFT).

Electronic Funds Transfer (EFT)

Electronic Funds Transfer is a safe and convenient method of paying bills or transferring funds from one account to another automatically. Common methods of transferring money or paying bills using EFT are standing orders and direct debits.

A *standing order* is used to make payments of a *fixed* amount from one account to another account on a regular basis, eg, monthly. Standing orders are typically used to: pay insurance premiums, mortgage repayments, or to make regular lodgements to other bank accounts. This facility ensures that payments are made on time.

A *direct debit* is used to make payments of *variable* amounts from one account to another account on a regular or irregular basis. For example, telephone bills and ESB bills must be paid regularly, but are of irregular amounts. A standing order/direct debit facility is set up by completing the appropriate form (mandate) stating:

♦ the name and bank account details from which payment is being made
♦ the name and bank account details of the account receiving the payment
♦ frequency of payment, date of each payment and the amount of payment (for standing orders).

A business may offer the facility of paying bills by EFT by sending its customers the appropriate mandate to complete. The business account details will be pre-printed on the mandate. There is a set-up fee and a transaction fee on each standing order/direct debit.

Standing orders/direct debits are cancelled only upon the written instruction of the customer to their bank.

Example

Bord Gáis sends the customer a direct debit mandate to complete.

The customer signs the form, giving their account name, number and bank details and returns the direct debit form to Bord Gáis.

Bord Gáis sends the direct debit mandate to the customer's bank authorising the bank to debit the amount of the gas bill from the customer's account.

Bord Gáis is credited with the amount of the bill.

Details of the direct debit transaction are shown on the customer's bank statement.

Advantages of Standing Orders/Direct Debits

1. Payments are automatically deducted from the customer's current account and paid into the account named on the mandate.
2. It is a safe method of ensuring that payment is made on time.
3. Details of the transaction are shown on the bank statement.
4. Special discounts may be obtained by paying bills on time.

Foreign Exchange

Since the introduction of the euro on 1 January 2002, the exchange to foreign currency is necessary only when travelling to non-eurozone countries. Non-eurozone countries quote daily 'buy' and 'sell' rates as determined by the central bank and the world trading markets.

The 'sell rate' is the rate at which the bank will sell foreign currency to the customer. The 'buy rate' is the rate at which the bank will buy foreign currency from the customer.

Purchasing Foreign Currency

When a customer is purchasing foreign currency, the banks' 'sell rate' is used to calculate the amount of foreign currency sold for €1. The euro quantity is multiplied by the sell rate.

Example

Miss Carty wishes to holiday in the US and has a budget of €3,000. If the banks' 'sell rate' is US$1.75, how many US$ can she buy? (Assume no commission.)

Solution

For every euro purchased, Miss Carty will receive US$1.75

For €3,000, Miss Carty receives US$5,250, ie, €3,000 multiplied by US$1.75.

Selling Foreign Currency

When a customer is selling back foreign currency to the bank, the 'buy rate' is used. The foreign currency amount is divided by the buy rate.

Example

Miss Carty returns from her holiday and discovers a US$50 bill in her handbag. The buy rate is €1.24. How many euros does she receive in exchange for US$50? (Assume no commission.)

Solution

Miss Carty will receive €40.32 for her US$50 bill, ie, US$50 divided by €1.24.

Traveller's Cheques

When travelling abroad it is advisable to use traveller's cheques rather than carry cash. Traveller's cheques are pre-printed cheques of a fixed value which can be exchanged in most countries for purchases or local currency. Traveller's cheques are purchased from a bank in most strong currencies, ie, euro, sterling, dollars, yen, etc. Traveller's cheques should be ordered in advance of travel.

When purchasing traveller's cheques, the customer signs the cheques at the bank. The customer is presented with a list of the cheque numbers. This list should be kept separate from the cheques (ie, at home) and is used to secure a refund in case of theft.

When purchasing an item with a traveller's cheque, the customer must countersign the cheque and personal identification is required (eg, passport). Change is given in local currency. A commission may be charged.

Unused traveller's cheques can be sold back to the bank at the current exchange rate or kept for future use.

Internet and Telephone Banking

Customers can now access their accounts 24 hours per day, 7 days per week, by using Internet or telephone banking.

The customer must complete the appropriate registration form to take advantage of these services. Once the customer is registered, their account can be accessed with telephone banking by entering the requested digits of their PIN. For Internet banking, the customer will receive a username and password separately by post which can be used to access their account.

Internet and telephone banking allow the customer to:

◆ check their account balance
◆ review recent transactions (eg, lodgements, withdrawals, standing orders, direct debits, etc.).
◆ check balance on credit card accounts and review recent transactions
◆ transfer funds to other registered accounts, eg, from a current account to a deposit account
◆ pay bills (eg, utility bills, credit cards, etc.)
◆ order a new cheque book
◆ request a statement
◆ change PIN
◆ 'top up' mobile phone credit.

Internet banking allows the customer greater transparency compared with telephone banking, as the customer can view their account while carrying out their banking transactions. The customer should ensure that there is no unauthorised access to their account and should:

- never reveal their username, password or PIN to anyone
- ensure that the bank has a secure website for transacting business. A secure address would display https:// as distinct from http (notice the 's')
- log out from the website when finished accessing the service or when leaving the desk, even for a short period.

Credit Unions

Like the commercial banks, the Credit Union provides their members (individuals and organisations) with loans and saving facilities. Unlike the banks, which operate as public limited companies, Credit Unions are registered as societies.

The Credit Union is based on a co-operative ethos and provides an important source of credit for members at fair and reasonable interest rates. To join a Credit Union, members must provide two forms of identification and lodge a small deposit to open an account. Savings and deposits are protected by the Irish League of Credit Unions up to a maximum of €110 million.

Every Credit Union branch is managed by a Board of Directors that oversees the business of the Credit Union on behalf of the members and are responsible for ensuring appropriate financial statements are provided at each year end.

Credit Unions are now part of the Irish Banking Clearing System and have developed a new 'Access Account', which operates like a bank current account. Members can now transfer funds electronically between their bank accounts and their Credit Union Access Account. Previously, transactions between bank accounts and credit union accounts were completed manually.

Facilities provided by Credit Unions

- Loans and Savings Accounts
- Credit Union Access Account
- Paypath (where wages can be directly lodged to a credit union account by an employer)
- Billpay (where bills, eg, gas, phone, mortgage, electricity, etc., can be paid electronically)
- ATM facility
- Foreign currency exchange
- Insurance (on savings and loans)
- Budget scheme to assist members in managing their funds.

Short Questions

1. List the EU member states that are participating in the eurozone.
2. List the three original EU member states that have not joined the eurozone.
3. State four benefits of the euro to Ireland.
4. What is the role of the Central Bank in Ireland?
5. Outline the facilities offered by commercial banks to customers.
6. List and briefly distinguish the four facilities available on one 'basic card' issued by the banks.
7. List four services available through an ATM machine besides the withdrawal of money.
8. Outline the information required by the bank before a current account can be opened.
9. What is a cheque? Explain the three parties to a cheque.
10. What is the effect of crossing a cheque? Distinguish between the various types of crossing.
11. What does 'endorsing' a cheque mean?
12. Distinguish between a cheque and a bank draft.
13. List the checks carried out when accepting a personal cheque for payment.
14. Explain the following terms: open cheque, stale cheque, post-dated cheque.
15. Outline the procedure to follow when preparing money for lodgement.
16. Describe briefly four methods by which a lodgement can be made.
17. Explain the term EFT.
18. Distinguish between a standing order and a direct debit.
19. State four advantages of a standing order/direct debit.
20. Distinguish between a credit card and a debit card.
21. Outline the procedure to follow when accepting a debit card or a credit card for payment.
22. Convert:
    a)   €500 into US$ assuming a 'sell rate' of US$1.57
    b)   US$70 into euro assuming a 'buy rate' of €1.50.
23. Explain the procedure involved in purchasing and exchanging traveller's cheques.
24. Distinguish between telephone banking and Internet banking, outlining the services available.
25. Explain why the balance on a bank statement may not be the 'true balance'.
27. What documentation is necessary to carry out a bank reconciliation?
28. Outline four services other than loans offered by Credit Unions.

Chapter 4 — Legislation in the Workplace

Since joining the EU, Ireland has introduced new legislation that protects the rights of employers and employees at work and provides for a safe working environment. Workplace legislation discussed in this chapter includes laws governing terms and conditions of employment, employee health, safety and welfare and the protection of personal information maintained by a business.

Ireland has also developed a number of State agencies, such as the Labour Court, Labour Relations Commissions, Equality Officers, Employee Appeals Tribunal and the Rights Commissioners to facilitate and mediate disputes that arise between employers and employees. Typical cases brought to these agencies involve disputes over dismissals, discrimination, pay and working conditions.

Decisions from the above bodies are seldom legally binding. However, employers and employees attend these bodies with the intention of resolving disputes through independent facilitators and usually accept their recommendations. If both parties do not accept the recommendations made, the case can be taken to the civil courts.

Employment Legislation

Employment legislation covers Acts of law devised to ensure that employees receive a contract detailing the terms of their employment, regulations controlling working hours, wages/salaries, as well as legislation to provide redress in cases of discrimination, unfair dismissal or redundancy.

Terms of Employment (Information) Acts 1994–2001

The *Terms of Employment (Information) Acts 1994–2001* applies to all employees who are in continuous work for at least one month. An employee is entitled to a written statement of the terms and conditions of employment within 2 months of commencing work. This statement should include the following details:

- Name and address of employer and employee
- Title and description of job
- Date of commencement of job

◆ Place(s) of work of employee
◆ Nature and duration of contract – ie, full-time, part-time, contract
◆ Rates of pay
◆ Methods of payment and frequency of pay
◆ Conditions relating to holiday leave and sick leave
◆ Pension contributions and entitlements
◆ Period of notice required by employee and employer.

Other information such as grievance procedures, company rules and regulations, shift-work regulations and probationary periods are often included in this statement.

Minimum Notice and Terms of Employment Acts 1973–2001

These Acts entitle employees who are in employment for 13 continuous weeks to receive minimum notice of termination from their employer as outlined below:

Length of Service	Notice required
13 weeks–2 years	1 week
2–5 years	2 weeks
5–10 years	4 weeks
10–15 years	5 weeks
Greater than 15 years	8 weeks

Employers are entitled to receive at least one week's notice from an employee. The contract of employment may include a clause outlining the notice required to terminate the contract for both employers and employees. Both employers and employees can receive payment in lieu of notice.

The minimum notice required does not apply to cases where the termination was due to gross misconduct by the employee. An employee is deemed to commit an act of gross misconduct if while at work s/he is drunk, under the influence of drugs, assaults or bullies a person at work, is found stealing from work or is guilty of a serious breach of the business' rules and regulations. In such cases, the employer can dismiss the employee immediately without notice.

Protection of Employees (Part-time Work) Acts 2001–2007

These Acts stipulate that a part-time employee cannot be treated in a less favourable manner than a comparable full-time employee in relation to conditions of employment. All the employee protection legislation applies to a part-time employee in the same manner as it already applies to a full-time employee.

A part-time employee is an employee whose regular hours of work are fewer than the normal working hours of a full-time employee. A part-time employee must have 12 months' continuous service completed if bringing a case of Unfair Dismissal against their employer.

Protection of Employees (Fixed-term Work) Act 2003

This Act protects fixed-term contract employees who are entitled to the same benefits from legislation as full-time employees. Fixed-term contract employees should not be treated in a less favourable manner, in terms of conditions of employment, than comparable full-time employees. In addition, if an employee has been employed under a fixed-term contract that spans more than 4 years, and receives another contract of employment, that contract is deemed to be a 'contract of indefinite duration', ie, a permanent contract.

Employee (Provision of Information and Consultation) Act 2006

This Act applies to businesses with at least 50 employees. The Act stipulates that employers should put in place appropriate systems for information and consultation with employees before organisational and structural changes occur in the business that would affect the employees directly and would lead to substantial changes in work practices.

Redundancy Payments Acts 1967–2007

These Acts provide employees with statutory compensation payments in the event of dismissals due to redundancy. These payments are tax free. Employees from the age of 16 with a contract of employment and with at least 104 weeks of continuous service (ie, two years) are entitled to receive a lump sum based on length of service calculated as:

◆ (two weeks' gross pay, subject to a maximum of €600 per week) x (the number of years in continuous service) plus

◆ an additional one week's gross pay.

If an employee has worked more than an exact number of years, the excess days are credited as a proportion of a year. For example, John worked for ABC Ltd for 10 years and 73 days or 10.2 years (73 days / 365 days = 0.2). His weekly gross wage on redundancy was €350. His statutory entitlement is: [(2 weeks x €350) x 10.2 years + €350] = €7,490.

The employee is entitled to two weeks' notice, with time off during the notice period to look for other employment.

The *Protection of Employment Acts 1977–2007* requires the employer to consult with employee representatives (eg, trade unions) at least 30 days before the proposed redundancies take place. The consultation should include:

◆ other courses of action

◆ the reason(s) for the redundancy

◆ details of the number of redundancies to take place

◆ criteria for selection of employees put forward for redundancy
◆ the time period involved for the redundancies and
◆ the calculation of the redundancy payments.

The Protection of Employment Act 2007 (Exceptional Collective Redundancies and Related Matters) established a Redundancy Panel under the Department of Trade, Enterprise and Employment. The Redundancy Panel consists of a Chairman, appointed by the National Implementation Body (a body that oversees industrial stability), a member appointed by the Irish Congress of Trade Unions (ICTU) and a member appointed by the Irish Business Employers Confederation (IBEC).

The Redundancy Panel investigates cases of collective redundancy to ensure that employers engage in genuine redundancies and do not intend to hire new employees on a lower rate of pay and under less-favourable working conditions. If the redundancies are not genuine, the employer will not receive a rebate of his/her contributions made to the redundancy fund. In addition, the employees can take a case of unfair dismissal to the labour courts.

Employment Equality Acts, 1998–2007

These Acts incorporate the *Anti-Discrimination (Pay) Act 1974*, which entitles men and women to equal pay for equal work. The *Employment Equality Acts 1998–2007* state that:

◆ The employer must not discriminate against employees in relation to access to employment, conditions of employment, training, promotion and classification of positions.
◆ The employer must not discriminate against employees, in relation to age, sex, marital status, sexual orientation, religion, colour, disability, nationality, ethnic origin or membership of the Travelling Community.
◆ Conditions of work laid down by employers must be related to the job, be justifiable and not discriminatory.
◆ Employees should not be victimised for exercising their statutory rights, ie, taking a case of discrimination under these Acts.
◆ Sexual harassment cases can be brought under these Acts.

Organisation of Working Time Acts 1997–2001

These Acts regulate working times for employees with regard to hours worked per week, hours worked at night, rest periods and holidays. The act states the following:

◆ The maximum number of hours an employee should work per week is 48 hours, which can be averaged over a 4-, 6- or 12-month period. For example, a hotel employee on a 6-month contract from May to October works the following hours per week: 60 hours during June, July and August and 20 hours during the off-peak months of May, September and

October. Over the 6-month period (ie, 24 weeks) the employee worked 960 hours (12 weeks x 60 hours) + (12 weeks x 20 hours) which when averaged over 6 months (24 weeks) totals 40 hours of work per week, which complies with the legislation.

◆ Employees who work at night (from midnight to 7 am) should not be expected to work more than 8 hours in any 24-hour period.

◆ Employees are entitled to a 15-minute rest break when more than 4.5 hours have been worked, and 30 minutes when more than 6 hours have been worked. However, many industry sectors have reached agreement on rest periods with employee unions and the labour court in cases where the statutory rest periods have implications for their industry.

◆ Full-time employees are entitled to 20 days' paid holidays in a year (ie, one week's paid holiday is given for every 3 months worked). A qualifying month requires the employee to work at least 117 hours per month, or 1,365 hours over a 12-month period.

◆ Part-time employees (who work fewer than 117 hours per month or 1,365 hours per year) are entitled to paid holidays based on 8% of the hours worked.

◆ Holidays must be taken within a 12-month leave period or within 6 months of the following year. The timing of annual leave is determined by the employer, who should take due consideration of the employee's work and family commitments.

◆ Employees are entitled to 9 paid public holidays. If the employee agrees to work the public holiday, s/he should receive another day's leave or an additional day's pay.

Where an employee is requested to be available for work and is then not required to work, the employee should be paid for 25% of the time s/he was required to be available.

Under the Organisation of Working Time (Records, Prescribed Form and Exemptions) Regulations 2001, employers are obliged to keep records of the number of hours worked by employees and maintain detailed records of the type of leave granted to each employee (eg annual leave, parental leave, public holiday leave, etc.) and any payments made in respect of leave taken by employees.

Payment of Wages Act 1991

This Act gives employees the right to a written statement of gross wages and deductions (ie, a payslip) from their employer. It also protects against the employer making unauthorised deductions from an employee's wages. Under the Act, an employee may be paid in cash, cheque, bank draft, postal/money order, by credit transfer or any other method recommended by the Minister of Enterprise, Trade and Employment.

An employer is authorised to make statutory deductions from employee wages such as PAYE, and PRSI. The employer can make other deductions from employee wages upon written consent from the employee, for example, for trade union subscriptions, medical insurance contributions, contributions to the social club, etc. The employer may make other deductions from wages where authorised by the terms of the employee's contract, such as deductions to pay for any breakages or till shortages that may be specified in the contract of employment.

National Minimum Wage Act 2000

This Act sets minimum payment rates for all employees except apprentices, family members and the Defence Forces. From 1 July 2007, the current minimum wage is set at €8.65 per hour for experienced adult workers (ie, a person over 18 years with at least two years' experience).

An inexperienced adult is entitled to 80% of the minimum wage rate in the first year of employment (€6.92), rising to 90% in the second year of employment (€7.79), and should receive the full minimum wage rate in subsequent years. Employees between 16 and 18 years of age and who have at least 1 year's continuous employment are entitled to receive 70% of the minimum wage rate (€6.06).

Trainee employees who are embarking on an approved training or study programme of at least three months' duration that takes place during normal working hours will receive €6.49 per hour for the first third of the course, €6.92 for the second third of the course and €7.79 for the final third of the course.

Many industry sectors in Ireland have conditions of employment and minimum rates of pay agreed with Joint Labour Committees which are documented in Employment Regulation Orders (EROs). EROs would apply to sectors like contract cleaning, hairdressing, hotels and catering. Other industry sectors such as electrical contracting, construction and printing have established agreed Registered Employment Agreements. These rates of pay should not be lower than the minimum legal wage.

Unfair Dismissals Acts, 1977–2007

These Acts apply to employees over 16 years of age with at least one year's continuous service. An Unfair Dismissal case can be taken by an employee through the Rights Commissioners, the Employee Appeals Tribunal (EAT) or the courts. The onus is on the employer to prove that there were substantial grounds for the dismissal. The claim must be made by the employee within six months of dismissal by sending a claim form (available from the Department of Enterprise, Trade and Employment, www.gov.ie) to the relevant body, ie, the Rights Commissioner, etc. A copy must also be sent to the employer. An employee can be fairly dismissed if:

- the employee was not qualified or competent to do the job s/he was employed to do
- the conduct of the employee contravenes company rules or is a danger to others at work
- the dismissal was due to unavoidable redundancy.

The dismissal is seen as *unfair* if it is shown that the reason for the dismissal was due to:
- religious or political beliefs
- gender or racial bias
- involvement of the employee in trade union activities
- pregnancy
- sexual orientation
- age.

Remedies for unfair dismissal

If it is agreed that the employee has been unfairly dismissed, the employer must:
- reinstate the employee to the original job, or
- re-engage the employee to an alternative similar position, and/or
- arrange financial compensation for the employee.

Employee Welfare Legislation

Employee welfare legislation includes Acts of law that are devised to give rights to expectant mothers, to enable parents of children under eight years of age to take unpaid leave and to ensure that the working environment is a safe and healthy place to work.

Maternity Protection Acts 1994–2004

These Acts provide protection at work for pregnant women and for those who have recently given birth. The entitlements include:
- a minimum maternity leave of 26 consecutive weeks
- an option of an additional 16 weeks' unpaid leave
- time off from work for antenatal care, postnatal care and for breastfeeding, without loss of pay
- that the mother be reinstated to her original job if it is reasonable to do so. Her status and rights at work should not be affected by availing of maternity leave.

Maternity leave can be postponed in the event of the newborn child requiring hospitalisation after birth.

Employers are not obliged to pay employees on maternity leave, unless paid maternity benefit is part of the terms and conditions of employment.

However, the employee may be entitled to receive maternity benefit from the Department of Social and Family Affairs.

The employee must:
◆ notify her employer in writing of her intention to take maternity leave at least four weeks before the maternity leave begins
◆ present a medical certificate indicating the expected week of birth
◆ take at least two weeks of the maternity leave before the birth and 4 weeks after the birth of the child.

Should the nature of the job or working environment affect the health of the expectant mother, she is entitled to take 'health-and-safety leave' during pregnancy. This leave is in lieu of maternity leave and can be taken from the beginning of pregnancy to 26 weeks after the birth.

If the mother becomes ill during her additional unpaid maternity leave, she can transfer the unpaid leave to sick leave with the agreement of the employer. In this case, the mother forfeits any additional unpaid maternity leave not taken.

The father of the child is also entitled to time off work without loss of pay to attend antenatal classes and to be present for the birth of the child.

Parental Leave Acts 1998–2006

These Acts entitle both parents to take unpaid leave of 14 weeks per child up to the age of eight, or where the child has a disability, up to the age of 16. In the case where a child is adopted between the ages of six and eight, parental leave may be taken up to two years from the date of the adoption order.

Parents generally must have at least one year's continuous employment to be eligible to take parental leave. However, the Parental Leave Amendment Act 2006 allows for parents who have completed three months' continuous employment to take one week of parental leave for every one month of work completed.

Parental Leave cannot generally be transferred between parents, unless both parents have the same employer and this is agreed.

Parental leave is restricted to 14 weeks' unpaid leave in a 12-month period, except in the case of multiple births. The leave should be taken as 14 consecutive weeks or as two separate blocks of at least six weeks each, with at least a 10-week gap between each block. In practice, parental leave can be negotiated with the employer to suit both parent and the workplace.

If a parent becomes ill while taking parental leave, s/he can revert to sick leave, which is generally paid leave. The remainder of the parental leave is suspended until after the sick leave period is finished.

Force Majeure leave (emergency leave) is also provided for in these Acts. Employees are entitled to paid leave for a period of three days in a 12-month period, or up to a maximum of 5 days in a 36-month period in case of injury or illness of an immediate family member.

Employees are also entitled to paid leave from work if they are summonsed by the Courts to perform Jury Service. (Juries Act 1976)

Safety, Health and Welfare at Work Act 1989–2007

These Acts place general duties and responsibilities on employers and employees to prevent accidents and to increase the safety levels at work. Manufacturers, designers and suppliers of materials also have a duty to ensure that the goods and materials produced will not adversely affect the welfare of others.

The Health and Safety Authority (HSA) was established under the 1989 Act and is responsible for enforcing the legislation, devising codes of practice and industry regulations, providing guidelines for safety statements and advising businesses on safety and welfare matters.

Employers have a duty to:

◆ provide and maintain a safe place of work with safe access to and egress from the building
◆ provide and maintain safe machinery
◆ prevent and/or reduce risks by implementing, providing and maintaining safe systems of work
◆ employ competent employees
◆ provide information, training and supervision to ensure that safety standards are met
◆ provide and implement a *safety statement*, outlining safety procedures and emergency plans
◆ provide welfare facilities.

Employees have a duty:

◆ to take reasonable care to perform tasks safely so that the health, safety and welfare of others are not affected
◆ to cooperate with employers in matters of safety by following procedures and using any protective clothing and safety guards provided
◆ to report unsafe conditions/practices to a supervisor or the Safety Representative
◆ not to interfere with, misuse or damage anything in the workplace that could endanger others
◆ not to engage in improper conduct that could endanger themselves or others at work
◆ not to be under the influence of alcohol or drugs, and to undergo testing for intoxicants if requested by an employer.

Safety Representative

Every business should have at least one employee safety representative who will negotiate with management on behalf of employees on safety and welfare issues and to ensure that safety measures are being adhered to. S/he can inspect the workplace to identify unsafe conditions/practices and can make oral or written submissions to management. The safety representative can also investigate accidents and can accompany the HSA inspector on an inspection tour of the premises. Management must provide the safety representative(s) with information and training to enable them to carry out their duties effectively.

The Safety Statement

The Safety Statement is management's written commitment to safety. Every business must have a safety statement that specifies how health and safety will be provided and implemented. Safety statements are normally prepared by a consultant, in conjunction with employers and Safety Representatives. The employer is primarily responsible in ensuring that the safety statement is implemented. The Safety Statement should be reviewed annually.

A *risk assessment* should be carried out in the preparation of the Safety Statement in order to identify and assess the risk of potential hazards in the workplace. This involves examining the structure and layout of the building, equipment, work practices and other physical elements, such as noise, dust, light and heat levels, that may have a negative impact on the health and welfare of employees. Common causes of accidents in the workplace include poor storage of materials, slippery floors, faulty/loose electric cables, frayed carpets and cluttered work areas.

The Safety Statement should specify:
◆ the hazards identified and the levels of safety required
◆ resources necessary to implement and maintain safety standards
◆ precautions that should be taken to prevent accidents
◆ the level of cooperation expected of employees in maintaining safety
◆ names, departments and responsibilities of elected safety representatives
◆ procedures for consultations between employer and employees
◆ reporting procedures for accidents

All incidents at work resulting in minor injuries should be reported internally. Accidents that result in more than three days' absence from work must be reported to the HSA.

Organisations with three or fewer employees can fulfil their Safety Statement obligations by adopting a Code of Practice designed by the HSA advisory body for that industry.

Data Protection Legislation

The Data Protection Act (DPA) 1988–2003

The *Data Protection Act (DPA) 1988–2003* applies to organisations that maintain information on individuals, in manual or electronic format. For example, a personnel file contains information on the employee's contract of employment, salary details and pension contributions, etc. The file may also hold sensitive information regarding the employee, such as health, family circumstances, disciplinary details, etc. Breaches of the Data Protection Act can result in a fine or a conviction.

The DPA Acts regulate the collection, processing, storage and disclosure of personal information through:

1. *A Data Protection Commissioner,* who enforces the legislation, investigates complaints, develops codes of practice for information-sensitive industries and maintains a register of *Data Controllers*, ie, the organisations or individual that controls the contents and use of personal data.

2. *The Data Controller,* who must ensure that data is:
   - obtained lawfully, ie, the individual should be aware of why the data is being collected, where it will be stored and for what purpose it will be used
   - used for the purpose for which is was collected
   - not used or disclosed for any unspecified or unlawful purposes
   - kept safe and secure to prevent unauthorised access or alteration
   - as accurate and as up to date as possible
   - complete, relevant and not excessive
   - not stored longer than is necessary.

   The Data Controller may be instructed by the Gardaí or a Government Minister to disclose personal information relating to an individual, where the information is required to investigate tax or criminal cases to prevent injury, serious loss or damage to others.

3. *Giving rights to the Data Subject:* ie, the person affected by the information. The Data Subject:
   - can request a copy of the information held and must receive that information within 40 days, unless the Government instructs the Data Controller to withhold the information
   - has the right to rectify any incorrect information.

Freedom of Information Acts (FOI) 1997–2003

The Freedom of Information Acts 1997–2003 place an obligation on public bodies (ie, public authorities and government departments) to publish information on their activities and to make an individual's personal information available upon request by that individual.

Every public body is obliged to produce a Freedom of Information Manual that outlines general duties and services provided by the body, a description of the records held and how members of the public can access these files if required.

Under the Acts, an individual has a legal right to:

◆ access information kept by public bodies and government departments
◆ have official information relating to him/herself amended where it is incomplete, incorrect or misleading
◆ obtain reasons for decisions relating to him/herself. For example, in the case of an individual not being successful at a job interview with a public body, the individual can obtain the results of his/her interview.

An application for information must be made in writing to the public body and the request must refer to the FOI Acts. The request should be as specific as possible, to allow the Information Officer of the public body to search for the information required. A request for information should be responded to within 4 weeks or the request is deemed to be refused. The individual can then appeal the refusal to a senior staff member in the public body and, if still not satisfied, can appeal to the Office of the Information Commissioner, which was set up under the FOI acts to investigate complaints and to carry out independent reviews on public bodies that do not comply with FOI legislation.

Short Questions

1. List four agencies available in Ireland that mediate over employment disputes in the workplace.
2. List six details that should be included in an employee's terms of employment.
3. List four conditions that are covered under the *Employment Equality Acts 1998–2007.*
4. State the entitlements of employees under the *Organisation of Working Time Acts 1997–2001* in relation to rest periods, holidays, total hours worked and night-time work.
5. What is the national minimum rate per hour for a 19-year-old with one year's experience?
6. Under the *Unfair Dismissals Acts 1977–2007,* state three cases in which a dismissal is regarded as fair and three cases where a dismissal is regarded as unfair.
7. What should:
   a) an employee do, if s/he has been unfairly dismissed?

    b)   an employer do, if it is found that the employee had been unfairly dismissed?

8. Explain the term 'gross misconduct' and outline two incidents in which gross misconduct may lead to an instant dismissal.

9. John started work at 16 years of age and has worked with the same company for 26 years. His gross weekly wage at the time the company closed down was €650. Calculate the statutory redundancy payment to which he is entitled.

10. Explain and give two examples of statutory and non-statutory deductions that may be taken from an employee's wages.

11. Under the *Maternity Protection Acts, 1994–2004*, state:
    a)   three rights of the expectant mother
    b)   three duties of the expectant mother.

12. What does the term '*force majeure*' mean?

13. State two entitlements that are covered under the *Parental Leave Acts 1998–2006*.

14. State four duties of employers and four duties of employees under the *Safety, Health and Welfare at Work Acts, 1989–2007*.

15. Explain the function of the HSA under the *Safety, Health and Welfare at Work Acts 1989–2007*.

16. What is a 'risk assessment'?

17. What is a 'safety statement'? State four points that a safety statement should specify.

18. Outline the role of the Safety Inspector and the Safety Representative under the *Safety, Health and Welfare at Work Acts, 1989–2007*.

19. State four duties of the Data Protection Commissioner under the *Data Protection Acts, 1988–2003*.

20. State four obligations imposed on the Data Controller under the *Data Protection Acts, 1988–2003*.

21. State two rights given to individuals under the *Data Protection Acts, 1988–2003*.

22. Explain the obligations placed on public bodies under the *Freedom of Information Acts, 1997–2003*.

Summary

A legally formed business may operate as a sole trader, partnership, company and co-operative or may be part of a franchise agreement. Each business form is specific in terms of set-up, control, ownership and the liability of the members.

    Every business needs money to start and grow the business. Business funds can be obtained through a variety of means, such as private funds, loans from financial institutions, investment by shareholders or venture capitalists, government support etc. The amount of funds required will be determined by the activity level of the business.

As the business grows it is generally necessary to divide the business activities according to business function, such as marketing, finance, human resources and production. *Marketing* is generally responsible for sales, market research and product promotion. *Finance* is responsible for preparing accounts and budgets, accounts payable, accounts receivable and cost control. *Human Resources* is responsible for manpower planning (ie, recruitment, selection and training), employee welfare and industrial relations. *Production* is responsible for producing the product to suit the market. However, as a business grows it may be necessary to reorganise the business activities according to product, geographic location or a combination of both. An *organisation chart* depicts the structure of a business by outlining the business functions and formal lines of communication.

Regardless of how the business functions are organised, an administration centre or office is central to the business's daily activities. The office is often the first point of contact with customers and is the central point for collecting, processing, recording, storing and communicating information. Once the location of the office is decided upon, the Office Manager must decide whether some office activities will be centralised, or whether it will be necessary to duplicate services within various departments.

The office manager must also plan the physical layout of the office space. Generally an *open-plan* office is preferred as an office layout, as it utilises space efficiently and facilitates the sharing of resources and equipment. Some offices adopt a landscaped approach in which furniture and partitions can be arranged to provide an element of privacy.

When the office design is completed, the office(s) must then be equipped as appropriate to the services provided. Office equipment such as workstations, photocopiers, scanners, telephones, desktop equipment, stationery items, filing cabinets, fax machines, binders, laminators, etc., may be shared among office staff, therefore the layout of the workstations and the location of the office equipment must be planned carefully to allow an efficient flow of work.

The administrators in the office may be required to perform routine banking activities on behalf of the business, and therefore must be familiar with banking services such as current accounts, electronic funds transfer, credit card and debit card facilities and foreign exchange. Traditionally businesses settle their accounts by cheque and while this is a safe and trusted method of paying bills (especially when the cheques are crossed), it does take time to prepare and process the payment. Modern banking facilities such as electronic funds transfer (EFT), telephone and Internet banking enable the business to pay its bills directly to the creditors' accounts, ensuring bills are paid on time with minimum effort. Using Internet banking the administrator can track the business transactions at any time, day or night and s/he is therefore aware of the business's cash flow at all times. Irish businesses trading with countries in the eurozone can trade more easily without experiencing fluctuations in foreign exchange rates.

As with every element of the business, within the office environment, workplace legislation plays an important role for both the business and the employees. Every business must be aware of current legislation regarding conditions of employment, health, safety and welfare of employees at work. Agencies such as the Rights Commissioners, Equality Officers and the Labour Court help to resolve disputes between employer and employees. While the majority of decisions of these agencies are not legally binding, both parties approach these bodies in the hope of resolving the issue without going to court. Disputes generally involve terms and conditions of work, pay issues, unfair dismissals and equality issues. Much of the current legislation (ie, Acts relating to Unfair Dismissals; Terms of Employment; Data Protection; Health, Safety and Welfare; Parental Leave) is a result of directives issued by the EU and reflects the changing work patterns in Ireland today.

Assignments

1. Using information from a local small/medium business (fewer than 50 employees) draw up an organisation chart showing the departments and key positions in the business. Write a brief description of the activities carried out in each department.
2. John and Joe are setting up a new recruitment business but are undecided as to whether to set up the business as a partnership, a private company or as a franchise. Write a report explaining the advantages and disadvantages of each and recommend one form, justifying your choice. Outline the necessary steps involved in setting up your chosen form of business.
3. The Marketing team is launching a new detergent. What promotion techniques would you recommend to the Marketing Manager and why? Remember, this product must be differentiated from similar products on the market.
4. Assume that an organisation is divided into four departments – production, finance, sales/marketing and human resources. Write a one-paragraph summary on each department, detailing the types of activity that would be handled by each of the four departments.
5. The Office Manager in a Travel Agent has been informed that the office is being relocated to a bigger site. S/he has asked the office staff for

suggestions to design the best layout. Write a report to the Office Manager outlining how the office should be designed. State whatever assumptions you wish regarding the building structure. Include drawings of the new office, indicating workstations, equipment, doorways, etc.

6. You have been asked to purchase a new photocopier for the office that is capable of handling complex jobs and a large workload. Research three different models that meet these specifications. In your report, document the features of each model and highlight the differences between the models. Recommend one photocopier, stating why you think it is most suitable for the office requirements.

7. There are various types of credit card on the market at present. Compare and contrast three credit cards in terms of annual cost, interest rates, credit periods, bonuses such as travel insurance, etc.

8. In your business, bills such as telephone and ESB are paid by cheque and are often overdue. Suggest three alternative methods of payment that your business could use to ensure that these bills are paid on time.

9. Compare the Internet banking services of the Irish commercial banks. Which bank offers the most suitable services and rates for you?

10. Locate your local Credit Union branch and compare the interest you would receive on savings of €2,500 over a five-year period from the Credit Union and two of the major Irish commercial banks.

11. What currency is used in the following countries? Using the current rate of exchange, calculate how much €500 is worth in:
    a) Bulgaria
    b) Saudi Arabia
    c) South Africa
    d) the US.

12. The *Safety, Health and Welfare Acts, 1989–2007* have made people more aware of safety levels at work. Look around your classroom (or your home) and identify five potential hazards; assess the risk level of injury (high, medium or low), and recommend how you could make that environment safer.

13. Examine the various state agencies and chart the different options an employee has if they wish to take a case for unfair dismissal against their employer.

14. Explain the implications of the *Data Protection Acts, 1988–2003,* for the Human Resources department of a business.

Unit 2 —
Office Duties

Introduction

Unit 2 provides an overview of the typical office duties carried out by the receptionist and office administrators. It examines the procedures and documentation involved in a business transaction (ie, the buying and selling of goods/services), and it concludes with an overview of the types of formal meetings that an administrator typically must convene on behalf of the business. Unit 2 is divided into four chapters:

Chapter 5 — Receptionist Duties

Reviews typical receptionist duties and examines procedures for dealing with visitors and operating the switchboard:
- Maintaining the Reception Area
- Receiving Visitors
- Dealing with Complaints
- The Switchboard and Features
- Operating the Switchboard
- Voicemail Answering Facility
- Telephone Charges
- Making National and International Calls

Chapter 6 — Administration and Accounting Duties

Discusses the typical administrative and accounting duties. It provides guidelines on how work can be planned and organised to ensure its completion in time for deadlines. Guidelines on how to deal with petty cash and the preparation of wages are also provided. Topics include:
- Planning and Organising Work
- Arranging Appointments
- Arranging Travel
- Preparing for Meetings and Conferences
- Accounting Activities
- Wages and Salaries

Chapter 7 — Business Transactions

Examines the documentation involved in a business transaction, from the initial enquiry to the final payment for the goods/services. Stock control is also examined, ensuring that every item of stock moving to and from the warehouse is accounted for. Topics include:

◆ Stages of a Business Transaction
◆ Procedure for Dealing with Incoming Orders (Supplier)
◆ Procedure for Dealing with Incoming Goods (Purchaser)
◆ Statement of Accounts
◆ Overview of Stages in Business Transactions
◆ Stock Control

Chapter 8 — Meetings

Discusses formal meetings in a company and the duties of the secretary and chairman in relation to the preparation and conduct of the meeting. Topics include:

◆ Types of Formal Meeting
◆ Convening Company Meetings
◆ Documentation for Meetings
◆ Duties of the Chairman and Secretary

Chapter 5 — Receptionist Duties

Large businesses will employ a receptionist to operate the switchboard and receive visitors. As the receptionist is often the first point of contact with the business, a smart personal appearance and good interpersonal and communication skills are essential.

The main duties of the receptionist are as follows:

◆ Maintaining the reception area
◆ Receiving visitors
◆ Dealing with complaints
◆ Operating the switchboard.

However, the receptionist is often required to assist with other routine administrative tasks such as:

◆ Accepting incoming deliveries from couriers
◆ Distributing correspondence
◆ Dispatching outgoing deliveries to couriers
◆ Posting general notices (on electronic or manual noticeboards)
◆ Filing
◆ Booking meeting rooms
◆ Photocopying, faxing or scanning documents.

Maintaining the Reception Area

The reception desk should ideally be placed facing the door, so that visitors are seen when entering the building. However, the reception desk should be some distance away from the waiting area, so that work can continue while visitors are waiting, but the receptionist should be able to view visitors at all times. The reception desk should not be left unattended.

The reception area should be kept neat and tidy and should have a no-smoking policy in keeping with legislation. Comfortable seating should be provided for the visitor, with reading material available. If it is policy to offer refreshments, these should be kept close at hand. The receptionist should have easy access to the following:

◆ telephone message pad
◆ appointments book

- diary
- visitor log book and visitor badges
- telephone and fax directories, internal telephone lists and emergency numbers (eg, doctor, guards, fire brigade, etc.)
- stationery
- calendar
- first-aid kit.

Today, a customised computer package designed for specific business requirements is generally used to maintain a diary, manage appointments and record telephone messages that can be distributed by email to the appropriate person.

Receiving Visitors

As the receptionist is the first point of contact with the business, it is his/her duty to welcome and screen visitors. The receptionist should always be pleasant but not too familiar with visitors, and should greet the expected visitor formally: eg, 'Good morning, how may I help you?'

If the receptionist is busy with a telephone call or another visitor, s/he should acknowledge any visitor approaching the desk and invite them to take a seat while they are waiting.

The following procedure may be used when dealing with expected visitors:

- Greet visitor pleasantly and check their name, the business they represent and whom they wish to see, with the details recorded in the appointments diary.
- Request that the visitor sign the visitor log book both on entering and exiting the building. (This is a security precaution in case of an emergency, so that the receptionist will have a record of who is in the building.)

Power Ltd, Main Street, Wexford						
Name	Company	Date of arrival	Time of arrival	Referred to	Signed	Time of departure
G Larkin	Glen Ltd	June 10	1000 hrs	L Kiernan	K Shea	1200 hrs
L Flynn	Carbury Products	June 10	1500 hrs	A O'Connor	K Shea	1510 hrs
G Deegan	ACT Ltd	June 12	1550 hrs	V Shanahan	K Shea	1640 hrs

Visitor log book

◆ Distribute a visitor badge, if policy. This may be necessary to allow the visitor access to restricted areas. The badge should be returned to reception on departure.

◆ Inform the person concerned by telephone that the visitor has arrived.

◆ Depending on the business's policy, direct the visitor to the appropriate office or call an office junior to accompany the visitor to the desired location.

Even though appointments are made in advance, emergency situations may occur that cause delays or even prevent the appointment from taking place. The receptionist should be discreet when dealing with this kind of situation. The receptionist should:

◆ apologise for the delay and inform the visitor of the approximate waiting time

◆ offer to reschedule the appointment, if the visitor is unable to wait or the appointment cannot be met

◆ if the visitor decides to wait, offer some reading material and refreshments if appropriate.

Often the receptionist will encounter visitors who do not have an appointment. These visitors may be:

◆ important clients who happen to be in the area

◆ sales representatives 'cold calling' in the hope of obtaining new business

◆ a customer with an urgent message or problem

◆ a personal emergency.

Whatever the reason for the visit, the receptionist must use his/her initiative and assess the urgency of the caller. In an emergency situation, inform the person concerned of the visitor's arrival immediately. In other situations, it may not be possible to meet unexpected visitors. The experienced receptionist will judge whether or not s/he can deal with the visitor's business. The receptionist should be polite at all times and should:

◆ greet the visitor and obtain his/her name, name of organisation and reason for his/her visit

◆ if s/he cannot deal with the enquiry, invite the visitor to sit in the waiting area, while s/he checks to see if the person requested is free to meet the visitor

◆ if the person required is unavailable to meet the visitor, suggest another appropriate person, or arrange another suitable time, and distribute the message to the appropriate person.

Dealing with Complaints

The receptionist will often have to deal with complaints. In situations like this, the receptionist must retain his/her composure and be polite at all times. Even though the nature of the complaint will differ from business to business, a general procedure to deal with complaints is to:

◆ listen attentively to the complainant and avoid unnecessary interruptions
◆ record details of the complaint carefully
◆ neither agree nor disagree with the complaint
◆ offer assistance or refer the problem.

The receptionist should keep the caller informed on progress, as appropriate.

The Switchboard and Features

The telephone is perhaps the most important means of communication for a business. A business will operate a switchboard to cater for the volume of calls and to enable calls to be transferred to the appropriate person.

A switchboard is a private local exchange used in businesses that have large volumes of incoming and outgoing calls. The switchboard is connected to the public telephone network and is used to direct incoming calls to the appropriate person's telephone extension. As the telephone extensions are not connected *directly* to the public telephone network, the switchboard reduces the number of telephone lines required in a business, thus making it possible for a telephone to be on everybody's desk.

The switchboard allows a number of incoming calls to be received at the same time and permits telephone extensions to make outgoing calls if a line is free. Extension users make external calls by dialling a single-digit code or pressing a line number that is free.

If a switchboard receives a high volume of incoming queries, Interactive Voice Response (IVR) technology may be installed. IVR technology recognises keypad and/or voice input from the caller and directs calls to the required department without the call being answered by the switchboard operator. For example, the caller may be required to 'press 1 for sales, press 2 for accounts,' etc., or the caller may be required to answer 'yes' or 'no' to a list of questions. IVR reduces the number of incoming calls handled by the switchboard operator.

A switchboard can also be linked to cordless telephone extensions, allowing calls to be made and received as long as the user stays within the coverage area of the switchboard. Cordless telephones are particularly useful where employee mobility is important, such as in hospitals, large factories, building sites, garages, airports and large stores.

An alternative to making telephone calls using the standard telephone network is Voice over Internet Protocol (VoIP), where telephone calls can be made over the Internet using a computer and software provided by a VoIP provider such as Skype. Costs of long-distance calls are significantly cheaper and many private individuals and businesses already use VoIP providers to make and receive long-distance calls. A business communication system should not rely totally on an Internet connection, VoIP systems will not replace the standard telephone network.

Features of a Switchboard

All the features and facilities of a switchboard are under software control and can be easily customised. Switchboards vary in their degree of sophistication, but will include some or all of the following features:

Hold and transfer: Calls are received through the switchboard and are routed to the appropriate telephone extension. The receptionist puts an incoming caller on hold and dials the appropriate telephone extension number to transfer the call. Sometimes, music is played to the caller while they are on hold. The person at the telephone extension can also transfer the incoming call directly to another extension if appropriate.

Direct dial in (DDI): A facility that allocates DDI numbers for each telephone extension, allowing a caller to dial directly to an extension without going through the switchboard, thus reducing the pressure on the switchboard. If the person is unavailable, voicemail is activated.

Voicemail: A facility that sets up an answering machine for each extension user. Using special software, extension users are given their own personal answering machine called a 'mailbox', where messages can be stored.

LCD (liquid crystal display): A panel on the telephone which displays the number dialled and the duration of the call.

Call status display: Coloured lights are displayed to indicate whether the calls are internal or external, transferred, picked up or forwarded.

Hands-free operation: Calls can be made without lifting the handset. The conversation is carried out via a built-in microphone and loudspeaker. A useful feature if information needs to be checked while on the telephone or if more than one person needs to hear the conversation.

Memory recall: Also known as 'last number redial'. By pressing a special key the *most recently* dialled number is dialled again. A useful feature when the number dialled is engaged.

Speed dialling: The switchboard can be programmed to store frequently used telephone numbers alphabetically by surname, business name, etc. The assigned name is then selected rather than dialling the telephone number.

Clear last digit: A function to erase a misdialled digit while entering a telephone number.

Call forwarding: Also known as 'follow me'. A diversion facility which diverts all incoming calls to another telephone number (internal or external, such as a mobile or home number). This facility could be used in the evening, when the switchboard operator is off duty.

Call waiting: A facility which alerts a person on the telephone to the presence of another incoming call. S/he can then put the call on hold, deal with the incoming call and return to the original call on hold.

Call barring: Telephone extensions can be prevented from making specific calls such as national, international or mobile calls.

Call logging: A metering facility to record the origin of incoming calls and the destination and duration of outgoing calls by extension number.

Call pickup: Allows someone at a telephone extension to answer a call ringing on another telephone extension. This is useful if the person requested is not at their desk and the call can be dealt with by someone else in the office.

Camp on busy: Allows automatic redial of an engaged telephone extension. This saves time trying to contact individuals and avoids the pitfall of forgetting to redial. When an extension number is engaged, the caller enters a code. When the extension becomes free, the caller's telephone will

Detailed switchboard

automatically ring. When the caller lifts the receiver, the extension number dialled previously is redialled automatically and the call can be completed.

Conferencing: A number of telephone extensions and, if required, a number of exchange lines can be connected. This allows more than two people to be involved in a conversation.

Uniform call distribution: Allows incoming calls to listed telephone numbers to be distributed evenly over a given number of lines. Useful for distributing calls to a 'helpline' or 'call centre'.

Operating the Switchboard

When dealing with enquiries over the telephone, the receptionist must always be pleasant, friendly and efficient and must speak clearly.

Handling Incoming Calls

- ◆ Keep a pen and telephone message pad close at hand by the telephone.
- ◆ Answer the telephone as soon as possible (eg, on the second ring).
- ◆ Greet the caller pleasantly and identify the business by name and state who is taking the call, eg, 'Good morning, Power Products Ltd, Lisa speaking.'
- ◆ Obtain the caller's name, business name and to whom they wish to speak. Sometimes the receptionist will make further enquiries as to the nature of the call, as s/he may be able to deal with the issue him/herself.
- ◆ Ask the caller to 'hold' while you connect them to the appropriate person.
- ◆ Dial that person's extension number and inform him/her of the caller's name, business name, nature of the call and the telephone line number.
- ◆ If the call cannot be taken, return to the caller and inform him/her that the person is unavailable at present and offer to take a message or to leave a 'voicemail'.
- ◆ If the person concerned is on another telephone call (as seen from the 'call status' feature), the receptionist should ask the caller if they wish to 'hold'. The call can then be put through when that line is free. The 'call waiting' facility could also be used to alert the person on the telephone call that another caller is waiting.
- ◆ If the caller is waiting longer than expected, the receptionist should return to the caller and offer to take a message.
- ◆ When taking a message, record the caller's name, organisation, telephone number, date and time of call and details of the message. Repeat essential details to the caller, such as telephone numbers and dates, to ensure accuracy.
- ◆ Distribute the message to the person concerned as soon as possible.

On-line telephone message pads can be set up to facilitate sending the message by email to the recipient.

Telephone Message Pad

For: _____

From: _____   Tel No: _____

Returned call: ☐   Will call again: ☐   Please call back: ☐

Message: _____

_____

Taken by: _____   Date: _____   Time:_____

Example 1

Receptionist: Good morning, Print Technology Ltd, Lisa speaking.

Caller: Hi, I want to speak to Mr Walsh please.

Receptionist: Who shall I say is calling?

Caller: Barry O'Brien.

Receptionist: Barry O'Brien — from?

Caller: From Highway Wholesalers.

Receptionist: (Checks the switchboard and sees that Mr Walsh is on another call.) I'm sorry, but Mr Walsh is on another call. May I help you?

Caller: I'm ringing in connection with my account from last month.

Receptionist: Ms Ryan also deals with accounts; would you like to speak to her?

Caller: Yes, thank you, I need to get this problem sorted out immediately.
(The receptionist should inform Ms Ryan of the caller's name, business name and nature of his query.)

Receptionist: I'm putting you through to Ms Ryan now.

Example 2

Receptionist: Good morning, Fitzgerald Insurances – Margaret speaking.

Caller: Hi, I wish to speak with Mary Drohan, please.

Receptionist: Who shall I say is calling?

Caller: This is Mrs Cooney.
(The receptionist checks to see if the person required is available and returns to the caller.)

Receptionist: I'm sorry, Mrs Cooney, but Mary is with a client. Can I take a message?

Caller: Yes, I'm calling to see if my motor policy is ready yet.

Receptionist: I believe that that policy is ready, but may I take your telephone number, and Mary will call you back when she is free?

Caller: OK, the number is 7635475 and I'll be here for another 20 minutes.

Receptionist: That is (writing down) Mrs Cooney at 7635475. I'll give Mary the message and if she can't contact you this evening she will telephone you tomorrow morning.

Caller: Thank you.

Note in this example, the name and telephone number of the caller are repeated to ensure that the receptionist heard the details correctly.

Voicemail Answering Facility

Voicemail is a telephone answering facility which allows telephone messages to be received when there is no one available to answer the telephone. Voicemail has largely replaced the traditional answering machine, (ie, with which messages are recorded on a tape). Voicemail is based on digital technology and is built into the telephone system. Employees are assigned their own private 'mailbox' on their extension phone where telephone messages are recorded. In general, voicemail operates as follows:

1. When an incoming call is received, the telephone switches automatically to voicemail after a certain number of rings.
2. A recorded greeting message is played inviting the caller to leave a message after the tone.
3. The caller states his/her message, which is recorded.
4. Messages can be played back from that telephone using a PIN number or messages can be accessed from a remote location by dialling the telephone number followed by the PIN number.

Advantages and Disadvantages of Voicemail

Advantages	Disadvantages
1. Messages can be received when there is no one in the office.	1. Voicemail is impersonal; people do not like talking to machines.
2. Messages can be picked up remotely.	2. The person leaving a message may forget to state their name and telephone numbers making the message redundant.
3. Forward contact numbers can be left.	
4. Calls can be screened. The receiver can cut in on urgent calls.	

Recording an Outgoing Message

1. Write down your message in advance, keeping it short.
2. Record the message in a quiet area; speak slowly and articulate each word.
3. The message should do the following:
    ◆ Greet the caller and state the name of the business.
    ◆ Apologise that there is nobody available to take the call.
    ◆ Ask the caller to leave their name, number and message after the 'tone'.
4. Play back the message to ensure that it is audible. If not, delete it and repeat the process.

Example 1 — Message Recorded

O'Flynn, Solicitors. We apologise there is no one available to take your call. Please leave your name, number and message after the tone and we will contact you as soon as possible.

Example 2 — Message Recorded

Hello, High Flyers Ltd. We regret that our office is closed. Opening hours are 9am to 1pm weekdays. Please leave your name, number and message after the tone.

In the above message, the opening hours of the business are stated. This is not usually required, but as the opening hours are not standard, it does provide the caller with useful information. 'Hello' is used as the greeting, as it is suitable for all times of the day.

Leaving a Message

1. Speak slowly and clearly, giving the following details:
   ◆ state whom the message is for
   ◆ give your name, business name and telephone number.
     (It is not necessary to state the date and time of the call, as this is automatically recorded on a voicemail facility.)
2. If the message is short, state your message. Spell out any words or figures that may be confusing. For example, the number '15' could sound like '50' and some foreign names are difficult to comprehend.
3. Do not leave a message if it is long, complex or confidential; just ask to be called back at a specific telephone number.

Example 1 — Leaving a Message

Good morning, this is Michael Carty from Shape-Up. Message is for Harry Smith, Sales Department. Please add two more boxes of All-Green Shampoo to my order. If you need further details, contact me at 234987 up to 6.00 pm. Thank you.

Here the caller leaves a message. This is very efficient as the receiver can act on the information and may not need to contact the caller again, saving time and money.

Example 2 — Leaving a Message

Good afternoon, this is Joe. Message is for Nora Shannon, Public Relations. Please call me at your earliest convenience.

In the above message, the caller's full name, business name and number were not given. This is acceptable if the receiver knows the caller very well. The caller does not state a message, maybe because it is too complex, private or the receiver is familiar with the issue from an earlier conversation.

If the receptionist receives general messages on his/her voicemail facility, the details should be saved and distributed as appropriate. Some voicemail systems facilitate the distribution of voicemail messages through email.

Telephone Charges

Since the deregulation of the telecommunications industry, Eircom no longer has a monopoly on providing fixed-line telephone calls. The telephone line, however, is still rented from Eircom by the other telephone providers. A list of authorised telephone providers is available from the Communications Regulations website at www.askcomreg.ie.

Most telephone service providers offer a *call bundle* for a monthly fee to suit the usage pattern of an individual or business that covers line rental and a certain number of free minutes of calls at certain times. All providers charge for calls not included in the *call bundle* at different rates during peak times (ie, day) and off-peak times (ie, evening and weekends). The charge for local, national, international and mobile calls can vary significantly between telephone service providers. Therefore, in selecting a telephone service provider and a call bundle, the following details should be considered over a few billing periods:

- ◆ *type of calls* commonly made: ie, local, national, international or mobile
- ◆ *time calls* are mostly made: ie, day, evening or weekends
- ◆ *number of minutes* used per month on local, national, mobile and international calls

This information is summarised on the telephone bill received from the telephone provider. With this information, the user can complete a questionnaire on the Communications Regulations website at www.callcosts.ie. Once submitted, the questionnaire returns a list of the telephone providers which best meet the needs of the individual or business.

A simple comparison of telephone charges from fixed lines based on two telephone call providers, Eircom using their call bundle Talktime 200 and BT Ireland using their call bundle BT Talk is given overleaf.

Eircom* –
Call rates from *fixed line* based on Talktime 200 bundle

Terms:
Bundle €33.99 which includes line rental at €25.47 per month
Call set-up fee/Minimum charge: 5.95c per call
200 minutes per month applies to local and national land-line calls at any time
Calls outside the 200 minutes, international and mobile calls are charged as detailed below:

Times	Local	National	International** UK, USA & Canada	Mobile Varies depending on operator
Peak Mon–Fri : 8am–6pm	5.19c	8.06c	10c	from 27.84c to 20c
Off Peak 1 Mon–Fri : 6pm–8am	1.33c	5.18c	10c	from 19.84c to 14.20c
Off Peak 2 W/end & Public Hols: Fri 12pm – Sun 12pm	1.33c	1.33c	10c	from 16.10x to 9.56c

★ **Website:** www.eircom.ie
Other International calls are priced differently

BT Ireland* –
Call rates from *fixed line* based on their BT Talk bundle

Terms:
Bundle €25.36 which includes line rental at €25.36 per month
Call set up fee/Minimum charge: 5c per call
All national calls are charged at the price of a local call and the charges for international and mobile calls vary as detailed below:

Times	Local	National	International** UK, USA & Canada	Mobile
Peak Mon–Fri : 7am–7pm	3c	3c	8c	21.09c
Off Peak Mon–Fri : 7pm–7am Weekend & Public Hols: Fri 7pm – Mon 7am	1c	1c	8c	13.56c

★ **Website:** www.btireland.ie
Other International calls are priced differently

Telemarketing and Premium Services

Telemarketing services are used by businesses to generate sales. The business pays the full cost or balance of the telephone charge depending on the number(s) they choose. Telemarketing numbers include:

◆ *Freephone – 1800*: Free at all times to the customer. The business pays the total telephone charge.

◆ *CallSave – 1850*: The call is charged at a fixed rate based on the local call rate of minute for any duration of a call. The business pays the balance of the telephone charge.

◆ *LoCall – 1890*: The call is charged at the local call rate per minute. The business pays the balance of the telephone charge.

However, as telemarketing numbers are *not* included as part of a call bundle provided by telephone service providers (ie, free local and national calls), it is advisable to use the landline number of the business to avail of the free calls. Furthermore, dialling these numbers from a mobile phone is a lot more expensive than dialling from a landline phone.

Premium services are used by businesses that provide information services to the public, ie, news, weather, sports results, horoscopes, entertainment, advice, etc., and typically operate 24 hours per day, 7 days per week. The cost of the call, which is paid totally by the caller, depends on the number dialled, which can change depending on the number dialled:

◆ *1512 –1518 Numbers*: call cost can range from 25c to €1.00 per minute at all times.

◆ *1520 – 1550 Numbers*: call cost can range from 15c to 95c per minute at all times.

◆ *1560 – 1590 Numbers*: call cost can range from €1.25 to €2.90 per minute at all times

Charges for premium calls vary between telephone providers, and dialling these numbers from a mobile phone is considerably more expensive. The charges above are based on the telephone provider Eircom.

Costing Telephone Calls

All calls made from fixed-line telephones outside of the telephone provider's call bundle limit are generally charged on a per-minute basis, subject to a minimum charge which depends on the telephone provider.

The cost of a telephone call will be the combination of the:
1. minimum call charge and
2. duration of call multiplied by cost per minute at the peak or off-peak rate.

Example — National Call

Cost a call made from Waterford to Cork on Tuesday at 5.00pm for 3 minutes 42 seconds, using BT Ireland as the telephone provider and their call bundle BT Talk.

The call has a minimum charge of 5c, plus the call is charged at peak rate for national calls, which is 3c per minute. The call is rounded to the nearest minute, so this call is of 4 minutes' duration. The cost of the call is 17c (5c + (4 minutes x 3c)).

Outgoing Calls

Before making a telephone call, the receptionist should:

◆ locate the telephone number from the telephone directory or other source, ie, letterhead, website or Eircom's online phonebook at www.eircomphonebook.ie. Dialling a directory enquiry number should be used as a last resort due to the cost involved, which can exceed a minimum charge of about 89c for one minute, depending on the telephone provider.

◆ plan the telephone call and identify the person or department s/he wishes to contact

◆ keep files and correspondence nearby for easy reference.

Making National and International Calls

Making Telephone Calls within Ireland

Ireland is divided into a number of telephone zones which are represented by an area code. For example, the telephone zone of Dublin to north Wicklow is assigned the area code of 01.

For other telephone zones, the area code also starts with a two digit number but specific areas with a telephone zone have other digits added. For example, the telephone zone for County Cork is 02, and the specific areas within this telephone zone are assigned another digit, ie, Cork City is 021, Mallow is 022, Bandon is 023, etc. The area codes are listed in the phonebook.

To make a local telephone call (ie, dialling within the same area code), the number to dial is simply the local number. To make a telephone call outside the local area code, the area code for the specific area is dialled first, followed by the local number.

Example

Joan is on her way from Waterford to Cork Airport. When she gets to Cork city, she discovers that she has forgotten her passport and needs to telephone home for it to be sent by courier. Her local number in Waterford is 382111. To dial from Cork, Joan dials the area code for Waterford, which is 051, followed by the local number, 382111.

Making International Calls from Ireland

When making an international telephone call from Ireland, an **access code** and an **area code** are required. The access code is necessary to enable the caller to **dial out** of Ireland. The access code from Ireland to all other countries starts with **00** and the remaining digits of the access code depend on the country being dialled. The access codes, area codes and time differences for each country are listed in the telephone directory.

To make an international telephone call, dial the number in the following order:

access code + **area** code + **local number**

Example

You are requested by your manager to contact a supplier in Manchester in Great Britain. She has given you the number of the company as 4410700. When you dial this number you discover that the number is incomplete. What do you do?

From the Telephone Directory locate:
the access code for Great Britain — 0044
the area code for Manchester — 161

The number you should dial is 0044 161 4410700.

Making International Calls to Ireland

When making an international telephone call to Ireland, the access code is 00353 from elsewhere in the EU. (From the US and Canada, dial 011353; from Austalia, 0011353; from New Zealand, 010353.) If the area code begins with **zero**, the caller should omit the first zero from the area code when making an international call to Ireland. For example, if dialling from France to Cork, the procedure is:

The number to dial will be 00353 21 + local number (omitting first zero from area code). The caller should also take note of the time difference between the country they are in and the country they are calling.

Short Questions

1. List four core duties of the receptionist and three other general tasks a receptionist may be required to do.
2. When scheduling an appointment, state the essential information that must be recorded by the receptionist.
3. Outline the procedure for dealing with expected visitors to the business.
4. How would you deal with a client/visitor who arrived without an appointment?
5. Outline a procedure for dealing with complaints.
6. Describe the following features of a switchboard:
   a) speed dialling
   b) camp on busy
   c) uniform call distribution
   d) voicemail.
7. Distinguish between the following features of a switchboard:
   a) call forwarding
   b) call pickup
   c) call logging
   d) call status display.
8. Explain what DDI is and how it operates.
9. Outline the procedure for dealing with incoming calls via a switchboard.
10. List two advantages of installing IVR technology on a business telephone system.

11. Explain the term 'VoIP' and describe how telephone calls are made using VoIP.
12. Design a telephone message pad suitable for use in the reception area.
13. List the essential points that an outgoing message on voicemail should contain.
14. List the essential points that should be dictated when leaving a message on voicemail.
15. State four advantages of voicemail.
16. Outline the procedure for making outgoing international calls.
17. Differentiate between telemarketing and premium services.
18. Explain the difference between the following telemarketing telephone numbers: 1800, 1850 and 1890.
19. Outline the range of codes that must be dialled when dialling from:
    a) Ireland to Paris, France
    b) Paris to Dublin.

Chapter 6 — Administration and Accounting Duties

With the speed of technological developments, the role of the administrator has changed from that of a decade ago. The administrator is expected to be competent in the use of computers and modern office technology.

The administrator should be:
- pleasant and courteous
- skilled in oral, written and electronic communication
- efficient and professional at all times
- tactful and discreet, especially when dealing with complaints
- willing to assist and show initiative.

Classifications of administrators include:
- **Personal Assistant (PA):** A personal assistant to a senior executive in the business is responsible for the day-to-day organising of events that take place in the executive's working day. The personal assistant becomes a specialist in his/her area. For example, the PA to the Marketing Manager may be responsible for preparing sales presentations and processing orders from the sales representatives. The PA deals with confidential correspondence, arranges the executive's appointment schedule, prepares travel itineraries and often has to deal with queries on behalf of the executive.
- **General Administrator:** The duties regularly carried out by general administrators are:
  1. Planning and organising work
  2. Arranging appointments
  3. Arranging travel
  4. Preparing for meetings and conferences.
- **Junior Office Assistant:** Most offices will employ a junior assistant to carry out general office tasks, such as word processing, handling the post, operating the switchboard, filing, photocopying and other general administration duties.

Planning and Organising Work

As the administrator's normal working day involves routine tasks and the preparation of work for a future date, it is vital that plans are made. Generally the administrator will plan in the short term, ie, on a day-to-day basis, but s/he will also make arrangements for dates in the future, for example, organising meetings, booking appointments, arranging travel or planning conferences.

However, even the best-made plans can go wrong in a dynamic office environment. Emergencies occur, new priority work may emerge, deadlines may change, but the routine work must also get finished. The administrator must therefore be organised to deal with these situations as efficiently as possible. S/he must plan, but must also be flexible to rearrange plans if necessary. To help plan the work, the administrator may use some of the following, either a manual or an electronic version:

◆ **Diary:** used to record details of appointments or meetings for some date in the future.
◆ **'To-do' List:** used to list work that needs to be completed that day.
◆ **Calendar:** essential to identify days, dates and months when planning for future events, such as meetings, arranging travel, conferences, staff holidays, etc.

Diaries

A diary is a vital tool for any administrator and a manual or an electronic format may be used.

◆ **Manual Diary:** When selecting a manual diary, the administrator should choose one with appropriate space to record the necessary details. For example, in a doctor's surgery, a one-page-per-day appointments diary may be sufficient, with times specified and space allocated to allow the administrator to write the appropriate details when scheduling appointments.

APPOINTMENTS

MONDAY   JANUARY 12 2010

	Patient	Telephone no	Doctor	Doctor
0900	Mrs Joan Doyle	4539412/086 937651	Dr Byrne	
0930	Mr Tom Dawson	3964145		Dr O'Sullivan
1000				
1030	Miss Nora Gaffney	5368423/085 453312	Dr Byrne	
1100	Mr Tadgh Coakley	4986541		Dr O'Sullivan
1130	Mr Paul Cooney	4965522/086 853367	Dr Byrne	
1200				
100				

An extract from an appointment diary for doctor's surgery

◆ **Electronic Diary:** Normally managed from a desktop computer, this diary is usually organised via an email system such as MS Outlook. The main advantage of an electronic diary is that it can be shared easily with others on the network, thereby reducing significantly the time taken to arrange meetings. A simple check of the electronic diary will indicate when other employees are available.

Information on the desktop diary can be transferred to a high-spec mobile phone (eg, Blackberry or Smartphone) or to a handheld electronic diary, known as a 'personal digital assistant' (PDA) and vice versa. These hand-held devices can be connected to the business network via a wireless network, thus enabling employees to monitor the desktop diary from off-site locations.

Generally, an electronic diary:

– contains planning tools: an address/contacts book, a diary, a to-do list and a calendar.
– can be viewed in different formats, eg: daily, weekly, monthly or yearly, to facilitate future planning.
– has no space restrictions as in a manual diary, as new pages can be added as required.
– allows reminders to be set in advance to notify the user of priority appointments/tasks.
– can have different levels of access for each working group. For example, 'read-only' access may be granted to allow certain groups of users to view but not edit any entry in the diary.

Handheld Diary (PDA)

How to plan

1. Record all known deadlines in a diary.
2. Estimate the time required to complete each task and record the start and completion dates in the diary. The administrator may plan to complete the task before the deadline, to allow for changes in the workload that may take priority.
3. The administrator should consult with his/her manager each day (if possible) to arrange a To-do list. Entries on the To-do list will include: unfinished tasks that must be completed, routine tasks and the new entries taken from the diary for that day.
4. The tasks on the To-do list should be prioritised in order of importance. For example:
   ◆ urgent work that must be completed immediately
   ◆ routine tasks that must be done, eg, dealing with correspondence
   ◆ work that will soon become a priority unless completed
   ◆ routine tasks that are less important and can be completed at some later stage.
5. As new work comes in, the order of the tasks on the To-do list may change as the new work may take priority.
6. When tasks are completed, they are ticked off the list.
7. Tasks not completed on the day will be:
   ◆ listed on the To-do list for the following day if it is a high-priority task, or
   ◆ listed in the diary and dealt with at a later date.

Arranging Appointments

In general, incoming appointments are arranged by telephone or the administrator may receive a written request for an appointment by post, fax or email. The administrator should keep a diary at hand, to check free times and dates. The nature of the business will determine the appointment details taken by the administrator.

If the appointment is **in-house**, ie, a visitor is coming to the business premises, the administrator should record the visitor's name, the time and date of the appointment, the contact number and whom the visitor wishes to see in the appropriate section of the diary.

Where clients are met **outside the premises**, eg, insurance representatives, auctioneers, etc., the administrator should take the client's name, contact number and the address of the meeting point. When arranging the appointment, allow time for travel.

In some cases a general diary may not be sufficient to record non-standard details. In such cases a customised form is designed either manually (ie, typed) or generated electronically (ie, created from a database).

The Enquiry Form displayed below details the information required by the booking office of a coach business. The enquiry form is used to record the overall details. The date and summary details are recorded in the appropriate section of the main diary.

ENQUIRY FORM — COACH HIRE

Day:_____   Date of hire: _____

Destination: _____

Pick-up points:_____   _____   _____

Pick-up time: _____   _____   _____

Number of passengers (coach size): _____

Luggage capacity:_____

Special requests (microphone, disability facilities, etc.): _____

_____

Price (if quoted): _____

Contact name:_____   Contact number:_____

Booked by: _____

Date of booking: _____

Arranging Travel

The administrator may be required to make travel arrangements on behalf of employees. The administrator must identify the:

◆ destination
◆ duration and purpose of the visit
◆ date and time of departure/return
◆ accommodation preferences (hotel, guesthouse)
◆ preferred mode of transport, (eg, air, rail, bus, sea or car).
◆ facilities required at the accommodation (special needs facilities, Internet access, fax, etc.)

If the person is travelling by air, then it is likely that the business has already established a working relationship with a reputable travel agent. If no arrangement exists, the administrator should consult with more than one travel agency to ensure the best value is obtained, in terms of both finance and quality of service.

The administrator may need to arrange for transport to and from the point of arrival, ie, it may be necessary to hire a car or a taxi.

Booking Accommodation

When the type of accommodation required is identified (eg, hotel or guesthouse, single or double room, Internet facilities, etc.) the administrator should research a variety of accommodation providers, using approved accommodation websites, guidebooks or the local tourist office.

Once accommodation has been identified, the administrator should:

◆ telephone, fax or email the accommodation providers to find a room that suits the requirements of the business traveller. If the accommodation is satisfactory, a provisional booking will be made. A deposit is generally required to secure the booking.

◆ request details of the booking to be forwarded (ie, email, fax, post).

◆ check the details received to ensure that the dates, room type, etc. correspond to the initial booking requirements.

◆ confirm the booking.

◆ contact the accommodation provider a day or two before the person is due to arrive to ensure that the accommodation details are in order and remind the receptionist of any special requests.

Preparing an Itinerary

If the person travelling has a series of appointments to attend, an itinerary is prepared by the administrator. An itinerary is a concise schedule generally produced on one page, outlining the details of meetings, contact information and travel arrangements for the duration of the trip.

Relevant correspondence, confirmation of bookings and the final itinerary should be given to the person travelling and copies should be retained in a travel file and kept by the administrator in the office for reference purposes.

TRAVEL ITINERARY

MR JAMES RYAN — Trip to England 8–9 February 2010

Mon 8 February	
0830 hrs	Check in at Dublin Airport — 0830 hrs.
1000 hrs	Depart Dublin Airport for Manchester — Flight No. IE 113.
1130 hrs	Arrive Manchester — Meet Ms Jane Carty at Terminal 2, Gate No. 11. Leave airport for Hilton Hotel, Stoke-on-Trent.
1400 hrs	Collected by Ms Carty at hotel to go to Wedgwood plant to meet senior executives. Tour of plant.
1600 hrs	Presentation to senior executives — Strategic Planning.

Tues 9 February	
0900 hrs	Depart hotel by taxi to manufacturing plant.
1100 hrs	Meet production managers — Demonstrations of new techniques.
1400 hrs	Depart factory for Manchester Airport — check in 1600 hrs.
1700 hrs	Depart Manchester Airport for Dublin.

Travelling Abroad

When employees are travelling abroad on business, the administrator should allow time to:

◆ check whether a visa is necessary

◆ advise the person travelling to update their passport if necessary

◆ check whether medical vaccinations are required before travel and make appointments if required

◆ book the travel tickets and print boarding passes as necessary

◆ arrange company credit/debit cards and foreign currency if required

◆ prepare any documentation necessary for meetings

◆ arrange car hire and insurance cover if necessary

◆ finalise accommodation arrangements

◆ prepare an itinerary for the person travelling.

Calculating Travel Expenses

Travel expenses are paid to employees who travel on behalf of the business. The business will pay for the employee's meals, accommodation, costs of transport and other costs associated with the travel.

Some businesses will give employees expenses before they travel, while other businesses will reimburse employees on their return. To claim travel expenses, the employee completes a Travel Expense Form and attaches receipts for expenditure incurred. The employee should check the business travel policy on allowable expenses before travelling.

When processing the claim form, the administrator must ensure that details are correct (ie, dates, number of days away, distance travelled) and that the claim form is signed by someone in authority, usually a department senior who can authorise payment.

Distance charts detailing the official distances between main destinations in Ireland are found in most road maps and on relevant travel websites, eg, www.goireland.com or www.myguideireland.com.

Example 1

Employees are paid 72c per kilometre for business travel. The expense form submitted by Mr O'Donnell shows he travelled from Tralee in Kerry to Cork city and returned that evening. Calculate how much should be paid to Mr O'Donnell for kilometres travelled. Use the distance chart below.

1. Check the kilometre section of the distance chart and locate Cork and Tralee.
2. The intersection point of Cork and Tralee is the distance travelled. Tralee to Cork is 117 km.
3. Mr O'Donnell travelled a return trip, so 117 km × 2 = 234 km travelled. He should receive €168.48 as his travel expenses (ie, 234 km × 72c).

Distance Chart

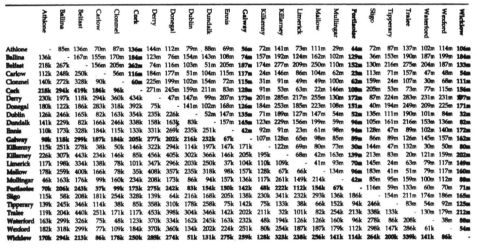

	Athlone	Ballina	Belfast	Carlow	Clonmel	Cork	Derry	Donegal	Dublin	Dundalk	Ennis	Galway	Kilkenny	Killarney	Limerick	Mallow	Mullingar	Portlaoise	Sligo	Tipperary	Tralee	Waterford	Wexford	Wicklow
Athlone	-	85m	136m	70m	87m	136m	144m	112m	79m	88m	69m	56m	72m	141m	73m	111m	29m	44m	72m	87m	137m	102m	114m	106m
Ballina	136k	-	167m	155m	170m	184m	123m	76m	154m	143m	108m	74m	157m	192m	124m	162m	102m	129m	36m	153m	190m	187m	199m	184m
Belfast	218k	267k	-	156m	205m	262m	74m	116m	103m	51m	205m	187m	174m	277m	209m	250m	110m	152m	130m	216m	275m	204m	187m	133m
Carlow	112k	248k	250k	-	56m	116m	184m	177m	51m	104m	115m	117m	24m	146m	86m	104m	62m	23m	113m	71m	157m	47m	48m	54m
Clonmel	140k	272k	328k	90k	-	60m	225m	199m	102m	154m	72m	115m	31m	91m	49m	49m	100m	62m	159m	24m	107m	30m	68m	111m
Cork	218k	294k	419k	186k	96k	-	271m	245m	159m	211m	83m	128m	91m	53m	63m	22m	146m	108m	205m	53m	73m	77m	115m	156m
Derry	230k	197k	118k	294k	360k	434k	-	47m	147m	99m	207m	173m	201m	285m	217m	255m	130m	172m	87m	224m	283m	231m	231m	197m
Donegal	180k	122k	186k	283k	318k	392k	75k	-	141m	102m	168m	126m	184m	253m	185m	223m	108m	151m	40m	194m	249m	209m	225m	171m
Dublin	126k	246k	165k	82k	163k	354k	235k	226k	-	52m	147m	135m	71m	189m	127m	147m	54m	52m	135m	111m	190m	101m	84m	32m
Dundalk	141k	229k	82k	166k	246k	338k	158k	163k	83k	-	157m	145m	123m	229m	156m	199m	59m	96m	105m	161m	216m	153m	136m	82m
Ennis	110k	173k	328k	184k	115k	133k	331k	269k	235k	251k	-	42m	92m	91m	23m	61m	98m	94m	128m	47m	89m	102m	140m	172m
Galway	90k	118k	299k	187k	184k	205k	277k	202k	216k	232k	67k	-	107m	128m	65m	98m	85m	89m	86m	89m	126m	145m	157m	162m
Kilkenny	115k	251k	278k	38k	50k	146k	322k	294k	114k	197k	147k	171k	-	122m	69m	80m	73m	30m	144m	47m	132m	30m	50m	80m
Killarney	226k	307k	443k	234k	146k	85k	456k	405k	302k	366k	146k	205k	195k	-	68m	42m	163m	139m	213m	83m	20m	121m	159m	202m
Limerick	117k	198k	334k	138k	78k	101k	347k	296k	203k	250k	37k	104k	110k	109k	-	41m	93m	70m	145m	24m	63m	79m	117m	149m
Mallow	178k	259k	400k	166k	78k	35k	408k	357k	235k	318k	98k	157k	128k	67k	66k	-	134m	96m	183m	41m	51m	79m	117m	160m
Mullingar	46k	163k	176k	99k	160k	234k	208k	173k	86k	94k	157k	136k	117k	261k	149k	214k	-	42m	85m	95m	159m	100m	112m	88m
Portlaoise	70k	206k	243k	37k	99k	173k	275k	242k	83k	154k	150k	142k	48k	222k	112k	154k	67k	-	116m	59m	133m	60m	70m	71m
Sligo	115k	58k	208k	181k	254k	328k	139k	64k	216k	168k	205k	138k	230k	341k	232k	293k	136k	186k	-	154m	211m	174m	186m	165m
Tipperary	139k	245k	346k	114k	38k	85k	358k	310k	178k	258k	75k	142k	75k	133k	38k	66k	152k	94k	246k	-	83m	54m	92m	125m
Tralee	119k	204k	440k	251k	171k	117k	453k	398k	304k	346k	142k	202k	211k	32k	101k	82k	254k	213k	338k	133k	-	130m	179m	212m
Waterford	163k	299k	326k	75k	48k	123k	370k	334k	162k	245k	163k	232k	48k	194k	126k	126k	160k	96k	278k	86k	208k	-	38m	88m
Wexford	182k	318k	299k	77k	109k	184k	370k	360k	134k	202k	224k	251k	80k	254k	187k	187k	179k	112k	298k	147k	286k	61k	-	54m
Wicklow	170k	294k	213k	86k	178k	250k	286k	274k	51k	131k	275k	259k	128k	323k	238k	256k	141k	114k	264k	200k	339k	141k	86k	-

Distance chart in miles and kilometres

Preparing for Meetings and Conferences

In many cases, the administrator will be involved in organising a conference or meeting on behalf of the business. This may involve:

◆ booking an appropriate hotel or conference centre, keeping in mind the size and layout of the room, audiovisual facilities, communication facilities (eg, Internet access, fax) and refreshments

◆ preparing and issuing booking forms for attendees

◆ obtaining literature on the local area for delegates, eg, lists of accommodation, tourist maps and other local information, which may be enclosed with the booking form

◆ preparing a checklist to confirm the number of delegates attending
◆ booking accommodation for delegates if required
◆ preparing essential paperwork for the conference (ie, speaker's notes, copies of presentations, reports, etc.)
◆ arranging name/title badges for delegates
◆ co-ordinating a social programme for delegates
◆ arranging for a representative to meet delegates on arrival, if required
◆ handling queries that may arise during the conference

The administrator should carry out a post-conference evaluation of how the conference was organised for future reference.

Videoconferences/e-Meetings

Meetings or conferences can also be carried out remotely by using a videoconferencing system (VTC). A videoconferencing system consists of a screen, camera, microphone, loudspeakers and videoconferencing software and the meeting is transmitted via an ISDN telephone line, or utilising Internet technology.

A VTC system allows participants in two or more offices or locations to communicate in real time with the benefit of video. As well as seeing and hearing the participants at the meeting, documents, diagrams, photographs, etc., can be displayed on-screen, allowing increased levels of collaboration between videoconference participants in remote locations.

High-quality, dedicated VTC systems can be very expensive, but desktop VTC systems are very affordable and can be added easily to desktop computers to facilitate e-meetings. A variety of video-conferencing software, such as Microsoft Netmeeting is available on most PCs to allow users to communicate orally and visually simultaneously.

Advantages

1. Meetings can take place 'face-to-face' without the participants leaving their offices, so savings on travelling time and cost can be made.

Videoconferencing system

2. Enables employees with conflicting schedules to 'meet'.
3. Remote expertise can be brought into a business, eg, guest speakers can provide their presentation through videoconferencing.
4. Can be used to interview potential employees.
5. Can be used to facilitate employee training.

Accounting Activities

The administrator may be required to carry out accounting-type activities such as maintaining the petty cash book, preparing lodgments, bank reconciliation statements and processing wages/salaries.

Petty Cash

A petty cash box is maintained in the office for purchasing or reimbursing employees for sundry items such as travel expenses, emergency stationery supplies, refreshments, etc. Petty cash operates on an **imprest system** in which an imprest (ie, a float) is received at the beginning of the petty cash period, usually weekly. The float is restored to the original amount at the end of the period. A typical procedure is:

a) An initial amount of cash is received from the Accounts Department for the petty cash float. The float is the opening balance on the petty cash book.

b) When there is a request for money from petty cash, a petty cash voucher is completed giving details of the amount, item purchased and date of expenditure. Receipts for expenses incurred are usually required and are attached to the petty cash voucher. The voucher is signed by both the recipient of the money and the person authorising the petty cash payment.

c) The vouchers are used to write up the petty cash book at the end of the petty cash period.

d) The petty cash book is totalled and balanced at the end of the petty cash period. More cash is requested from Accounts to restore the imprest to the original amount for the next period.

PETTY CASH VOUCHER		
Voucher no 34	**Date** Feb. 7 '10	
Details	**Amount**	
	€	c
Stamps	8	25
	8	25
Signed by	*Carol Ryan*	
Authorised by	*Jack O'Reilly*	

Example

The imprest at the beginning of the petty cash period is €60. During the week, three vouchers were signed for:

stamps (€20.55)

stationery (€11.50)

cleaning agents (€15.90).

The total spent for the week was €47.95, leaving a balance of €12.05. €47.95 is required to restore the imprest to €60.

The petty cash book

				PETTY CASH BOOK				
Received	Date	Details	Voucher no	Total payment	Post	Stationery	Travel	Sundries
60.00	Feb 1	Accounts						
	Feb 1	Stamps	34	20.55	20.55			
	Feb 2	Stationery	35	11.50		11.50		
	Feb 4	Cleaning	36	15.90				15.90
		Cash	€47.95	€20.55	€11.50			€15.90
	Feb 5	Balance c/d		€12.05				
€60.00				€60.00				
€12.05		Balance b/f						
€47.95	Feb 8	Accounts						

The petty cash book analyses each petty cash transaction, which is displayed on the right-hand side of the petty cash book. The left-hand side of the book records the money received. The balance on the petty cash book is the original amount of imprest minus the total of the petty cash vouchers. This balance should match the amount of cash remaining in the petty cash box. The sum €47.95 represents the amount of money received to restore the imprest to €60 for the next period. The petty cash book for the above example is written up as follows:

Wages and Salaries

The administrator may be required to process wages and salaries for all the employees. Every employee is entitled to a wages slip from their employer, detailing gross pay, the various statutory and voluntary deductions and net pay.

Employees who are paid a **salary** receive a fixed amount of money on a fortnightly or monthly basis. Employees who are paid a **wage** may be paid on the following basis:

- **a basic hourly rate:** employees are paid a basic rate per hour. Any hours worked above the standard week (ie, 38 hours) are paid at overtime rates, ie, a rate higher than the basic rate. Businesses will generally have a range of overtime rates, for shift work, bank holidays and Sundays. Typical overtime rates are time and a half, double time or triple time.
- **a basic wage plus commission:** employees are paid a basic wage (ie, a standard week of 38 hours) and can earn more depending on their performance, eg, sales representatives are often awarded commission on the volume of sales over a specific target.
- **a piece rate:** employees are not paid a basic wage, but according to the quantity of output produced.

Tax Credit System

The procedure for calculating tax on an employee's wage/salary is based on the tax credit system. An employer needs a *Certificate of Tax Credit and Standard Rate Cut-off Point* for each employee, which details the weekly/monthly 'tax credit' and the weekly/monthly 'standard rate cut-off point'.

- The tax credit reduces the amount of tax to be paid for each week/month and is based on an employee's personal circumstances (ie, single, married, widowed, etc.) and relief for certain expenses such as rent relief, tuition fees, service charges and trade-union subscriptions.
- The standard rate cut-off point is the amount of income each week/month to be taxed at the low rate of tax (known as the standard rate – currently 20%). Any income above the standard rate cut-off point is taxed at the higher rate of tax (currently 41%).

If an employer does not have a Certificate of Tax Credit and Standard Rate Cut-off Point for an employee, s/he will deduct tax at the emergency rates as obliged by law. Therefore, the employee will pay more tax than is necessary and will remain on emergency tax until the employer receives the Certificate. Any overpayment of tax is refunded.

Obtaining a Tax Credit Certificate

a) If an employee has just started work, s/he must complete **Form 12A** obtainable from the Tax Office or can be downloaded from the Revenue website, www.revenue.ie. Form 12A requests the employee's personal details, the employee's income amount from 1 January last and the employer's details. The employee selects the relevant options on the form for *tax credits* (ie, single, married, etc.) and *reliefs* (ie, rent paid, tuition fees, trade-union subscription and service charges).

The tax office then calculates the tax credits and the standard rate cut-off point for the employee and issues this certificate to both the employee and the employer.

b) A P45 is given to employees on termination of their employment. When an employee takes up a new job s/he should give the new employer the P45, which states the tax credits and the standard rate cut-off point. Without these details, the employee will have to pay emergency tax.

Calculation of Wages/Salaries

Before looking at how wages are calculated, it is important to understand the following terms:

♦ **Gross pay:** consists of the total income earned by the employee *before* any deductions are made. If the employee is paid by the hour, the gross pay is calculated by multiplying the total hours worked by the rate per hour.

Example 1 — Gross Pay

James worked a total of 38 hours at €10.50 and 3 hours' overtime paid at time and a half. His weekly gross wage is:

38 hours × €10.50	=	399.00
3 hours × €15.75	=	47.25
		€446.25

♦ **Taxable Income:** is the amount of income on which an employee is taxed. It is calculated by deducting pension contributions, known as Superannuation Contributions (SAC) from Gross Pay as SACs are not subject to tax.

♦ **Gross Tax Liability:** is the *sum* of the tax calculated on *taxable income*. It is calculated by:
(a) applying the standard rate of tax (currently 20%) to the weekly/monthly standard rate cut-off point and
(b) applying the higher rate of tax (currently 41%) to the balance of income.

♦ **Net Tax Liability:** is the *gross tax liability* minus the weekly/monthly tax credits.

♦ **Net Pay:** consists of Gross Pay minus all deductions. It is the employee's take-home pay.

Income Levy

An income levy is a supplementary tax which applies to gross income above the threshold of €15,028 per annum (€1,252.33 per month). The income levy rates are progressive depending on gross income earned. The current income levy rates are:

♦ 2% on income from 0–€75,036 per annum (€6,253 per month)
♦ 4% on income from €75,036–€174,980 per annum (€14,582 per month)
♦ 6% on income in excess of €174,980 per annum

Example 2 — Calculation of Net Pay

John's gross monthly pay is €4,000. He pays €250 per month into an approved Superannuation fund. His monthly standard rate cut-off point is €3,062.58 and he is entitled to tax credits of €316.75 per month.

Gross Pay	4,000.00	4,000.00
Less SAC	250.00	
Taxable Income	3,750.00	
Taxed as:		
€3,062.58 @ 20%	612.52	
€687.42 @ 41%	218.84	
Gross tax liability	831.36	
Less Tax Credits	316.75	
Net tax liability	514.61	
Less Deductions		
Income Levy (2% of Gross Income)	80.00	
PAYE	514.61	
SAC	250.00	
Total Deductions	844.61	844.61
Net Pay		**€3,155.39**

John's take-home pay (net pay) will be €3,155.39.

Pay related social insurance (PRSI)

An employee must contribute to a social insurance scheme to provide funds to the Government for its social programmes, ie, unemployment benefits, medical cards, etc. Different PRSI rates apply to certain classes of employment. Employers also pay a PRSI contribution for every employee. PRSI is calculated on 'Taxable Income' (ie, Gross Pay less SAC).

We will now calculate John's PRSI deduction and net pay. Assume John pays PRSI at 5%; how much PRSI does he pay and what is his net pay?

Example 3 — Calculation of Net Pay (deducting PRSI)

Gross Pay	4,000.00	4,000.00
Less SAC	250.00	
Taxable Income	3,750.00	
Taxed as:		
€3,062.58 @ 20%	612.52	
€687.42 @ 41%	218.84	
Gross tax liability	831.36	
Less Tax Credits	316.75	
Net tax liability	514.61	
Less Deductions		
Income Levy (2% of Gross Income)	80.00	
PAYE	514.61	
SAC	250.00	
PRSI (5% of Taxable Income)	187.50	
Total Deductions	1,032.11	1,032.11
Net Pay		**€2,967.89**

John will pay PRSI of €187.50 and this reduces his net pay to €2,967.89.

Deductions from wages

An employer will deduct two types of deduction from gross pay. These are:

a) *Statutory deductions:* deductions that an employee is obliged to pay by law from wages, ie, tax (known as PAYE or **P**ay **A**s **Y**ou **E**arn), PRSI and Income Levy.

b) *Voluntary deductions:* deductions that the employee is not obliged by law to pay from wages. However, many employees subscribe to group schemes to pay VHI contributions, to donate money to charities, to save or to pay their trade-union subscriptions directly from their wages.

The payroll administrator should ensure that the employee has signed a form authorising voluntary deductions to be made from his/her wage/salary.

We will now calculate John's net pay assuming he pays the following voluntary deductions: VHI contributions of €40, contribution to saving scheme €60.

Example 4 — Calculation of Net Pay (continued)

Gross Pay	4,000.00	4,000.00
Less SAC	250.00	
Taxable Income	3,750.00	
Taxed as:		
€3,062.58 @ 20%	612.52	
€687.42 @ 41%	218.84	
Gross tax liability	831.36	
Less Tax Credits	316.75	
Net tax liability	514.61	
Less Deductions		
Income Levy (2% of Gross Income)	80.00	
PAYE	514.61	
SAC	250.00	
PRSI (5% of Taxable Income)	187.50	
VHI contributions	40.00	
Saving scheme	60.00	
Total Deductions	1,132.11	1,132.11
Net Pay		**€2,867.89**

Payslip

Most payslips are generated using computerised payroll packages. The details necessary for calculating pay are entered once, ie, name of employee, employee work number, PPS (Personal Public Service) number, SAC contribution, standard rate cut-off point, tax credits and the voluntary deductions.

At the end of each week/month, the payroll administrator only enters the standard and overtime hours worked and the payroll package automatically calculates the total gross pay, PAYE due, PRSI due, total deductions, net pay and provides a running total of the pay and tax details to date since the start of the tax year.

Every employee is entitled to receive a payslip which summarises the calculations of take-home pay. The payslip for John would read as follows:

PAYSLIP	APPLEWOODS SUPPLIES		PPS No. 6743212 S
John Creedon 0008976			Tax Period 2
Date: 28 February 2010			

Gross Pay Analysis		Deductions		Year To Date	
Basic Pay	4,000.00	PAYE	514.61	Gross Pay	8,000.00
O/T		PRSI	187.50	Taxable Income	7,500.00
Holiday Pay		SAC	250.00	Standard Rate	
Other		Income Levy	80.00	Cut-off Point	6,125.16
		VHI	40.00	Tax Credits	633.50
		Savings Scheme	60.00	PAYE	1,360.22
Total Gross Pay	€4,000.00		1,132.11	PRSI	375.00
				Income Levy	160.00
Hourly Rate					
Hrs @				Tax credits per month	316.75
Hrs @					
				NET PAY	€2,867.89

Short Questions

1. Briefly describe three classifications of administrator.
2. List four main duties of a general administrator.
3. Describe three aids used by an administrator in planning and organising work.
4. List four main features of an electronic diary.
5. Outline a procedure for planning and organising work, taking into account events in the future, day-to-day activities and unexpected urgent activities.
6. When taking appointments/messages, state the essential information that must be recorded.
7. Why is a general appointments diary not suitable for all appointments? Give an example.
8. What steps would you follow when booking accommodation for your manager?
9. What is an itinerary and what details are generally recorded?
10. List the main duties an administrator may have when arranging for a conference to be held in another location.
11. Describe how videoconferencing operates.
12. List three advantages of videoconferencing.
13. Why is a petty cash system maintained? What document is used to record money issued?
14. Distinguish between wages and salaries.

15. In the payment of wages, distinguish between a piece rate and a basic rate plus commission.
16. What is Jane's gross wage if she is paid a basic hourly rate of €10.00 and works a standard week of 38 hours, plus three hours overtime paid at time and a half?
17. Briefly describe the tax credit system.
18. Distinguish between Form 12A and a P45.
19. Distinguish between the following:
    a) gross pay and net pay
    b) gross tax liability and net tax liability
    c) statutory deductions and voluntary deductions
    d) PAYE and an Income Levy.
20. Explain the term 'taxable income'.
21. List six items of information on a payslip.

Chapter 7 — Business Transactions

business transaction takes place between two organisations, one of which is purchasing goods or services, the other selling. From the time of the initial enquiry to the dispatch of the goods, several stages are involved in the process.

In a small business, one person may be responsible for monitoring stock levels, making enquiries to suppliers for new stock, assessing quotations and placing the orders. When the goods are received, the same person may be responsible for checking the goods received against the delivery document that comes with the goods and against the copy of the order to ensure that the goods that arrived were actually ordered. When the business is billed for payment by means of an invoice, the invoice will be checked against the record of the goods received to ensure that the goods have actually been received before payment is made and that the correct amount has been charged.

The documents produced at the various stages of a business transaction are typically generated by a computerised accounting system, ie, SAGE, TAS Books, etc. An account is created for each customer, details of the various transactions are entered on the system and the necessary business documents such as invoices, credit notes, statements, etc., can be printed. Documents can be tracked by customer name or reference number, and various monitoring reports can be generated to assist the business in managing its finances. In a large business, this process will be split among several individuals who work in different departments.

Stages of a Business Transaction

The stages of a business transaction are as follows:

Purchase Requisition

A purchase requisition form is used when there is an internal request for goods to be purchased. It is signed by the head of the department requesting the goods and sent to the Purchasing department for the goods to be ordered. If details such as supplier's name, catalogue number and price are not known by the department sending the request, a brief description of what is required is recorded. The purchasing department will source the information required.

In the purchase requisition shown here, the supplier's name, price and catalogue numbers are unknown.

Distribution of Purchase Requisition:
◆ Original to Purchasing Department
◆ Copy to the file of the Department that sent the requisition.

PURCHASE REQUISITION				Ref No. AB231
Department	Admin Department			
Supplier's name (if known)				
Address				

Qty	Details	Cat. No.	Unit Price
2	Exhibition Display Stand — three-panel concertina, self-standing		
2	LCD Multimedia Projector — portable		

Signature	Date
John Murray	12 March 2010

Purchase requisition form

An Enquiry

An enquiry is a request from a buyer to a seller requesting a formal quotation to establish price and terms and conditions of trade such as trade discounts, cash discounts, delivery dates and whether delivery costs are paid or not. In practice, it is usual to obtain quotations from at least three suppliers to establish best purchasing terms. The quotations received from various suppliers will be compared before any particular supplier is decided upon.

The buyer in the purchasing department sources the supply and the price of goods by contacting appropriate suppliers, generally by letter, fax or email to maintain a record. The buyer can identify possible suppliers from the Golden Pages, trade journals, internal files on past suppliers and the Internet. Details for the enquiry are taken from the Purchase Requisition.

Distribution of an Enquiry:
◆ Original to various suppliers
◆ Copy in Buyer's File.

A + J Rudd Ltd
34 Main St
Blackrock   **Tel No: 353 1 2875640**
Co. Dublin   **Fax No: 353 1 2876543**
                                 email: purchases@ajrudd.ie
                                 web: www.ajrudd.ie

12 March 2010

Office Supplies Ltd
Wexford Industrial Estate
Wexford

Dear Sir/Madam

Please forward a quotation for the items below, including your terms of trade
and delivery terms. Include a catalogue for reference if available.

2   Exhibition Display Stand – three-panel concertina, self-standing
2   LCD Multimedia Projector – portable

Yours faithfully

Brendan Kelly
Purchasing Dept

An enquiry — generally sent by letter, fax or email

Quotation

The enquiry will be handled by the Sales Department of the supplier, who will
send a quotation in reply by letter, fax or email.

A quotation is an offer to supply goods/services at the stated price and
under the terms and conditions stated in the quotation. An order form is
generally sent with the quotation.

Distribution of Quotation:
◆ Original to Customer
◆ Copy in File (Sales Department of Supplier)

Quotation No. 1460

Office Supplies Ltd
Wexford Industrial Estate
Wexford

Tel No: 353 53 564396
Fax No: 353 53 564987
email: sales@officesupplies.ie
web: www.officesupplies.ie
VAT No: 159 4321 67

16 March 2010

Attention of Mr Brendan Kelly

A+J Rudd Ltd
34 Main St
Blackrock
Co. Dublin

In reply to your enquiry dated 12 March, the prices for the items requested are listed below. Our full catalogue of office supplies can be viewed on www.officesupplies.ie.

Qty	Description	Cat. No.	Unit Price
2	Exhibition Display Stand – three-panel concertina, self-standing	B2345	€2,000
2	LCD Multimedia Projector – portable	B3347	€1,050

VAT — Standard Rate of 21% not included

Terms: Trade Discount   25% for orders over €4,000 (before VAT)
             Cash Discount   5% for payment within 10 days of invoice date
                              2.5% within 1 month
Delivery: within 7 days of receipt of order — delivery paid

We look forward to receiving your order.

Sandra Jones
Sales Department

Quotation

Terms and Conditions of Trade

The terms and conditions of trade stated on business documents may include the trade discount, cash discount, delivery costs and methods of payment required such as cash with order (CWO).

♦ **Trade discount:** an allowance given by a seller to a buyer for bulk purchasing to encourage customers to buy in large quantities. It is deducted on the invoice before VAT and does not depend on the time of payment.

♦ **Cash discount:** an allowance given in addition to trade discount to encourage prompt settlement of an account. Cash discount is offered as it improves the cash position of the supplier, enabling the supplier to pay its debts on time. The supplier may offer different rates of cash discount for accounts settled within a stated period. For example, s/he may offer 5% for accounts settled within 10 days of the invoice date and 2.5% for accounts settled within one month. It is deducted by the buyer when payment is being made.

If the terms of sale were stated as *net two months*, this means that no cash discount will be given and payment must be made within two months.

♦ **Delivery terms:** The cost of delivery and delivery times are important considerations when ordering goods. Some suppliers offer free delivery for an order over a certain amount. The supplier generally quotes 'delivery paid' or 'delivery not paid', and indicates the delivery time as 'x' days from the date the order was placed.

♦ **CWO (cash with order):** The purchaser must forward the payment with the order before the order will be processed.

♦ **VAT number:** Registered businesses must quote their VAT (Value Added Tax) registration number on **all** business documents. The trader submits a VAT return to the Government detailing the VAT on sales and the VAT on purchases every two months, or can opt to settle their VAT account at the end of their accounting period. If the VAT on sales exceeds the VAT on purchases the trader pays the difference, otherwise a refund is claimed.

♦ **Reference number:** a unique number placed on business documents which is used to trace correspondence. For example, if a business has placed many orders with the same supplier, a query about a particular order can be traced immediately by quoting the order reference number.

♦ **E&OE:** means 'errors and omissions excepted'. This means that the seller has the right to correct the information stated on the documentation. For example, if there is an error in arithmetic or if an item has not been charged for, the seller can send a supplementary invoice to correct the mistake.

Order

The purchasing officer evaluates the quotations from the various suppliers. The cheapest may not necessarily be the best. Quality, the terms and conditions of trade and delivery terms are other important factors to take into account. An order will be placed with the supplier that offers the best overall package.

The buyer will use the supplier's order form (printed or on-line) or an order form will be generated through the buyer's computerised accounting system. The order is sent by the buyer in the Purchasing Department to the Sales Department of the supplier. The order gives full details of the goods to be supplied, including catalogue reference number, quantity, quality, colour, size, unit cost and total cost.

Order No. A221

A + J Rudd Ltd	**Tel No: 353 1 2875640**
34 Main St	**Fax No: 353 1 2876543**
Blackrock	**email: purchases@ajrudd.ie**
Co. Dublin	**web: www.ajrudd.ie**
	VAT No: 284 3455 89

Quotation No: 1460

20 March 2010

Office Supplies Ltd
Wexford Industrial Estate
Wexford

Please supply the following:

Qty	Description	Cat. No.	Unit Price	Total Price
2	Exhibition Display Stand – three-panel concertina, self-standing	B2345	€2,000	€4,000
2	LCD Multimedia Projector – portable	B3347	€1,050	€2,100
				€6,100

Terms of Sale:	As on quotation no. 1460
Trade Discount	25% for orders over €4,000 (before VAT)
Cash Discount	5% within 10 days of invoice date
	2.5% within 1 month
Delivery paid	

Brendan Kelly
Purchasing Department

Order form

Distribution of Order:

◆ Original to the Sales Department of the supplier
◆ Copy in buyer's file (Purchase Department)
◆ Copy to stores (of the Purchasing business) — notification of goods to be received, for checking with Delivery Note.

Procedure for Dealing with Incoming Orders (Supplier)

When an order is received from a new customer, a credit check is normally run on the buyer's credit status. When dealing with a new customer, the seller may request references from a bank or an existing supplier of the customer to reduce the risk of a bad debt. The seller may request payment from a new customer by one of the following means:

(i) requesting cash with the order (CWO)

(ii) submitting a pro-forma invoice, which is an imitation invoice rather than a real invoice. It is used to request payment in advance of delivery from a first-time customer or where no credit facility is allowed. (A pro-forma invoice is also used when goods are sent 'on approval', eg, in a mail-order business. If the goods are retained, payment is made in accordance with the pro-forma invoice.)

(iii) requesting that the buyer furnish a percentage of the cost of the order before delivery is made, and the balance on delivery.

Preparation of Invoice

If the order is approved, an invoice is prepared by the Sales Department in duplicate form for distribution. An invoice is a bill requesting payment. It is sent by the Sales Department of the supplying firm to the Accounts Department of the purchasing firm. It is usually sent after the dispatch of the goods, though in some cases the invoice is enclosed with the goods. An invoice will contain the following information:

◆ name and address of both the buyer and the seller
◆ date and VAT registration number
◆ quantity, description and catalogue/reference number of product
◆ the unit cost of each item, the total cost of each item and the overall total cost
◆ trade discount
◆ the VAT rate and VAT amount shown separately
◆ terms of sale such as cash discounts and delivery terms as quoted on quotation
◆ E&OE at the bottom of the invoice.

Distribution of Invoice:
- ◆ Original to buyer (Accounts Department)
- ◆ Copy held in Sales Department to answer queries
- ◆ Copy to Accounts Department to record the sale on the customer's account
- ◆ Copies to Stores omitting price details.

Stores will keep one copy as proof of authorisation to release the goods. The other copies, known as a 'delivery' or an 'advice note', are sent with the goods.

Delivery Note

Delivery Note No. D1675

Office Supplies Ltd
Wexford Industrial Estate
Wexford

Tel No: 353 53 564396
Fax No: 353 53 564987
email: sales@officesupplies.ie
web: www.officesupplies.ie
VAT No: 159 4321 67

Order No: A221

27 March 2010

A+J Rudd Ltd
34 Main St
Blackrock
Co. Dublin

Qty	Description	Cat. No.
2	Exhibition Display Stand – three-panel concertina, self-standing	B2345
2	LCD Multimedia Projector – portable	B3347

Not Examined

Received by: *John Hegarty*

Delivery note

A delivery note contains the same details as the invoice except that the price details are omitted.

A two-part delivery note accompanies the goods and the delivery person requests that the customer sign the delivery note. The top copy is given to the customer and the other copy is returned to the supplier as proof of delivery.

Before signing, the customer (Stores Department) checks the goods against the delivery note, ensuring that all goods listed on the delivery note are received. If the goods are found to be faulty, or goods are missing, this is recorded on the delivery note before signing.

It is rarely possible to examine goods in detail immediately they are delivered. The most that can be done normally is to check that the correct number of items are received and that there is no obvious damage. In this case, 'not examined' should be recorded on the delivery note.

Distribution of Delivery Note:
◆ Top copy given to customer
◆ Duplicate copy held by delivery person who returns it to the supplier.

Advice Note

An advice note contains the same information as a delivery note. An advice note may be sent in advance of the goods to inform the buyer that the goods are being dispatched, detailing delivery arrangements, expected time of arrival (ETA), etc. An advice note may also be sent when the goods are not sent by the supplier's transport, for example, by post or rail. It is packed with the goods to enable the receiver to check them upon arrival. It does not have to be signed.

Procedure for Dealing with Incoming Goods (Purchaser)

When the goods are delivered to the Stores Department, the following procedure is carried out:
1. The contents are checked against the delivery note or advice note.
2. The goods are then checked against the copy of the order to ensure that the goods received were ordered, and also that all the goods ordered were received.
3. A goods received note is prepared by the Stores Department.

Goods Received Note

When the goods are received, a goods received note is prepared by the Stores Department, noting any discrepancies such as shortages, damages or incorrect goods received. A copy will be sent to the Accounts Department to be compared with the incoming invoice before payment is processed.

Distribution of Goods Received Note:
◆ Original to Accounts Department (to check against incoming invoice)
◆ Copy held in the Stores Department to update stock records.

Leabharlanna Fhine Gall

Goods Received Note No: 12343

A + J Rudd Ltd

Supplier: Office Supplies Ltd
Date Received: 27 March 2010
Delivery/Advice Note No: D1675

Order No.	Description	Qty Received
A221	Exhibition Display Stand – three-panel concertina, self-standing	2
	LCD Multimedia Projector – portable	2

Received by:	Date:	Entered in stock by:	Date:
D. Foyle	27/3/10	P. Connolly	27/3/10

Inspected by: Harry Dineen	Date: 27/10/05

Shortages: *None*
Damage recorded: *None*

Goods received note

Checking Invoice Received

The invoice is usually sent after the dispatch of the goods, though in some cases the invoice is enclosed with the goods. When the invoice is received by the Accounts Department of the purchasing firm the following checks are made:

1. Check invoice against the goods received note (from Stores) to ensure that goods have actually been received in good condition before making payment.
2. Check all calculations, total unit cost, trade discount and total cost.

If errors are discovered on the invoice, the Accounts Department will contact the supplier, who will rectify the error by sending a credit note or a debit note as appropriate.

Cash discount is deducted (if applicable) at the appropriate rate and the payment is sent to the Accounts Department of the supplier before expiration of the credit period, to claim the discount.

Distribution of Received Invoice:
◆ Original held in Accounts Department.

Invoice No. 1675

Office Supplies Ltd
Wexford Industrial Estate
Wexford

Tel No: 353 53 564396
Fax No: 353 53 564987
email: sales@officesupplies.ie
web: www.officesupplies.ie
VAT No: 159 4321 67

Delivery Note No: D1675
Order No: A221

28 March 2010

A+J Rudd Ltd
34 Main St
Blackrock
Co. Dublin

Qty	Description	Cat. No.	Unit Price €	Total Cost €
2	Exhibition Display Stand – three-panel concertina, self-standing	B2345	2,000	4,000.00
2	LCD Multimedia Projector – portable	B3347	1,050	<u>2,100.00</u>
				€6,100.00
	Deduct: 25% Trade Discount			<u>1,525.00</u>
	Net goods value		**Sub Total**	4,575.00
	ADD: VAT @ 21%		**VAT**	<u>960.75</u>
			Total	**€5,535.75**
	Terms: 5% within 10 days			
	2.5% within 1 month			
	Net 2 months			
E&OE	Delivery Paid			

Invoice

Calculating Cash Discount

To claim the cash discount, the invoice must be paid within the time specified by the terms of trade. The date is taken to be the date of the invoice.

Example

Calculate how much A + J Rudd Ltd will pay, if they pay Invoice No. 1675 on:

a) 4 April 2010
b) 20 April 2010
c) 6 June 2010

Solution

a) As the invoice is paid on 4 April, which is within 10 days of the invoice date, A + J Rudd Ltd is entitled to deduct a discount of 5%. They will therefore pay €5,535.75 less 5 per cent (€276.79), which is €5,258.96.

b) As the invoice is paid on 20 April, which is within one month of the invoice date, A + J Rudd Ltd is entitled to deduct a discount of 2½ per cent. They will therefore pay €5,535.75 less 2.5% (€138.39), which is €5,397.36.

c) As the invoice is not paid until 6 June, which is after the date when the invoice should be paid (ie, net 2 months), A + J Rudd Ltd pays the full amount owing of €5,535.75. Under the Prompt Payments Act 1997 suppliers who are not paid on time are entitled to charge interest at the rate of 2.5% per month on unsettled accounts.

Credit Note

A credit note is sent by the seller to the Accounts Department of the purchasing firm when goods were overcharged, goods were charged for but not received, goods are returned or packing cases are returned. The credit note reduces the original invoice charge, ie, the buyer pays the original invoice less the amount of the credit note.

Distribution of Credit Note:
◆ Original to Customer (Accounts Department)
◆ Copy to Sales Department
◆ Copy held in Accounts Department to record on customer's account.

In this particular example, one of the LCD Multimedia Projectors failed to operate and was returned to the seller, Office Supplies Ltd, on 30 March. The accounts department of Office Suppliers Ltd will enter a credit on the customer's account, generate a credit note and forward it to the customer.

Credit Note No. C2343

Office Supplies Ltd
Wexford Industrial Estate
Wexford

Tel No: 353 53 564396
Fax No: 353 53 564987
email: sales@officesupplies.ie
web: www.officesupplies.ie
VAT No: 159 4321 67

Invoice No: 1675
Order No: A221

30 March 2010

A + J Rudd Ltd
34 Main St
Blackrock
Co. Dublin

Qty	Description	Cat. No.	Unit Price €	Total Cost €
1	LCD Multimedia Projector — portable	B3347	1,050	1,050.00
	Deduct: 25% Trade Discount			262.50
	Net goods value		**Sub Total**	787.50
	ADD: VAT @ 21%		**VAT**	165.37
			Total	**€952.87**
E&OE				

Credit note

Debit Note

Traditionally, an error in an invoice resulting in an *undercharge* was corrected by means of a debit note, which was sent by the seller to the Accounts Department of the purchasing firm for the additional charge. It had the same effect as an invoice, so today, businesses generally just send a revised invoice for the additional charge instead of a debit note.

For example, assume that the VAT rate on Invoice No. 1675 was charged at 13.5% instead of 21%. There is an undercharge of €343.12 calculated as follows:

Net Goods value of €4,575 x VAT @ 21% = €960.75
Net Goods value of €4,575 x VAT @ 13.5% = €617.63
Vat deficit = €960.75 minus €617.63 = €343.12

Distribution of Debit Note:
- ◆ Original to Customer (Accounts Department)
- ◆ Copy held in Accounts Department to record on customer's account.

Debit Note No. D343

Office Supplies Ltd
Wexford Industrial Estate
Wexford

Tel No: 353 53 564396
Fax No: 353 53 564987
email: sales@officesupplies.ie
web: www.officesupplies.ie
VAT No: 159 4321 67

Invoice No: 1675

Order No: A221

30 March 2010

A + J Rudd Ltd
34 Main St
Blackrock
Co. Dublin

Ref.	Description	Amount €
Invoice No. 1675	VAT charged at 13.5% instead of 21% Undercharge	€343.12
E&OE		

Debit note

Statement of Accounts

At the end of the month, the Accounts Department of the supplier firm sends a Statement of Account to the customer. The statement of account is a copy of the customer's account in the sales ledger, also known as the debtor's ledger. These details are entered from source documents such as invoices and credit notes sent to the customer and payments received from the customer.

The statement does not contain particulars of the goods supplied but shows the balance at the beginning of the month, all transactions during the month (ie, invoices, credit notes, payments received) and the balance due.

Statement

Office Supplies Ltd
Wexford Industrial Estate
Wexford

Tel No: 353 53 564396
Fax No: 353 53 564987
email: sales@officesupplies.ie
web: www.officesupplies.ie
VAT No: 159 4321 67

31 March 2010

A + J Rudd Ltd
34 Main St
Blackrock
Co. Dublin

Shows all increases in amounts owed, eg, invoices, debit notes.

Shows all decreases in amounts owed, eg, credit notes and cheques received.

Date	Ref. No.	Details	Debits €	Credits €	Balance €
28 Mar	1675	Invoice	5,535.75		5,535.75
30 Mar	C2343	Credit Note		952.87	4,582.88

Statement

When the statement is received by the Accounts Department of the purchasing firm the following checks are made:
1. Details of the statement are compared with the details entered for the creditor in the purchaser's ledger.
2. Calculations on the statement are checked.
3. The balance on the statement is paid, less the appropriate cash discount on invoices listed, if those invoices are paid within the time period to avail of cash discount.

Overview of Stages in Business Transactions

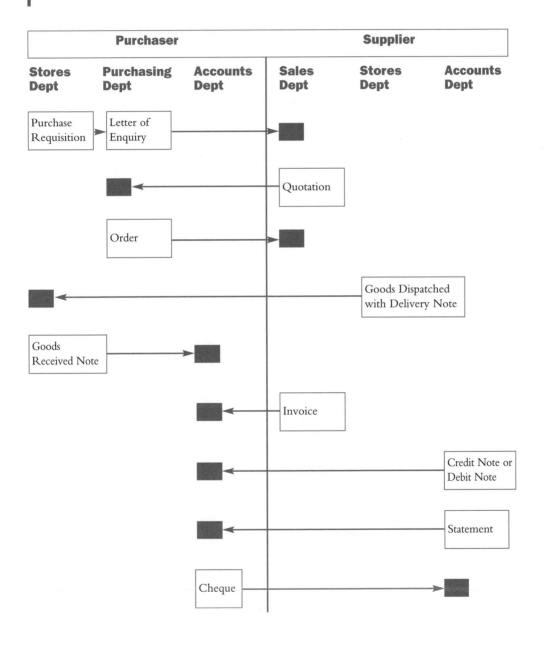

Stock Control

Stock control means monitoring the level of stock held in a business. A stock control system is necessary to ensure that the business has sufficient stock to meet anticipated needs, while at the same time not holding more stock than is necessary.

Maintaining large amounts of stock represents money tied up in the business that could be used elsewhere. A business may have taken out a loan to purchase stock and will have to pay back the loan with interest. Stock costs to the business also includes: insurance costs (in the event of fire or theft), storage costs (ie rent of warehouses), and security costs (eg alarms costs, security guards etc.). Stock may go out of date, lose its value or deteriorate over time and thus be of no value to the business. On the other hand, having insufficient stock available ('stock-out') when it is needed is also unsatisfactory. Delays ('bottlenecks') can occur in production, which may result in customer orders not being processed on time. This may lead to a loss of customers who may purchase from a competitor instead. What is needed is a balance between these two extremes.

In a small business, the stock of stationery and supplies may be the responsibility of the administrator. S/he will be responsible for monitoring stock levels, ordering supplies and dealing with incoming supplies. In a large organisation, stock control will be the responsibility of the Stores Department which will monitor stock levels and notify the Purchasing Department, via a purchase requisition, when new supplies are required.

Stock Control System

A business will set a minimum stock level, a re-order level and a maximum stock level for each item of stock, based on the rate at which stock is used over a given period and the time it takes for an order of new stock to be delivered. Mathematical formulae may be used in complex situations to determine the optimum amount of stock that should be ordered, known as the economic order quantity (EOQ).

Minimum stock level: Stock cannot safely be allowed to drop below this level. To avoid this happening, a 're-order level' is set above the minimum stock level. The minimum stock level is the 'buffer stock' and it is used in case of emergencies. It is set at a level so that an order will be received before the buffer stock is depleted.

Re-order level: When stock falls to the re-order level, an order is placed. The quantity ordered is the difference between the re-order level and the maximum stock level. It is set at a level such that the order will be received before the minimum stock level is reached.

Maximum stock level: This is the largest amount of stock that should be stored. Above this level it is uneconomical to hold stock.

The example below illustrates a simple stock control system using a stock control card for inkjet printer cartridges. The firm has set the maximum level at 30 cartridges, the re-order level at 10 cartridges and the minimum level at seven cartridges based on knowledge of usage and the 'lead time'. Lead time is the time it takes from ordering the stock to the actual delivery of the stock. The unit size of one means that the cartridges can be ordered as a single item.

The balance on 1 July was 17 cartridges. On 3 July and 10 July, cartridges were issued to departments, reducing the stock to nine cartridges on 10 July. As nine cartridges is below the re-order level, an order was placed to replenish the stock. The quantity ordered was 20 cartridges, which is the difference between the re-order level of 10 and the maximum level of thirty. The stock was received on 15 July and brought the stock level to 29 cartridges. Another issue took place on 17 July. This system ensures that the business holds an economical amount of stock.

Stock Control Card

Item:	Inkjet Printer Cartridges		
Code No:	D0034	**Maximum Level:**	30
Unit Size:	1	**Re-Order Level:**	10
Location:	A34	**Minimum Level:**	7

Date	Issued to/ received from	Quantity issued	Quantity received	Balance
1-7-10				17
3-7-10	Marketing Dept	3		14
10-7-10	Accounts Dept	5		9
15-7-10	Johnstown Supplies		20	29
17-7-10	Office Admin	1		28

Stock control card

To avoid losses due to obsolete or perished goods, the 'First In, First Out' (FIFO) system of issuing stock is used. The FIFO system operates by distributing the goods according to the earliest date at which they were delivered.

For example: assume 20 items were received on 4 June and 25 items on 28 June. If a requisition for goods was received on 8 July for 30 items, the stock will be issued from the delivery received on 4 June first, and the balance of 10 items will be issued from the later delivery.

Computerised stock control

Today, the stock control procedure is normally automated using an accounting/stock control computer package. This package will display stock control cards for each item of stock in a manner similar to the manual system.

The accounting/stock control package will be set up initially with details of each stock item and the minimum, re-order and maximum levels entered. The issue and receipt of stock are entered from the source documents (ie, requisition form, goods received note) received by the Stores Department and the balance of stock is automatically calculated. The system will indicate when the re-order level or the minimum level is reached.

Stock control systems can be incorporated at the point of sale (ie, the cash register). This type of control system is typically used in supermarkets, where there is a high volume of stock passing through the point of sale. All items are bar-coded at the point of manufacture and are entered into the purchaser's stock control system when they are delivered. When an item is passed through the point of sale, a barcode scanner scans that item as sold and the amount of stock held of that item is decreased accordingly. Thus, an up-to-date list of stock remaining can be obtained instantly. Modern stock control systems can automatically generate a new order for the stock item when the minimum re-order level is reached.

Stocktaking

While a stock control system ensures that the business holds an economical amount of stock and will not suffer a stock-out, procedures also need to be put in place to check that the amount of stock stated on the records actually is in stock. A stocktake confirms the accuracy of the stock records.

A stocktake is simply a physical count of the stock that remains in the storeroom. A stocktake is carried out once a year or more frequently, depending on the type of stock and values involved. The value of the stock may be a significant asset on the balance sheet. The business may operate a constant stocktake where areas of stock are checked periodically throughout the year, or it may operate random 'spot checks' on certain items of stock to ensure that stock records are being maintained properly and to reduce the risk of pilfering.

When a stocktake is carried out, the physical stock is counted and recorded on a *stock list* or on a handheld barcode device. The stock list will have the following information pre-recorded: reference number of stock item, item description, location of stock item and value of the item. The stocktaker records only the *actual count* of each stock item. This information is then entered into the computerised stock system where the value of stock remaining is automatically calculated. If a manual stock control system is in use, the stocktaker will also calculate and record at a later date the total value of each stock item for financial accounting purposes.

The quantity of stock recorded for each item is compared to the balances stated on the individual stock control cards. Discrepancies are investigated; these can arise for the following reasons: (a) stock was stolen; (b) stock was issued and not recorded; (c) stock was received and not recorded; (d) breakages or spillages were not recorded.

Rally's Mail Order Ltd **Main Street** **Wexford** Stock of Stationery as at 17 July 2010			This column is completed by the stocktaker. ↓	This column is completed by the stocktaker or automatically calculated by the computer. ↓		
Ref. No.	**Item Description**	**Location**	**Quantity in stock**	**Value per item €**	**Total value €**	**Signature**
P675	A4 Bond Paper	A45	40	7.50	300.00	
D0034	Inkjet Printer Cartridges	A34	28	38.00	1,064.00	
E89	DL Envelopes	B23	30	4.50	135.00	
	etc.					
total						

Stocktake list

Short Questions

1. Outline the main stages of a purchasing transaction, from the initial enquiry to the time when the goods are paid for.
2. Outline the main stages of a selling transaction, from the receipt of the enquiry to the time when payment is received.
3. List four common terms of trade offered by a supplier to a buyer when sending a quotation for goods.
4. Distinguish between trade discount and cash discount. What does 'net one month' mean?
5. Explain what the following terms mean:
   a)   delivery terms
   b)   CWO
   c)   E&OE.
6. Distinguish between:
   a)   a purchase requisition form and an order form
   b)   an invoice and a pro-forma invoice.

7. A buyer is offered goods by the two suppliers below. What does each term mean, and what factors will the buyer have to take into account in deciding which of the quotations to accept?

Supplier 1	Supplier 2
15% trade discount	25% trade discount
Ready delivery	1 month delivery
Cash — one month net	5% cash discount within 10 days

8. Distinguish between:
   a)   a delivery note and an advice note
   b)   a credit note and a debit note.

9. What checks are made on an incoming invoice?

10. An invoice shows a total amount of €3,500. A cash discount of 5% is offered if the invoice is paid within two weeks and 2% if paid within one month. Calculate the amount a customer should pay if s/he pays:
   a)   within two weeks
   b)   within one month
   c)   after one month.

11. What is a 'statement of account'?

12. Identify four costs associated with maintaining high levels of stock.

13. What is meant by the term 'stock-out'? List two possible reasons for a stock-out and describe how it can affect the business.

14. What is the relationship between the following in a stock control system:
   a)   minimum stock level
   b)   re-order level
   c)   maximum stock level?

15. Distinguish between stock control and stocktaking.

16. Explain the term FIFO. Give an example.

Chapter 8 — Meetings

Formal Meetings are conducted according to specific rules relevant to the legal form of business. For example, club and society meetings are governed by the club or society Charter, while company meetings are governed by the Companies Acts and the individual company's Articles of Association.

Types of Formal Meeting

The main types of formal meeting are:
- ordinary meetings
- extraordinary general meetings (EGMs)
- class meetings (or specific group meetings)
- annual general meetings (AGMs).

Ordinary Meetings

Ordinary meetings are held regularly to discuss routine issues that must be dealt with in the normal course of the business; for example, a meeting with Department Heads at the beginning of each month to discuss budgets, production plans and sales.

Extraordinary General Meetings

Extraordinary general meetings are convened to discuss urgent, non-routine business matters. Companies have a legal requirement to extend specific notice of an extraordinary meeting to shareholders, along with any information that may be deemed necessary to allow the shareholder make an informed decision before voting on a resolution at the meeting.

Class Meetings

Within a company, there may be several classifications of shareholder, eg, Ordinary Shareholders and Preference Shareholders, each with different voting rights attached. Class meetings are meetings that are specific to a certain class of shareholders.

Annual General Meetings

A company must hold its first Annual General Meeting (AGM) within 18 months of incorporation. After the first year, a company has a legal obligation to hold an AGM within six months of the end of their accounting year. The main business of the AGM is to:

◆ consider the audited accounts
◆ consider the directors' and auditors' reports
◆ appoint directors to the Board
◆ appoint auditors and decide their remuneration
◆ consider whether a dividend should be declared.

Convening Company Meetings

Company meetings are convened by the chairman of the Board of Directors, in accordance with the Companies Act and the Articles of Association. Shareholders can also request the directors to call a meeting. If a meeting is not properly convened, ie, if improper notification is given to shareholders, or if information necessary to consider a *special resolution* is not given, then any business carried out at the ensuing meeting may be considered null and void.

If the Board of Directors refuses to call a meeting, the Minister can intervene and direct that the meeting be held.

Quorum

Every meeting must have a quorum, (ie, a specified number of members present) before the meeting can start. The quorum for the meeting is determined by the Articles of Association. The normal quorum requirement is three members present for public company meetings, two members present for private company meetings and one member present for a single-member company. If the appropriate quorum is not present, and the meeting goes ahead, the business of the meeting may be declared null and void. If a quorum is not present after thirty minutes of the due commencement time of the meeting, the Chairman can adjourn the meeting and reschedule it for another date.

Resolutions

Resolutions are motions that are voted upon by shareholders. There are two types of resolution: 'Ordinary' and 'Special'. An Ordinary resolution requires a simple majority vote to succeed (ie, over 50% of the votes cast), while a Special resolution requires a 75% majority vote to succeed.

Voting at Meetings

At a company meeting, the voting rights of the shareholder are determined by the classification of shares held. Voting may be carried out by a show of hands, secret ballot or shareholders may call for a *poll* (ie, where votes are cast according to the number of shares held). In clubs or societies normally each member has one vote only.

Shareholders who cannot be present at a meeting may be allowed to vote on a resolution by *proxy*. This means that they can nominate another person, usually the chairman, to vote as directed by them at the meeting.

Documentation for Meetings

1 — Notice of Meeting

A Notice of Meeting must be sent out to everyone who is entitled to attend the meeting. The notice may be issued in hard-copy or electronic format (ie, posted, sent by email or put on a website). If the meeting is an AGM, then 21 days' notice must be given to members. The same period of 21 days' notice is also required when a 'special resolution' is to be passed. For EGMs, 14 days' notice of the meeting is required for public companies, and seven days' notice for private companies unless a shorter term is agreed by the members.

The Notice of Meeting should contain the date, day, time, location and type of meeting called. It is usual to send out an Agenda with the Notice of Meeting and any extra information that members may need to decide on resolutions. A proxy form may be included if the member is entitled to appoint a proxy to vote at the forthcoming meeting.

Example of Notice of Meeting

Springclean Ltd
14 Manor West
TRALEE
Co. Kerry

31 May 2010

Notice is hereby given that the Annual General Meeting of Springclean Ltd will take place on Wednesday 16 June 2010 at the Grand Hotel, Tralee, at 8.30 pm.

AGENDA
1. Apologies
2. Minutes from previous meeting
3. Matters arising from the Minutes
4. To receive and consider the Financial Statements and Reports of the Directors and Auditors for the year ended 31 December 2009. (Resolution 1)
5. To consider a declaration of a final dividend. (Resolution 2)
6. To reappoint the following Directors who retire by rotation in accordance with Article 34 of the Articles of Association. (Resolution 3)
   Mr J. Hegarty, Mr J. Creedon, Mr M. Connors
7. To authorise the Directors to fix the Auditors' remuneration. (Resolution 4)
8. Any other business (AOB)
9. Date and time of next meeting

Dervilla Spring
Company Secretary

2 — Agenda

The Agenda sets the order of business for the meeting. The Chairman must deal with the items on the Agenda in that order, unless agreement is reached by the meeting to change the order.

Normally, apologies from members who cannot attend the meeting is the first item on the agenda. Minutes from the previous meeting are read by the Secretary and any matters arising from those minutes are dealt with at this point. The meeting continues in accordance with the items on the Agenda. If a member wishes to raise an issue that is not on the Agenda, s/he may do so under Any Other Business (AOB). The meeting may deal with the issue then, or decide to place the issue on the agenda for the next meeting.

When the meeting is concluding, a date and time for the next meeting may be decided. This may not always be possible, so the Chairman may decide the time and date of next meeting and notify the members in due course.

3 — Proxy Form

A proxy form may be sent with the notice of meeting to allow the shareholder to nominate another shareholder and to direct him/her to vote on their behalf in their absence.

Springclean Annual General Meeting Form of Proxy

Name (in full): _____

Address: _____

I/We being an ordinary shareholder of the above-named company hereby appoint the duly appointed shareholder to be Chairman of the meeting:

_____

As my/our proxy to vote for me/us on my/our behalf at the Annual General Meeting of the company to be held at 8.30pm on 16 June 2010 at the Grand Hotel, Tralee, and at any adjournment thereof. I/we direct my/our proxy to vote on the resolutions set out in the notice convening the meeting as instructed below and in respect of other resolutions that may arise at the meeting as the proxy thinks fit.

		For	Against
Resolution 1	To adopt the Accounts	❑	❑
Resolution 2	To declare a dividend	❑	❑
Resolution 3	To re-elect the directors (as named)	❑	❑
Resolution 4	To authorise Directors to fix auditors' remuneration	❑	❑

Signature: _____ **Date:** _____

4 — Minutes

The minutes of the meeting are the legal record of events that take place at the meeting. It is vital that the Secretary transcribes correctly the details of the meeting. Every company is required by law to keep records of minutes and Resolutions at their registered office for a period of 10 years. The documents may be kept in hard-copy or electronic format and can be inspected by the shareholders at any time.

When the minutes of the previous meeting are agreed by the meeting, it is normal to have members to propose and second the minutes. The Chairman can then sign the minutes as being a true record of the events of that previous meeting. The minutes now become a legal record and cannot be adjusted without the consent of the meeting. A resolution is normally required to amend the minutes.

Example of Minutes

Springclean Ltd

Minutes of the AGM of Springclean Ltd held on the 16 June 2010 at the Grand Hotel, Tralee, Co. Kerry.

Present

K. Woods (Managing Director)	J. Creedon (Director)
D. Spring (Company Secretary)	M. Connors (Director)
J. Hegarty (Director)	D. Browne (Auditor)

and 30 shareholders

1. **APOLOGIES FOR ABSENCE**

   Apologies were received from Mr O'Donnell (Director).

2. **MINUTES OF THE LAST MEETING**

   The minutes read by the Company Secretary, proposed by Mr M. Connors and seconded by Mr J. Creedon, approved by the meeting and signed by the Chairman as being a correct record.

3. **MATTERS ARISING FROM THE MINUTES**

   There were no matters arising from the minutes.

4. **AUDITOR'S REPORT**

   Ms D. Browne outlined the financial position of the company to the shareholders for the past trading year, stating that the accounts had been prepared in accordance with normal accountancy standards and practice.

5. **DIRECTOR'S REPORT**

   Mr Woods outlined the activities of the company during the year. The company had succeeded in reaching its target growth of 20% with the acquisition of Brightclean Ltd in September. This has proved to be extremely advantageous in obtaining lucrative cleaning contracts in the hospitality industry. As a result, the company is intending to expand its employee base by ten during the next quarter. Each shareholder was given a full copy of the Director's Report.

6. **ELECTION OF DIRECTORS**

It was proposed by Mr Woods and seconded by Ms O'Neill, that Denise O'Connell be elected as a Director to the Board. This resolution was passed by the meeting.

7. **APPOINTMENT AND REMUNERATION OF AUDITORS**

It was proposed by Mr M. Connors and seconded by Mr J. Creedon that Ms D. Brown be retained as auditor to the company with a 2% increase in remuneration. This was agreed unanimously by the meeting.

8. **DIVIDEND**

Mr Woods recommended a dividend of 5% on ordinary shares which was agreed by the meeting.

9. **ANY OTHER BUSINESS**

There were no other issues raised and the meeting was closed by Mr Woods at 10.30 pm.

Chairman: _____   Date: _____

Duties of the Chairman and Secretary

The Chairman

The Chairman has a duty to control the meeting, to manage discussions fairly and to abstain from influencing any debates. A Chairman must ensure that the timing of the meeting is adequate, so that each issue is discussed in an equitable fashion. A realistic agenda should be set and sufficient time allocated for any debate that may ensue at the meeting. In the case of a debate, the Chairman should allocate equal opportunities to both parties to voice their opinions, rule on *points of order* (queries regarding correct procedures) and must decide when to call for a vote. The Chairman usually abstains from voting, but in the event of a tie, will have a casting vote.

The Chairman can adjourn the meeting if a quorum is not present or where there is unruly conduct at the meeting.

The Secretary

The Secretary sends out notices of the meeting, prepares documentation, will book the venue and make any other arrangements necessary for the smooth running of the meeting. At the meeting, the Secretary is responsible for taking the minutes.

Short Questions

1. What regulations govern formal meetings conducted at clubs or societies and companies?
2. List four main types of formal meeting.
3. Distinguish between an ordinary general meeting and an extraordinary general meeting.
4. What is a class meeting?
5. List four obligations on companies in relation to convening an AGM.
6. List four items that are usually dealt with at an AGM.
7. What is a quorum and what are the consequences of an insufficient quorum?
8. What is a resolution? Distinguish between an ordinary and a special resolution.
9. Distinguish between the terms 'poll' and 'proxy'.
10. List three documents that are normally sent out with the notice of a meeting.
11. Outline the format of the minutes of a meeting.
12. List three duties of the chairman and three duties of the secretary in relation to meetings.

Summary

The office of any business is a busy place, and many routine tasks are performed there, including dealing with telephone calls, visitors, arranging appointments, preparing meetings, processing expenses and calculating wages. Personnel in the office who perform these tasks include receptionists, personal assistants, general administrators and office juniors. The receptionist is often the first point of contact with a business, and it is vital that a professional impression is given when taking telephone calls, greeting visitors and handling queries. The receptionist's main task is to operate the switchboard and distribute messages. This has been made easier with facilities on the switchboard such as IVR and DDI. If a call is not answered, voicemail is generally activated.

Office technology has greatly improved routine administrative tasks. Dealing with everyday correspondence is made easier with the use of specialised software and email is commonly used to circulate messages both internally and externally. Arranging appointments can be made easier by using an electronic diary that allows the administrator to view and book time slots for appointments. Arranging travel can create quite a lot of paperwork, eg, forms authorising travel, quotations for 'best price', expense forms and receipts which must be compiled before calculating the appropriate expenses. This procedure can be automated by employees completing an on-line form and emailing the completed form to the administrator. Expenses can then be calculated by using an electronic distance chart and calculator.

Another common office task is maintaining a petty cash system, ie, a small cash fund from which sundry items are purchased for the office. Petty cash is usually maintained using the imprest system, and the administrator responsible for petty cash will obtain a float from the finance department at the beginning of every petty cash period. The administrator will only issue cash from petty cash when a completed voucher and receipt for the expense incurred is received.

In a smaller business, the office may have responsibility for accounts payable, accounts receivable and payroll, and a specialised accounts administrator may be required to perform these functions. Accounts payable deals with payments to be made to suppliers, and accounts receivable deals with payments received from customers. Most offices have a computerised payroll system into which details such as the 'standard rate cut-off point' and voluntary deductions are entered once for each employee. Payslips are generated at the end of each pay period, ie, weekly, fortnightly, etc.

Another duty of the administrator may be to organise and prepare for meetings. In some cases, there is a legal requirement to hold specific meetings, eg, a company must hold an Annual General Meeting to outline the activities of the company over the past year to the members and interested parties. Other types of meeting that the administrator may help to convene are Ordinary, Extraordinary and Class meetings.

When a meeting is to be convened, notification of the meeting is sent out to members, and an agenda and a proxy form is attached if necessary. At the meeting the chairman controls the conduct of the meeting and the secretary of the meeting takes the 'minutes', which are a record of the events of the meeting. This is a legal record and cannot be altered once approved by the meeting and signed by the Chairman. Rules and regulations regarding the running of the meeting (eg, voting procedures, resolutions, quorums, etc.) are determined by the Companies Acts and the Articles of Associations in the case of a company, and by a Charter in the case of a club or society.

Assignments

1. You work in Kerry and you are responsible for arranging a trip for a senior executive who must make a presentation to head office in Grafton Street, Dublin city. The meeting starts at 10 am Monday and the executive must attend another meeting in Dublin on Tuesday which ends at 5.30 pm.

   a) Outline the best means of transport for this trip. Use appropriate references to source this information.

b) Review three hotels in Dublin city and check price and availability of a single en suite room for the Monday night. Choose one of these hotels and prepare a fax or email as a provisional booking request.

c) Prepare an itinerary for the executive, detailing his departure time, connect time for other transport, the meetings he is attending and the return departure time.

2. Mr Buckley travels on a daily basis from Limerick city to Waterford city on business. At the end of the week he submits a claim form for travel expenses. However, on checking his claim form, his travel expenses are calculated incorrectly. Use a distance chart to calculate his total travel expenses for five days of travelling, assuming he is paid 70c per kilometre.

3. Your company is hosting this year's annual conference. You are assigned full responsibility for arranging the whole weekend. Fifty delegates are expected. Design a plan to cope with all aspects of the weekend — both formal and social. Make any assumptions you wish.

4. Write up procedures for a new junior receptionist for the following:

a) maintaining the reception area

b) handling incoming telephone calls

c) receiving visitors.

5. The following is a record of a telephone conversation between a junior administrator, Niamh Kelly at Health Care Products Ltd, and Mr Griffin, an important client from Shape Up Ltd:

Administrator: Hello.

Mr Griffin: Is that Health Care Products Ltd?

Administrator: Ya.

Mr Griffin: Is Mr Shannon there please?

Administrator: Hang on, I'll check…. No, sorry, he seems to have taken an extended lunch.

Mr Griffin: What time do you expect him back?

Administrator: He should be back shortly.

Mr Griffin: Can I leave a message please?

Administrator: Sure, just a second while I get a pen.

Mr Griffin: Tell him I can meet him tomorrow as arranged and to call me.

Administrator: (Writing down) OK, all right. Thanks. Bye.

a) State where you think the administrator went wrong in the way she handled this call.

b) Rewrite the telephone conversation in the way it should have been handled by the administrator. You may adjust Mr Griffin's responses based on what the administrator states.

c) Draw up a typical telephone message form and write the message which you would pass to Mr Shannon.

6. Compare the costs of making a telephone call from a fixed-line telephone in Kerry to: (a) Dubai (b) Finland and (c) Galway, during office hours, using three different telephone providers.

7. Mary earns €8 per hour for a 35-hour week. The overtime rate is double time. Her Tax Credit is €60 per week. She pays tax at 20%, PRSI at 5%, pays €7 per week into an approved pension fund, and €2.50 per week into the company social fund. She is exempt from the Income Levy as her gross income is under the limit. This week she worked 38 hours. Calculate Mary's:
   a) basic pay
   b) gross pay
   c) taxable income
   d) net tax liability
   e) take-home pay.

8. Prepare a petty cash book for the following sundry cash transactions. Decide the columnar headings. The imprest from accounts is €50. Balance the petty cash book on 30 June.
   June 1   €2.60 for stationery
   June 3   €5.80 for fax paper
   June 6   €4.50 for office staff bus fares
   June 8   €13.50 for cleaning
   June 15   €6.90 for canteen supplies

9. You work as the company secretary in an Irish-based Internet company called 'WhereEire.com' which supplies the tourist market with local tourist information. The Director has asked you to prepare the documentation for the first AGM. Make whatever assumptions you wish, prepare the Notice of Meeting and the agenda for the AGM.

10. Assign the roles of chairman, secretary, directors and shareholders to class members and using the documentation prepared in the previous question, let the meeting take place according to the agenda. Remember the secretary should write up the minutes after the event.

11. Locate your local Credit Union branch and tabulate the interest rates on savings of €5,000 over a period of 5 years and compare with the interest rates on savings at two other Irish commercial banks.

Blank documents are provided at the back of the book for the following exercises. These should be photocopied.

12. Joan Butler is employed as an office clerk in M & M Construction Ltd, Dundrum, Co. Dublin. She requests the following items to be purchased by the Purchasing Department:
   2 packs Sigma Purchase Orders
   1 pack Sigma Delivery Notes
   1 pack PaperMate 2000 Fine (Blue).

a) Complete the necessary document that she will send to Michael McGrath, the Purchasing Officer.

b) Complete the order (Order No. O231) sent by the Purchasing Officer, Michael McGrath, to Collins Stationery Supplies Ltd, Monasterevin, Co. Kildare. (Refer to price list on page 136.)

13. From the information provided compile the quotation that is sent by Mr John Doyle, Sales Dept, Stationery Supplies, 44 White Street, Cavan, in reply to a letter of enquiry received from Ms Jane Hanley, Purchasing Dept, 5 High Street, Cavan.

Quotation number Q531

Cat No. 231   40 lever-arch files @ €3.50 each

Cat No. 235   20 box files @ €6.00 each

Cat No. 211   10 boxes of manila folders at €8.50 per box

Delivery 1 week from receipt of order

Cash discount 5% within 1 week.

14. (i) Show how the following items will appear in a statement of account dated 30.5.10.

1/5/10	Balance b/f	€55
4/5/10	Sales Invoice — 008	€975
15/5/10	Credit Note — Returns	€70
27/5/10	Cheque	€55
28/5/10	Sales Invoice — 009	€1,420

(ii) If the terms of sale on invoice 009 are 'Cash Discount: 3% within 2 weeks, net one month', state how much the cheque payable will be if a cheque is sent:

within 2 weeks;

after 2 weeks but within 1 month;

after 1 month.

15. On 11 March, Printer Supplies Ltd, 12 Main Street, Kildare, supplied to Copypress, Westgate, Wexford, the items ordered on Order No. O451. On 18 March, Copypress returned 1 can of damaged cleaning fluid.

Order No. O451

10 cans of cleaning fluid at €5.50 per can excluding VAT of 21%.
Terms of sale were: 10% trade discount and 2.5% cash discount within 1 month.

---

a) Complete the invoice number I231 sent on 11 March.

b) Complete the credit note number C390 sent on 20 March.

c) Complete the statement of account number S200 sent on 31 March.

d) How much will Copypress pay if the statement is paid on 27 April?

16. Joseph Moran is the manager of the Purchasing Department in MEC Office Supplies Ltd. He receives the following quotation on 3 August 2010.

Quotation
Curragh Supplies Ltd, Kilcullen, Co. Kildare

Tel: 353 45 852329   **VAT Reg No:** 883294U
Fax: 353 45 852330   **Date:** 3 August 2010

MEC Office Supplies Ltd
Industrial Estate
Co. Laois

Qty	Code	Description	Unit Price €
20	3000	Treasury tags (box size 100)	6.35
4	4012	Two-ring A4 binders (packet 10) 2.27	15.00
2	3002	Dl 8⅝" x 4¼" window gummed	19.00

VAT 21%

Terms: 5% 1 Month   Carriage Paid

a) Complete the delivery note sent with the goods by Curragh Supplies Ltd.
b) Complete the invoice sent by Curragh Supplies Ltd.
c) Complete the cheque that Joseph Moran sends on 20 August.

16. You work for Office Equipment Supplies Ltd and the following goods were ordered by Marcol Systems Limited.

Order No.: x11

Marcol Systems Limited
Eagle House
Naas
Co. Kildare

Tel: 353 45 852000   **VAT Reg No:** 659844d
Fax: 353 45 852001   **Date:** 13 October 2010

Office Equipment Supplies Ltd
Evin Blue Industrial Estate
Dublin 1

Qty	Code	Description	Unit Price €
5	1933	3.5" DS/DD IBM PS2	€12.32
3	1934	3.5" DS/HD IBM PS2	€11.30
5	1827	3.5" DS/DD Apple Mac	€12.32
1	1600	3.5" 3 Drawer Unit	€81.26

Terms: Trade Discount 15%, VAT 21%, Discount Cash 2.5% 1 Month, Delivery 14 days

a) Complete the invoice sent by you on 25 October. All goods ordered were delivered.

b) If the invoice is paid on 12 November, how much will the buyer have to pay?

17. Complete the statement sent on 30 March from the details given. The supplier is Shannon's Supplies Ltd, Kilrush, Co. Clare and the purchaser is Kathleen Carty, Church Street, Athlone, Co. Westmeath.

		€
Balance outstanding from last month		425.50
4 Mar	Goods supplied on Invoice P2341	70.15
6	Goods returned — Credit Note CN523	20.10
7	Goods supplied on Invoice P2352	60.05
9	Cheque received	425.50
16	Goods supplied on Invoice P2370	15.00
18	Cases returned — Credit Note	12.00
26	CN547 Goods supplied on Invoice P2381	45.00

18. On 30 June 2010, Hegarty & Co. Ltd, Delgany, Co. Wicklow received a statement from Collins Stationery Supplies Ltd, Monasterevin, Co. Kildare. The balance due was €527.

On 2 July, Nuala Lennon, the Purchasing Manager for Hegarty & Co. Ltd, ordered the following goods from the price list she received.

10 packs Bic Crystal Medium (Black)

15 packs Bic Crystal Fine (Red)

20 packs Bic Crystal Medium (Blue)

5 packs Bic Clic Stic Ball Pen (Blue)

	Price List		
	Collins Stationery Supplies Ltd **Monasterevin** **Co. Kildare**	Means €7.30 for a pack of 50.	
Code	**Description**		**Unit Price €**
0124	PaperMate 2000 Fine (Blue/Black)		7.30/50
0125	PaperMate 2000 Fine (Red)		1.70/12
0126	PaperMate 2000 Medium (Blue/Black)		7.30/50
0127	PaperMate 2000 Medium (Red)		1.77/12
0128	Zebra Ball Pen (Black/Blue/Red)		6.12/10
0129	Zebra Refills (Black/Blue/Red)		2.06/10
0130	Bic Clic Stic Ball Pen (Blue/Black/Red)		8.00/25
0131	Bic Soft Feel Stic (Blue/Black/Red)		4.25/12
0132	Bic Crystal Fine (Blue/Black/Red/Green)		3.10/20
0133	Bic Crystal Medium (Blue/Black/Red/Green)		3.20/20
0136	Pentel Fountain (Black/Blue/Red/Green)		18.70/12
0137	Pentel Ultra Fine (Black/Blue/Red/Green)		12.90/12
0200	Sigma Purchase Orders		6.86/50
0201	Sigma Delivery Notes		5.40/50
0202	Sigma Invoice Sets		5.40/50
0203	Sigma Statements		6.80/50
0204	Sigma Memos		6.25/100

All Prices are excluding VAT at 21%

Terms: Trade Discount 15%, Cash Discount 2% 2 weeks

Net 1 Month

Required:

a) Complete the order form sent by Nuala Lennon on 2 July.

b) Complete the delivery note sent by Collins Stationery Supplies Ltd on 6 July.

c) Complete the invoice sent by Collins Stationery Supplies Ltd on 6 July.

d) On 8 July, Nuala Lennon wrote to Collins Stationery Supplies Ltd stating that 2 packs of the Bic Crystal Fine (Red) were damaged. Complete the Credit Note sent to Hegarty & Co. Ltd.

e) Complete the cheque sent on 20 July by Hegarty & Co. Ltd to clear their account.

f) Complete the statement sent by Collins Stationery Supplies Ltd on 31 July.

19. The details for receipt and issue of compact disks are given below. The unit size is 1 packet (20 disks per packet). Draw up an appropriate stock card recording the details.

    July 1   25   packets in stock
          6   4   packets issued to Personnel Department
          9   6   packets issued to Office
          9   2   packets issued to Accounts Department
          12   1   packet issued to Advertising Department
          13   20   packets purchased
          20   8   packets issued to accounts

20. You have just taken over a position as stationery clerk, and have found that your predecessor kept records on scraps of paper. Your job is to set up a stock control system. From the information recorded on the scraps of paper given below:
    a) show how you would record the details for overhead transparencies;
    b) state when you will place an order for more supplies.
       Inkjet overhead transparencies: min and max level — 5 and 25 boxes
       Unit size of 1 box (50 sheets per box)
       Balance on 2 June was 10 boxes
       1 box issued to Human Resources Department on 5 June
       5 boxes issued to Office Services Department on 9 June
       Received from Star Stationery Limited on 11 June — 20 boxes
       4 boxes issued to Marketing Department on 23 June.

21. a) An invoice was sent by Astra Business Systems to Ideal Office Supplies on 14 April 2005, for goods on Order No. A125. All goods ordered were delivered. You are required to write up the invoice.
    b) Ideal Office Supplies returned two Olivetti Inkjet JP370 printers which were damaged in transit. Complete the credit note that was issued on 20 April in response to these returns.
    c) An opening unpaid balance of €2,579.50 was brought forward on the statement from March. On 18 April a cheque for €2,450.52 was received from Ideal Office Supplies. Cash discount of 5% had been deducted from the amount owing. Complete the statement of account that was sent to Ideal Office Supplies on 30 April, showing details of *all* transactions that occurred during the month of April.
    d) A cheque was received from Ideal Office Supplies in full settlement of the balance due on the April statement. Complete the cheque and the stub dated 12 May 2010.

Order

Ideal Office Supplies
Silver Springs
Delgany
Co. Wicklow

No. A125

To:

Date: 2 April 2010

Astra Business Systems
Santry Hall Industrial Estate
Dublin 9
Please supply:

Qty	Code	Description	Unit Price €
3	672/1125	IBM Aptiva P75 Mini Tower computer	1,599.00
2	672/0755	Apple Performa 6200	1,329.00
5	671/2000	Olivetti inkjet JP370 printer	299.00
1	671/2017	Sharp JX 9200 laser printer	349.00

Terms: Trade Discount 15%, VAT 21%, Cash Discount 5% 1 month, Delivery 14 days.

Astra Business Systems
Santry Hall Industrial Estate
Dublin 9

Price List

Code	Description	Unit Price €
672/1091	IBM Aptiva Cyrix 586 computer	1,429.00
672/1125	IBM Aptiva P75 Mini Tower computer	1,599.00
672/0755	Apple Performa 6200	1,329.00
671/2031	Citizen ABC mono printer	119.00
671/1324	Citizen inkjet Projet 2c colour printer	248.50
671/2000	Olivetti inkjet JP370 printer	299.00
671/2017	Sharp JX 9200 laser printer	349.00

Terms: Trade Discount 15%, Delivery 14 days, VAT 21%, Cash Discount 5% 1 month.

Unit 3 — Computers and Networks

Introduction

Unit 3 provides an overview of the components of a computer system and clarifies the terminology encountered when buying a computer. The features of business application software and how these tools assist office workers are reviewed.

Very few office computers operate as stand-alone computers; they are generally networked. The various ways in which computers can be networked to facilitate communication within and outside the business are outlined. Access to the Internet is also explored, as well as techniques to search the web.

The unit concludes with a discussion of Information Systems implemented by a business to assist in the decision-making process at the various levels of management.

Unit 3 is divided into four chapters:

Chapter 9 — Computer Basics and Peripheral Devices

Reviews the components of a computer system and the various peripheral devices on the market such as printers, scanners and storage media (ie, magnetic, optical and solid-state). It concludes with a guide to buying a computer.

◆ Computer Systems
◆ Components of a Computer System
◆ Storage Media
◆ Printers
◆ Scanners
◆ Guide to Buying a Computer

Chapter 10 — Computer Applications

Examines the features of common computer applications used in a business and how computer viruses are transmitted and controlled.

◆ Word Processing
◆ Spreadsheets
◆ Databases

◆ Desktop Publishing
◆ Computer Viruses

Chapter 11 — Networks and the Internet

Reviews private and public networks, as well as explaining the differences among LANs, WANs, the Internet, intranets and extranets. It provides guidelines on how to use the Web and tips on how to make searching for information more productive:

◆ Types of Network
◆ The Internet
◆ The World Wide Web
◆ Understanding Web Addresses
◆ Searching the Web
◆ Intranet and Extranet

Chapter 12 — Information Systems

Discusses the different levels of decision making from operative level to senior management level and the information required to make such decisions. It looks at information systems implemented by a business to capture, process and distribute information to enable timely and informed decisions to be made at the appropriate level of management:

◆ Operational Support Systems
◆ Management Support Systems
◆ Designing an Information System

Chapter 9 — Computer Basics and Peripheral Devices

Computer Systems

A computer is an electronic device that accepts data or other input, processes the data/input in accordance with the computer software used and displays the results on a screen.

Every office, large or small, requires a computer to process and store information. Simple routine office work such as processing correspondence, maintaining a database of customers, preparing invoices, statement, and other documentation, and corresponding immediately via email are just some of the tasks made easy by computer technology. There are many different types of computer systems, such as desktop computers, laptops and netbooks:

Netbook   *Laptop*

◆ **Desktop Computer:** a computer made up of many separate parts, in including the processor, screen, keyboard and mouse, and is set up in a permanent location. Desktops are the preferred choice for office workers who use computers regularly, as bigger screens and more ergonomically designed keyboards are available.

◆ **Laptop Computer:** a portable computer that integrates the processor, screen, keyboard, mouse, etc. It performs the same tasks as a desktop computer, although it is typically less powerful at the same price. Laptops are used by office employees who work off-site, ie, sales representatives, company executives, etc. Their use enables employees to maintain contact with the office via email and complete their work while out of the office.

◆ **Netbook Computer:** a very portable computer, generally about half the size of standard laptop with the screen size ranging from seven inches to 10 inches. Generally, netbooks are a good deal cheaper than laptops, but have lower-power processors, do not have CD/DVD player, have their own versions of software and are intended primarily for light computer use such as browsing the Internet, emailing, and basic use of general applications such as word processing and spreadsheets. Netbooks are used by office employees who need to access their email and perform basic computing tasks off-site.

Regardless of its type, a computer has many components which accept data/input, processes the data/input and outputs the results. These physical components of a computer are known as the *'hardware'* and are discussed below.

Components of a Computer System

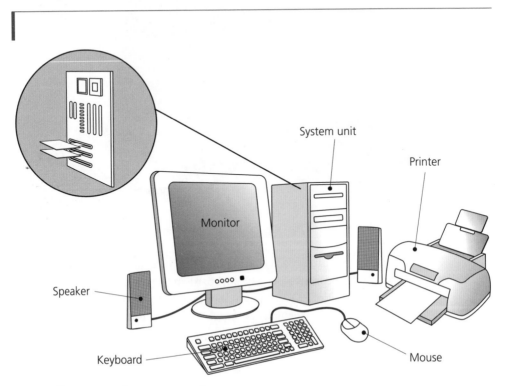

Components of a computer system

A typical computer configuration consists of the following components:

◆ **Input devices** enable data to be entered or selected on a computer. Examples of input devices are Human Interface Devices (HDI) such as a keyboard, mouse, tracker ball, touch pad, stylus or joystick and Data Capture Devices such as a scanner, digital camera, webcam or microphone.

◆ **Output devices** display the results of the computer processing. Examples of output devices are the monitor which displays the results of processing, speakers for audio and a printer which provides a printed copy, known as a 'hardcopy' of the information.

◆ **Storage devices:** the memory inside a computer is temporary storage which holds your data as you work on it. However, in order to keep your work for future use, it must be saved to a permanent storage medium, such as the hard disk, USB Flash drive, CDs, DVDs, the network drive, etc.

◆ **System Unit:** contains a motherboard which houses all the internal circuitry of the computer, such as the processor, memory chips, disk drives, audio and video cards, network cards and Universal Serial Bus (USB) ports. USB ports are used to attach input, output and external storage devices to the computer. The system unit can be a horizontal unit or a vertical unit, known as a 'tower'.

View of motherboard of a computer

The Central Processing Unit (CPU): is considered the 'brain' of the computer and carries out processing tasks by:

◆ retrieving the software instructions and data from memory

◆ processing the data as directed by the software

◆ placing the results back into memory.

Intel Core i7 processor

The word 'peripheral' refers to the components of a computer system other than the processor. It refers to equipment that could be added to a computer system to enhance its capability, such as a printer, scanner and extra storage devices. A keyboard, mouse, monitor and disk drives are also classified as peripheral devices, even though they are included with most computer systems.

Common Units of Measures Used with Computers	
Storage Capacity	**Speed**
The unit of measurement for capacity is a byte	The unit of measurement for speed is a Hertz (Hz)
A *byte* is one character	A *hertz* is one cycle per second
A *kilobyte* (KB) is approximately a thousand bytes	A *kilohertz* (kHz) is a thousand cycles per second
A *megabyte* (MB) is approximately a million bytes	A *megahertz* (MHz) is a million cycles per second
A *gigabyte* (GB) is approximately a thousand megabytes	A *gigahertz* (GHz) is a thousand megahertz
A *terabyte* (TB) is approximately a thousand gigabytes	

Storage Media

Files are stored on *magnetic* storage media (ie, disks and tapes), *optical* storage media (ie, CDs, DVDs and Blu-ray) and *solid-state* storage media (ie, USB disks).

Magnetic Storage Media

Magnetic storage media can be divided into two categories: *disks* and *tapes*.

Magnetic disk:

Magnetic disks are the most widely used as they provide direct access (also known as 'random access') storage. This means that the storage device can access where the information is stored on the disk directly and retrieve it, ie, it does not have to read from the start of the disk.

The most common type of magnetic disk in use today is the hard disk. A hard disk is embedded into a computer and generally provides vast capacity for storage ranging from 100GB to over 1TB. A portable hard disk can also be purchased and attached via a USB port at the back or side of the computer. Portable hard disks are widely used today for many reasons including making a backup of computer files, or working at another computer as one is not restricted to a computer having an appropriate drive, such as a CD drive.

Older portable storage technologies involving magnetic disks were widely used in the past in the form of floppy disks or zip disks. These are outdated and unlikely to be seen in a modern office. Furthermore, these magnetic disks are not as portable as their modern equivalents in the sense that one is dependent on a computer having an appropriate drive in which to insert these disks.

Magnetic tape:

Magnetic tape is a *serial access medium,* which means that the tape drive cannot retrieve the file directly but must work its way through the tape until it reaches the file required. For this reason, magnetic tape is not used for on-line storage.

Magnetic tape was widely used before optical storage media became popular for 'backup', ie, making a copy of the files stored on the hard disk in case they become corrupt or are deleted by mistake. A backup is carried out by attaching a tape drive to the computer and software is used to transfer the selected files from the hard disk to tape. The files can be transferred back to disk when required.

Portable magnetic storage media is more prone to damage from incorrect storage and mishandling than optical or solid-state storage media. Portable magnetic storage media should not be stored near magnetic fields, ie, a telephone, TV or photocopier; or exposed to extremes of temperature, sunlight and moisture.

Optical Storage Media

Optical storage media can be divided into three categories: *compact disk* (CD), *digital versatile disk* (DVD) and *Blu-ray* disk. Unlike magnetic media, optical media are not prone to damage from magnetic fields and are less prone to extremes of temperature. However, optical disks are prone to scratches.

Compact disk (CD)

There are three types of compact disk: CD-ROM, CD-R and CD-RW, all of which have a storage capacity of 700MB.

◆ **CD-ROM** (Compact Disk Read-Only Memory): A disk that contains pre-recorded data. CD-ROMs are widely used to store music and office materials such as reference manuals, catalogues, training courses and software applications. It is a read-only storage medium, which means that the data can be retrieved and read, but no changes can be made to the pre-recorded data stored on the disk.

◆ **CD-R** (Compact Disk, Recordable): a blank disk used for recording purposes. Once the information has been recorded and the file closed, no changes can be made to the data on the disk. CD-Rs are generally used for backing up files and archiving data. A CD-R may also be referred to as a CD-WORM (Write Once, Read Many Times).

◆ **CD-RW** (Compact Disk, Rewritable): a blank disk used for recording data, but unlike a CD-R the data recorded can be changed on that disk.

Digital versatile disk (DVD)

Like CDs, there are three corresponding types of DVD disks: DVD ROM, DVD-R and DVD-RW. Each DVD type performs the same function as the equivalent CD. However, the storage capacity of DVDs is 4.7GB, which is approximately 6 times greater than that of CDs. However, despite the significant capacity of the DVD, CD formats are still widely used today, as the recordable formats are cheaper and have ample capacity for general use.

Blu-ray disk (BD)

The latest improvement in optical disk storage since 2008 is the Blu-ray disk which is mainly used for storing high definition (HD) video, audio and the latest Play Station games. A Blu-ray disk has a capacity of 25GB, which is approximately 6 times greater than that of DVDs. Like CDs and DVDs, there are three corresponding types of Blu-ray disks: BD-ROM, BD-R and BD-RE (erasable and re-writable).

A mini-compact Blu-ray disk is also available, with BD-R and BD-RE versions for use with compact camcorders and other compact recording devices. The mini Blu-ray disk has a capacity of up to 7.5 GB.

Most computers have an optical drive as standard that is capable of reading all formats of optical media, ie, CDs, DVDs and Blu-ray disks. Such optical drives are known as 'combo' drives and are generally described as 'CD/DVD-RW with Blu-ray' which means they can read all formats of optical media but can only record/write ('burn') to both CD-R/RW and DVD-R/RW (ie, recordable/rewritable disks). Optical drives designed to record on a BD-R or BD-RE disk are not currently that prevalent on modern computers due to the cost of a BD R/RW drive. The cost of such drives will obviously decrease as the technology is adopted.

Solid-state storage media

Solid-state storage devices (SSD) are based on 'flash memory' technology. There are many forms of SSDs, such as the various sizes of 'memory card' used in electronic devices, ie, digital cameras, MP3 players, PDAs and USB drives.

A USB drive is a portable device used to transfer data between computers and has the following features:

◆ more robust and reliable than magnetic or optical media, as SSDs have no moving parts

◆ small – the size of a lighter or smaller

◆ can store from 256MB to 32GB of data, depending on the type

◆ has a faster access rate than magnetic or optical media, ie, data can be retrieved faster

USB plug that goes into USB port

USB drive

◆ are more portable in terms of accessing files between computers. For example, files stored on optical media can be accessed only on a computer with an optical drive. However, a USB drive can be used with any computer as all computers have a USB port.

USB drives are intended to be used as portable devices from one computer to another, or as a back-up device. They are not intended to be used like a hard disk (or other forms of magnetic media) onto which information is constantly written, as there is a restriction on the number of times information can be written to the disk. The restriction is very generous, however, allowing more than 100,000 writes. After that, the disk may not function correctly and some data may be lost.

The correct use of an USB drive is to transfer the files to the hard disk before working on them, and then transfer the finished files back to the USB drive.

Printers

Printers are vital in the office for producing hard copies of information and are normally connected to the computer network in an office to facilitate shared printing among users. Printers are categorised into two groups: impact printers and non–impact printers, according to whether the print mechanism makes contact with the paper.

Impact Printers

An impact printer is an older technology than non–impact printers such as the inkjet and laser printers. An impact printer has a printhead that makes contact with the paper, and because of the contact, it is noisy.

An example of an impact printer is the *dot matrix printer*, which operates by a printhead pressing a combination of pins against an inked

Dot matrix printer

ribbon as the printhead moves across the page. The characters appear as a matrix of dots. The greater the number of pins in the printhead, the better the quality.

Unlike non-impact printers, dot matrix printers can print on *continuous stationery* and *multi-part stationery*. 'Continuous stationery' consists of pages joined together by perforations which can be separated easily when printed. 'Multi-part stationery' (also known as 'NCR' — No Carbon Required) consists of two or more layers of paper joined together at the top by a peelable seal. The output is printed once, but the printout consists of the original printout and one or more copies which are used as receipts or delivery documentation.

Non-impact Printers

The printhead does not make contact with the paper and because of the non-contact they are virtually silent. Examples of non-impact printers are inkjet printers and laser printers.

An *inkjet printer* consists of a printhead with a series of nozzles that squirt tiny drops of ink onto the paper to form each character. The output produced is slightly moist, therefore the pages should be allowed to dry for a few seconds to avoid smudging.

Inkjet printers are very popular with home users and small businesses due to their low initial cost and their versatility in terms of colour and photographic printing.

A *laser printer* creates an electronic charge on a drum that attracts ink powder that is subsequently fused onto the paper. Laser printing is a more complex technology than inkjet printing so the initial cost is higher. Standard laser printers do not print in colour and

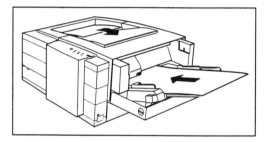

Laser printer

the cost of a colour laser printer is only justified where very high-quality colour output is required.

Both inkjet and laser printers are available as multi-functional printers (MFP) that incorporate a printer, fax, scanner and photocopier. An MFP is useful for small- to medium-volume output and is ideal for an office that does not have huge volumes of printing, faxing, scanning and photocopying.

Choosing a Printer

There are many different models of printer available on the market. When selecting a printer consider the following points:
◆ Budget constraints
◆ Where will the printer be located? — consider the noise level and size of printer
◆ What will the printer be used for? — consider colour capability, quality, paper types and sizes supported
◆ Is speed important?

♦ What volume of work is expected from the printer per time period (ie, week/month)?

♦ Before making the purchase decision, research the price of consumables for the printer, ie, ink, toner, specialised paper, etc., and the estimated number of prints per ink or toner cartridge.

Features of Printers			
Features	**Dot Matrix**	**Inkjet**	**Laser**
Noise Level	Noisy	Virtually silent	Almost silent
Initial Cost	Cheap, older technology	Relatively cheap and middle of the range printer	Expensive and top of the range printer
Running Cost	Medium: replacement cost of ribbon	Medium: replacement cost of ink cartridge	High: replacement cost of toner
Quality	Near-letter quality (NLQ)	NLQ	Letter quality
Speed	Slow	Prints one character at a time. Relatively fast	Prints one page at a time Very fast
Colour Capability	Poor	Most models good quality and cheaper than a laser	Some models excellent quality but very expensive
Volume of Output supported	Medium workload	Medium workload	High workload

Scanners

A scanner takes an image of a page or object, converts it into digital format and inputs it into the computer. A scanner eliminates the need to key in data manually and thereby reduces the risk of input error. Any type of document can be scanned, ie, text, pictures, diagrams, handwritten documents, etc.

The scanned image is known as a 'bitmap' image and cannot be edited easily. To edit a bitmap image, the document is opened with special software known as 'Optical Character Recognition (OCR)'. The OCR software 'reads' the scanned image and converts it into a text file that can be edited. OCR software can recognise a wide range of fonts and generally keeps the format of the document.

There are many types of scanners available and the choice depends on the requirements of the user such as the volume of data to be scanned, the quality required and the type of material to be scanned, (eg, single pages or pages from bound material, ie, books, magazines, etc.). The main types of scanner used in an office are:

◆ **Sheet feed scanner:** Consists of a document holder to store the page(s) to be scanned. As it can accommodate only single pages, articles from bound material must first be photocopied before scanning.

◆ **Flatbed scanner:** Consists of a glass plate similar to a photocopier, thus facilitating scanning from bound material.

◆ **Multi-purpose scanner:** Like a flatbed scanner with added attachments such as a sheet feeder for batch scanning, as well as facilities such as double-sided scanning and negative scanning. It is used when the volume of scanning is high, ie, in an electronic document-management system (EDM).

Multi-purpose scanner

Guide to Buying a Computer

Buying a computer can be very challenging, as advertisements list technical specifications describing the computer's components and features. The type of computer you buy depends on what you intend to use it for.

Computers are generally classified into three categories:

1. **Entry Level PC:** A budget computer capable of running office applications, ie, word processing, database, spreadsheet, desktop publishing and the Internet.

2. **Multimedia PC:** A mid-range computer capable of running more memory-demanding applications such as video- or photo-editing software.

3. **Top of the Range PC:** A computer capable of handling many sophisticated multimedia and gaming applications.

When purchasing a computer, decide which **category** suits your needs by reading reviews in magazines, on the Internet, talking to a sales assistant, etc. Once you have decided on a category, list the main features required and pay particular attention to:

◆ processor manufacturer and family name
◆ memory
◆ monitor size and resolution
◆ hard drive
◆ optical drive.

Even with a high-performance processor, a computer system with a limited hard drive and a small amount of memory is likely to be slow, especially with tasks such as starting programs, loading files, and scrolling through long documents. The final decision should not be made on price alone.

Processor

The processor (or CPU) is the core component in a computer and has a significant effect on price. For the latest processor, the price will be at a premium. However, for most users it is best to scale back a level or two and put the money into more memory and a bigger hard drive. Advertisements generally list the processor manufacturer and the family name that indicates the features of a processor such as architecture, speed and efficiency:

◆ **Manufacturer:** The two major manufacturers of PC processors are Intel and AMD. Intel is considered the industry leader, having led the development of the microprocessor.

◆ **Family Name:** Processors are assigned family names to identify their architecture. Within a family there is a graduation from lower to higher specification. For the desktop system, Intel produces the following family processors which are listed in order of increasing performance: Intel® Core™2 Duo, Intel® Core™2 Quad, Intel® Core™ i5 and Intel® Core™ i7 processors. These processors have superseded the older Intel® Pentium® and Celeron® processor families. AMD produces the: Athlon™, Sempron™ and Phenom™ processors.

For the laptop computer, Intel produces the Intel® Centrino® 2 processor and AMD produces the Athlon™, Sempron™ and Turion™ processors.

Memory

The memory of the computer is the computer's temporary working area. Programs and data, which are generally stored on the hard drive, must first be loaded into memory so that the processor can process the data. Memory is also referred to as random access memory (RAM), as the processor can directly retrieve the data.

The memory size, type of memory and speed of transfer from memory to the CPU all have an impact on the computer's overall level of performance:

◆ **Memory Size:** Determines how quickly an application performs and how many applications can run concurrently. The minimum amount of memory recommended for a mid-range computer is 3GB. For heavy multimedia usage, ie, video editing, flash animation, photo editing, etc., 4 GB of memory is recommended.

◆ **Type of Memory:** In new systems this is generally DDR2 SDRAM (Double Data Rate2-Synchronous Dynamic Random Access Memory) and transfers data more quickly. The computer is configured to accept one type of memory, so you can't swap your memory from one type to another later. However, more of the same type of memory can be added.

◆ **Speed:** Relates to how fast the data is transferred from memory to the CPU. It is measured in MHz and is often quoted in advertisements after the memory type '4 GB Dual Channel DDR2 SDRAM at 533 MHz'. 400 MHz is the minimum recommended memory speed. 'Dual Channel' memory systems have memory chips installed on the motherboard in two channels.

If the computer does not have enough memory the machine will be slow, as the programs and data will have to be swapped from memory to the hard disk many times. When this happens, the computer is using so-called 'virtual memory'.

More memory can be added later up to a stated maximum dependent on the computer specification. However, it is advisable to get as much memory as you can afford with your initial purchase.

Display Screen/Monitor

The display screen or monitor is the main point of interaction with the computer, so it is important that the size and quality of the monitor match the user's requirements.

There are two types of monitor on the market today: the traditional monitor – 'CRT' (based on Cathode Ray Tubes technology) and the more modern model known as 'Flat Screen' (based on LCD technology – 'Liquid Crystal Display'). A CRT monitor is big and boxy, while a Flat Screen monitor is slim and therefore saves a great deal of desk space.

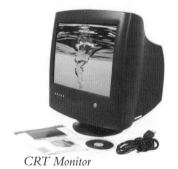

CRT Monitor

Flat Screen Monitor

Desktop systems now come with a Flat Screen as standard. Factors that affect the readability of a monitor are its size and resolution:

◆ **Size:** The recommended screen size is 19 inches. However, with a 'CRT' monitor the 'viewable area' of the screen will be smaller than the size specified, due to a black border around the screen. Advertisements may state the two measurements, eg, 19" (18" vis) monitor – 'vis' meaning viewable area. For a 'Flat Screen' monitor, the size specified is the actual size.

◆ **Resolution:** Characters and images displayed on the screen are constructed of dot patterns (dots of light) called pixels. The resolution is the number of pixels that can be displayed per inch on the screen and it affects the clarity of the display. At higher resolutions everything on the screen appears smaller but sharper, allowing more of the file to be displayed, thus avoiding horizontal scrolling. Advertisements generally state a monitor's maximum resolution. For high definition resolution of cinema quality, the monitor must support a resolution of 1920 x 1080.

The quality of the monitor display depends on the graphics card inserted in the computer. The amount of memory on the card (known as 'video memory') determines the maximum resolution and colour depth. A graphics card with 128 MB is fine for working with general business applications, but for the latest games and video applications at least 256 MB is recommended.

Hard Drive

The hard drive consists of a pack of disks stored inside the computer. As the hard drive is used as the main storage for programs and data files, a high-capacity drive is recommended. Most computers today have at least a 120 GB hard drive as standard.

Apart from the size of the hard disk, the speed of the drive, which is determined by the *rotational speed* of the drive is also an important factor to consider.

Rotational speed is the speed at which the drive spins, measured in revolutions per minute (rpm). Rotational speed determines how quickly data can be retrieved, known as the *access rate* (ie, how quickly a file can be opened, an application started, etc.). A hard drive with a rotation speed of at least 7200 rpm is recommended.

Optical Drive

Most mid-range computers come with a 'combo' optical drive and are generally described as having 'CD/DVD-RW with Blu-ray', which means they can read all formats of optical media and can write ('burn') to both CD-R/RW and DVD-R/RW. Such a drive is recommended because it helps to 'future-proof' your PC.

Sound

With the proliferation of multimedia applications, a sound system has become an essential piece of computing equipment. A basic computer sound system includes a sound card which is inserted into an expansion slot at the back of the computer and speakers which plug into the sound card.

The quality of the sound is a combination of both the sound card and speakers. Computer advertisements typically specify the sound card manufacturer and model. The models vary, but generally state: 'Sound Blaster compatibility' (the accepted standard).

Short Questions

1. Explain what a computer is.
2. Describe three types of computer systems.
3. Describe four components of a computer system.
4. Distinguish between human interface devices and data capture devices.
5. List three elements found on the motherboard and explain their functions.
6. What functions does a CPU perform?
7. What is a peripheral device? Give two examples.
8. Distinguish between magnetic storage media, optical storage media and solid-state storage media, and give an example of each.
9. Outline the storage capacities of the following optical media: CD, DVD and Blu-ray.
10. How does magnetic tape differ from a magnetic disk? What is magnetic tape used for?
11. Distinguish between a CD-ROM, CD-R and CD-RW.
12. Contrast the advantages of a USB drive as a portable storage media with optical storage media.
13. What factors should be taken into account when selecting a printer?
14. Distinguish between an impact printer and a non-impact printer, and give examples.
15. Distinguish between continuous stationery and multi-part stationery.
16. Compare and contrast an inkjet and a laser printer, using the following features: noise level, quality, speed, running cost and volume of output supported.
17. Differentiate between a sheet feed scanner, flatbed scanner and a multi-purpose scanner.
18. What is OCR software used for?
19. Distinguish between the measurement units a 'byte' and a 'Hertz'.
20. Outline what the following measurement units are: KHz, MHz, GHz, KB, MB, GB, TB.
21. List the family names of processors manufactured by both Intel and AMD.
22. List and briefly describe three factors to consider when assessing the capability of the main memory of a computer.
23. Describe two features that affect the quality of a computer screen.

Chapter 10 — Computer Applications

omputer application packages are software programs written to carry out specific tasks. These tools help to make office workers more efficient. For example, a business might store its rules and procedures manual or its price list on digital media. When these documents need updating, they are retrieved from disk, updated, saved and printed or uploaded to a network.

Typical computer application packages used by businesses are word processing, spreadsheets, database and desktop publishing. Computer application packages vary in the functionality they offer depending on whether they are an integrated package or an application suite:

◆ **An integrated package** is one program which will have more than one application, normally word processing, spreadsheets, databases, graphics, email and scheduling applications such as PIM (Personal Information Manager – ie, diary, to-do-list, calendar, etc.). Integrated packages cover the basics in each application and are suitable for small businesses or home users. An example of an integrated packages is MS Works Suite 9 and Corel Home Office.

◆ **An application suite** is a bundle of single applications from the same software developer sold together as one unit. A single application includes very advanced features not available in an integrated package. Single applications are generally sold as an application suite as it is more cost-effective, owing to the fact that the user interface is shared between applications. For example, editing and formatting features are similar across the applications. Examples of business application suites are:

- *MS Office 2007 Standard* includes MS Word (word processing), MS Excel (spreadsheet), MS PowerPoint (presentation) and MS Outlook (email and an electronic diary).
- *MS Office 2007 Professional* includes all the applications in the standard version, plus MS Publisher (desktop publishing) and MS Access (database).
- *Corel WordPerfect Office X4 Standard* includes WordPerfect (word processing), Quattro Pro (spreadsheet), Corel Presentations (presentation), Corel Visual Intelligence (visual data analysis), WordPerfect Mail and Digital Notebook.

- *Corel WordPerfect Office X4 Professional*: includes all the applications in the standard version plus Corel Paradox (database).

Word Processing

Word processing is a software application used for producing general office correspondence (ie, letters, memos, reports, etc.), mail merges (ie, sending personalised letters to individuals on a mailing list) and for producing booklets, leaflets and newsletters. Examples of wordprocessing applications are MS Word and Corel Word Perfect.

Features

Word processing provides features for editing, formatting, page layout and inserting graphics that enhance a document. Other features greatly increase efficiency in the production of personalised letters and long documents such as manuals.

Editing features

Editing refers to making revisions and may involve:

◆ **Deletion and insertion** of text.

◆ **Cut and paste:** Used to move text within a document or between documents.

◆ **Copy and paste:** Similar to 'cut and paste', except that the original copy is not moved and remains in its original position unchanged. Used to copy data from one application to another, eg, a statistical chart from a spreadsheet program into a document, etc.

◆ **Find and replace:** Used to directly locate and update text in a document, rather than scrolling through the document looking for the specific text to be changed.

◆ **Spellchecker:** Used to check the spelling of a document against an inbuilt dictionary. The user can: ignore the word (if it is correctly spelt but not in the dictionary), add the word to the dictionary (useful for technical or legal words), or select the correct spelling from a suggested list.

◆ **Grammar:** Used to identify sentences that contain grammatical errors and to suggest ways to improve the sentence.

◆ **Thesaurus:** Used to find a different word with the same meaning (synonyms), eg, 'busy' can be interchanged with 'occupied', 'engaged' or 'employed'.

Formatting features

Formatting refers to changing the appearance of a document, and may involve changing:

◆ **Font and size:** Different 'fonts' can be selected, ie, Times New Roman, Arial, etc., and the size of the font can also be changed. Fonts are measured in 'points' and normally a font size of 12 points is used in business documents.

◆ **Font style:** Used to emphasise particular words or to enhance the appearance of text. For example, underline, **bold**, *italics*, superscript (where the character is above the typing line, eg, $10°$) and subscript (where the character is below the typing line, eg, H_2O).

◆ **Line spacing:** Spacing between lines of text can be adjusted to single, line-and-a-half, double or treble spacing.

◆ **Justification:** Refers to the alignment of the text on the page. There are four main types: left, right, full and centred, as illustrated below.

Left justification. Text is automatically aligned flush with the left margin producing a ragged right margin. This is the default justification used.	**Right** justification. Text is aligned flush with the right margin, producing an even right margin but a ragged left margin. Generally used to draw attention to a small amount of text in a poster or flyer.
Full (even) justification. Text is aligned flush with both the left and right margins, producing an even look. Generally used in printed material.	**Centred** justification. Text is centred horizontally across the page. Used for displaying menus, invitations, etc.

◆ **Bullets:** Symbols used to separate and emphasise items in a list. Examples of bullets are: • ⇨ ◆ Bullets are used where it is not necessary to list items in any particular order.

◆ **Automatic numbering:** Used where it is necessary to list items in a particular order. Items typed in a list are automatically numbered; if changes are made to the list, ie, deletion, reordering, etc. the list will be automatically renumbered.

◆ **Tabs:** Used to align columns of text. When the tab key is pressed, the cursor is taken from point 'A' to point 'B'. Four types of alignment are available:

left — extends text to the right from the tab stop.

right — extends text to the left from the tab stop. Used to align non-decimal numbers.

decimal — aligns decimal numbers on the decimal point.

centred — centres text at the tab stop.

Left	Right	Decimal	Centred
there	10,234	12.34	there
the	23	123.56	the

◆ **Table facility:** A more sophisticated feature than tabs used to display text or figures in columns and rows. For example, columns and rows in the table can be merged or split to suit the data being presented, and minor calculations can be performed within the table.

Page Layout features

Page layout features offer choices in how the page appears, and incorporate features used to ensure consistency within long documents.

◆ **Page layout:** The layout of the page can be changed, ie, the orientation of the paper (portrait or landscape) and the paper size (ie, A4, A5, etc.) and margins of the page. A left margin of 3.75cm is recommended when a document is to be bound.

◆ **Header/Footer:** A 'header' is text that is keyed in once and appears automatically in the top margin of every page, eg, chapter headings. A 'footer' is text that is keyed in once and appears automatically in the bottom margin of every page, eg, page numbers and date revised.

◆ **Orphans/Widows:** An 'orphan' is a facility to ensure that the first line of a paragraph does not start at the end of a column or page. A 'widow' ensures that the last line of a paragraph is not brought onto a new column or page.

◆ **Templates:** Are pre-designed documents into which you type your text. Common templates include: memos, reports, faxes, curriculum vitae, etc. Templates can be customised to suit the business's needs.

◆ **Style sheet:** A 'style' is a collection of formatting attributes (ie, typeface, size, indents, etc.) defined by the user, named and saved. When the named style is applied to selected text, the program applies all the formatting attributes in the named style to the selected text.

For example, a style could be defined to have all subheadings in the following format – Arial 14 point, bold and in green. When the style is selected, all of the above formats will be applied to the subheadings at once. This speeds up formatting, as each individual format does not have to be applied separately. In addition, any changes made to the style will automatically change all the subheadings formatted with that style.

◆ **Table of contents:** When styles are created for heading levels, a table of contents can be generated automatically. A table of contents is used to give an outline of the contents in a publication with the corresponding page numbers.

◆ **Graphical features:** allow the user to insert images, charts, shapes and symbols to enhance the visual design of the document.

◆ **Image insertion:** Images can be inserted from a range of sources such as personal, scanned images and clip art. Clip art is a library of pictures available with the application, online or on optical media, eg, CD-ROMs, etc.

◆ **Drawing facility:** Used to insert and manipulate common shapes such as lines, boxes, circles, etc., which can be shaded using patterns and colour.

◆ **Diagram facility:** Pre-designed diagrams, eg, organisation charts, pyramids, etc., can be inserted and manipulated.

◆ **Image manipulation:** Images can be changed in size and shape and can be rotated. Text can be positioned all around the image, over the image, down one side of the image, etc.

◆ **WordArt:** Offers a variety of unusual ways to position and display text on the page. For example, text can be positioned vertically on the page, letters can be stretched and patterns, colours and shadows can be added.

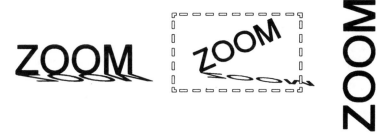

A sample of effects allowed with WordArt

◆ **Reverse Video:** Text is normally printed with black characters on a white background, but this can be changed (reversed) to white text on a black background. Other colours can be used.

Other Features

Other valuable features in word processing that greatly increase productivity in the office are:

◆ **Macros:** Frequently performed tasks or frequently typed text can be automated by creating a macro. A macro is a series of commands that are grouped together and assigned to a specific key. For example, a macro could be created to insert a name and address that is used regularly and assigned a keystroke, eg, ALT + R. Every time the user needs to insert the same name and address, the keystroke assigned to the macro, ALT + R is pressed and the name and address is inserted. Macros are generally specific to the individual computer user, depending on the nature of their work.

◆ **Mail merge:** A facility used to create a series of personalised standard letters by combining the standard letter with another file which contains the names and addresses. Mailing labels for envelopes can also be produced from the file that contains the names and addresses.

◆ **Send to:** A facility used to send a document directly from the word-processing program as an email attachment or a fax. (The computer must have an Internet connection or a fax-capable modem.)

Spreadsheets

A spreadsheet is a software package for financial modelling and analysis of results. For example, spreadsheets may be used for: preparing budgets and forecasts, job cost estimates and to carry out 'what-if' questions, such as, 'What effect will a 2% reduction in price have on profits assuming a 5% increase in sales?' Graphs such as pie charts, bar charts, etc. can be produced to visualise the data entered in the spreadsheet.

Spreadsheets are essentially used for any documentation that requires a lot of computational work. Office work that involves dealing with numerical calculations such as managing budgets is simplified with the use of spreadsheets. The major advantage is the automatic recalculation of results when a number used in the calculation is changed. Examples of Spreadsheet programs are: MS Excel, Lotus 123 and Corel QuattroPro.

Layout

A spreadsheet consists of rows and columns. Rows are numbered 1, 2, 3, etc., and the columns are lettered A, B, C etc. The intersection of a row and a column is known as a 'cell'. Each cell is referenced by a column letter and a row number. For example, cell F3, as shown in Figure 10–1 represents the wages figure for May.

	A	B	C	D	E	F
1		January	February	March	April	May
2	Income					Cell F3
3	Wages	900	900	900	900	900
4	Bonus	150	0	50	200	0
5	TOTAL INCOME	=SUM(B3:B4)	900	950	1,100	900
6						
7	**Expenses**					
8	Rent	400	400	400	400	400
9	Food	360	320	340	360	345
10	Clothes	50	15	10	30	0
11	Miscellaneous	80	20	25	50	55
12	TOTAL EXPENSES	=SUM(B8:B11)	755	775	840	800
13						
14	**SAVINGS**	=B5-B12 145	175	260	100	

Figure 10–1 Typical spreadsheet to manage income and expenditure

To perform calculations automatically, a *formula* is inserted in the cell where the answer is required. A formula is indicated by an equals sign and the cell references are used rather than the actual data in the cells.

Spreadsheets have built-in formulae called *functions*. The SUM function is used in cell B5; =SUM(B3:B4) to calculate total income and in cell B12 to calculate total expenses. The sum function adds all numbers in a range. For example, in figure 10-1 the sum function used to calculate total expenses is =SUM(B8:B11) which adds all the numbers in the range from B8:B11 inclusive. The results of the formulae are actually displayed in the cells as in, for example, C5, D5, E5 and F5, which display the results for total income.

Therefore if the numbers in the cells are changed, the answer is automatically recalculated. For example, if the food expense figure for April were changed to €400, the total expenses figure for April would be updated automatically to €880 and savings for April to €220.

There is no built-in function in a spreadsheet for subtraction. To calculate total savings the following formula is entered in cell B14: =B5-B12 which subtracts total income from total expenses.

Features

Specific features of a spreadsheet include:

◆ **Automatic recalculation:** When rows/columns are inserted/deleted or figures are changed, the formulae adjust automatically to take account of the changes.

◆ **Copying formulae:** A formula entered for one column or row can be copied to other columns or rows and the cell references in the formulae will adjust automatically. For example, in Figure 10–1 if the formula for the January savings =B5-B12 is copied to February, it will read =C5-C12. This is known as a *relative reference* as the formula adjusts when it is moved.

◆ **Protect facility:** A command that allows cells to be protected from unauthorised or accidental alterations. For example, the formulas in the spreadsheet (Figure 10–1) can be 'locked' while the other cells may be left unlocked for updating.

◆ **Charting facility:** Graphs such as pie charts, bar charts, etc. can be created from the data entered in the spreadsheet. Displayed below and overleaf are pie charts and a bar chart created from the spreadsheet in Figure 10–1.

A pie chart is generally used to show:

a) the breakdown of one category of information over one time period, eg, Figure 10–2 shows the breakdown of the expenses for January; or

b) the relationship of one item of information within a category over numerous time periods, eg, Figure 10–3 shows the relationship of the miscellaneous expenses between January and March.

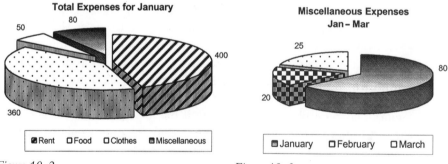

Figure 10–2   Figure 10–3

A bar chart is generally used to show:

a) the breakdown of one category of information over numerous time periods, ie, the breakdown of the *expense* category showing the amounts spent on rent, food, clothes and miscellaneous items for January to March; or

b) the *relationship* between categories of information over numerous time periods, eg, Figure 10–4 shows the relationship of the income, expenses and savings for the months January to March.

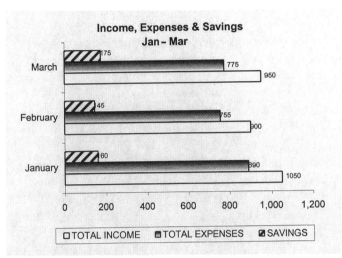

Figure 10–4

Databases

A database is a collection of related records. A database provides a structure for storing data in such a way that it can be manipulated, ie, searches can be performed for specific information, or the information can be sorted by a specific category, ie, surname, country, etc. For example, a business could search a database of customers by county or age to target a specific segment of the market to promote its products. Other uses of databases include: telephone directories, library databases, customer and supplier records and personnel records. Examples of databases in use are MS Access and Corel Paradox.

It is important to understand the terminology used in a database. Shown opposite is the structure of a database to record information about staff.

PERSONNEL DATABASE	
Title:	Mr
First Name:	Jerry
Surname:	Kelly
Address 1:	15 Main Street
Address 2:	Blackrock
County:	Dublin
Date of Birth:	10/11/75
Telephone No.:	01-2864532
Position:	Sales Assistant
Salary:	€45,000

Figure 10–5

Field: Each category of information in a database is known as a field. For example, in the personnel database, Figure 10–5, 'Title' is a field, 'First Name' is a field, etc. Each item of information is entered into a field to facilitate searching or sorting the database. For example, notice that the name information is split into two fields, First Name and Surname, rather than entering the whole name under one field. This is a design decision — the way the data is split up into specific fields determines the way the database can be manipulated; the personnel database can now be searched and sorted by surname.

Record: A record is a collection of related fields; it consists of all the fields for one unit of information. The record for Jerry Kelly is shown in Figure 10–5.

Database: A database is a collection of related records. In the Personnel database, there will be many records giving similar details for all employees.

Features

Specific features of a database include:

◆ **Queries:** A facility used to search the database for specific information and display the results, eg, a search for all employees who live in Blackrock.

◆ **Reports:** A facility used to generate professional reports from the information in the database. Reports are generally constructed from queries as the information has been filtered.

◆ **Merging information:** Information stored in a database can be merged with other applications. For examples, names and addresses stored in a database can be merged with a wordprocessing package to produce personalised letters.

◆ **Multi-user:** Some database packages are multi-user, which enables many users on a network to view the database concurrently. The database is stored in one location, ie, on a server.

◆ **Security:** Multi-user databases are controlled via passwords and 'access rights'. Passwords are used to block access to the system. Access rights are used to control what users can view or alter within the system, eg, controls can be set up so that particular users see only certain areas of the database.

Desktop Publishing

Desktop publishing software takes word processing one step further by providing more sophisticated features to lay out, format and manage complicated publications, ie, books, magazines, newspapers, brochures, etc., for both print and electronic media. DTP is now commonly referred to as digital publishing due to the development of programmes which facilitate a design to be either printed or published digitally, such as an email newsletter, electronic PDF books, etc.

DTP techniques require the layout of a page to be planned in advance, by creating boxes, known as 'frames', in which the various elements of a page are placed, eg, headlines, images, body text, 'boxed' story, etc. Once the page layout has been designed, the data can be entered. In DTP, large amounts of text are not generally typed directly into the columns or frames; the text is imported from a word processing file. This is because DTP is a page-layout program and is not designed as a primary typing program. Examples of DTP software include MS Publishing and Adobe InDesign.

Features

Specific features of DTP include:

◆ **Master pages:** A master page is a page created containing *design elements* such as headers, footers and frames that are common to most of the pages in the publication. New pages added to the publication can be based on a particular master page, thus avoiding the need to re-create the common design elements. Master pages ensure consistency across pages in a publication.

◆ **Style sheets:** Like those used in word processing, styles are set up for the various text elements in a publication, ie, headings, captions, body text, etc. Styles ensure consistency among similar text elements in a publication.

◆ **Templates:** A template is a pre-designed document into which content is imported from other files. In DTP, the user generally designs a template by saving the *master pages* and *style sheets* as a template, thus providing the structure for further publications.

For example, in the production of a magazine, a template with master pages and style sheets is created and saved. So when a new issue is required, the template is recalled and the new text, graphics, etc. are inserted.

Features

◆ **Control of typography:** Refers to increased control to manage text within the frames of a publication. For example, there are greater options to control widows/orphans, hyphens, headers/footer, line-spacing, etc., than in a word processing program.

◆ **Leading:** Refers to line spacing, ie, spacing between lines of type, and it can be adjusted in points, allowing immense flexibility. In word processing, line spacing is limited to single, line-and-a half or double.

◆ **Kerning:** Refers to letter spacing, ie, spacing between letters in a word and can be applied to selected pairs of letters to improve readability, especially at large point sizes. For example, at larger point size, the shape of some letter pairs, such as Wo, Ya, and Tu makes the space between the letters seem too big, while the shape of other letters, eg, Mi and Li, makes the letters seem too close together. In word processing, letter spacing is applied to the whole word.

Computer Viruses

A computer virus is a program written intentionally by vandals known as 'hackers' to corrupt, destroy or change files or programs on a computer, and/or to change the performance of a computer. A computer virus is easily transmitted from one computer to another unless the latest version of anti-virus software is installed. A computer can become infected with a virus when the user:

◆ Downloads and opens/runs an infected webpage or program from a website

◆ Opens an email message or an attachment to an email from an unknown source

◆ Uses infected removable storage media, ie, optical media, USB drives, etc.

In order to spread through a computer system or network, a virus must be activated, ie, the file that contains the virus must be opened or executed. Once activated, a virus duplicates itself and infects programs or files according to the virus' program. Some common signs that a virus has infected a computer are:

◆ The computer runs more slowly than normal

◆ The computer crashes/shuts down frequently

◆ The computer stops responding or 'freezes'

◆ Applications on the computer fail to respond correctly

◆ Storage media drives are inaccessible or the media appears to be blank

◆ Unusual messages appear on the screen

◆ Programs or files disappear

◆ Some files cannot be opened.

The most common method of transmitting a virus is by email or email attachment. For example, if an email is received with an attachment that has a virus, once the attachment is opened, the virus enters the email system and (without the user knowing) duplicates itself by automatically emailing everyone listed in the user's email contacts.

If the user saves the attachment to the hard drive and opens the file to edit it, the hard drive becomes infected. If the file is copied to another computer via USB drive, both the USB drive and the other computer will be infected once the file is opened. Unless everyone detects and removes the virus with anti-virus software from the computer and storage media, the virus will continue to spread. A good anti-virus program will monitor a computer and screen incoming emails for suspicious content.

Protecting against Viruses

There are many software programs on the market to combat viruses. Examples of anti-virus software include: Norton Anti-Virus, McAfee Anti-Virus Scan and Virex. Anti-virus software scans the computer and removes viruses or notifies the user if viruses cannot be removed due to out-dated anti-virus software. To protect your computer against viruses, pay particular attention to the following:

◆ Install the latest version of anti-virus software on your computer
◆ As new viruses are written daily, set the options on the anti-virus software to download updates automatically and to scan the computer on a regular basis, preferably daily
◆ Set the anti-virus software to scan incoming and outgoing emails automatically
◆ Scan all removable storage media on a regular basis before opening any files
◆ Never open emails or email attachments from unknown sources
◆ Do not download files or programmes from the Internet if you are unsure of the website
◆ Back up your computer files on a regular basis so that your files can be restored should a virus corrupt your hard drive

Short Questions

1. Distinguish between an integrated package and an application suite.
2. Describe and give an example of usage of the following features in word processing:
   a) search and replace
   b) justification
   c) right tabs
   d) reverse video.
3. Describe and give an example of usage of the following features in word processing:
   a) mail merge
   b) orphans/widows
   c) drawing facility.
4. Distinguish between a font's typeface, point size and style.
5. Explain the difference between, and advantages of, a document template and a style sheet.
6. Distinguish between a spreadsheet formula and a function.

7. Describe what the following features in spreadsheets do:
   a)   relative references
   b)   protect facility
   c)   charting.
8. Give an example of when it is more suitable to use a bar chart rather than a pie chart.
9. Distinguish between a field, a record and a database as used in a database program.
10. What is a multi-user database and what security measures are incorporated?
11. Distinguish between desktop publishing and word processing.
12. Distinguish between leading and kerning.
13. Distinguish between a master page, a style sheet and a template.
14. List four common computer software application packages and state the main use of each.
15. What is a computer virus? How are they controlled?
16. List four common signs that a virus has infected a computer.
17. State three ways that a computer can become infected with a virus, and outline six ways to prevent this from happening.

Chapter 11 — Networks and the Internet

A network is a collection of computers connected together using different technologies such as cables, a wireless link known as Wi-Fi, the telephone network or satellite, depending on the geographical distance between computers. A network typically consists of a 'server' or 'hub', ie, a dedicated device that manages and distributes resources to network users. Security is vital on computer networks to prevent unauthorised users accessing the network. The basic protection is a password and 'firewall' software, which determines access rights within the network.

A typical network layout, where each computer is connected to a central 'hub' via cable, is shown in Figure 11-1.

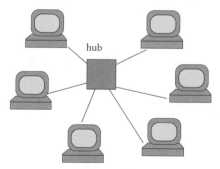

Figure 11–1: Graphical representation of a small network linked by cables

Types of Network

Networks can vary in size from a local area network (LAN), to a wide-area network (WAN), to the worldwide network known as 'the Internet'.

LAN — (Local Area Network)

A LAN is a network within a limited geographical area (ie, a single building or group of buildings) such as a small office/home office (referred to as SOHO), office buildings, universities, airports, hospitals, or manufacturing complexes. A LAN enables the computers linked to the network to share files and peripheral devices (ie, printers, scanners, etc.) and communicate with each other via email. A LAN is usually connected to the Internet.

A LAN can be connected using either cables or Wi-Fi. A wireless LAN is abbreviated to WLAN, the 'W' representing 'wireless'. Cable has been the traditional choice, but wireless technology is universally used today in office buildings and in public areas such as airports, hotels, cafés, etc. Such buildings are equipped with Wireless Access Points (WAP) devices, referred to as 'Hotspots'. A WAP device has an aerial, and a built-in radio transmitter/receiver which enables Wi-Fi-enabled computers to communicate with each other on the network via radio signals.

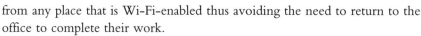

A WAP device

WLANs enable employees to be in regular communication with their business while travelling. For example, employees can access their business WLAN or the Internet from any place that is Wi-Fi-enabled thus avoiding the need to return to the office to complete their work.

WAN — (Wide Area Network)

A WAN is a network which covers a wide geographical area, for example, one which spreads across a country or between countries. Communication is through the telephone network and satellites where necessary. A WAN may use either the public telephone line or a private telephone line. Private telephone lines are leased from a telecommunications provider if the business requires a permanent connection between networks.

A WAN is installed where there is a high volume of inter-branch communication. For example, a business with many branches spread throughout the country may install a WAN to enable branches to access the head-office database, transfer files between branches, send email on a private network, etc.

A typical set-up for inter-branch communication could be as follows: each branch has a LAN installed and each LAN is connected to Head Office via a private telephone line known as a Digital Subscriber Line (DSL), giving a permanent connection between networks as displayed in Figure 11-2.

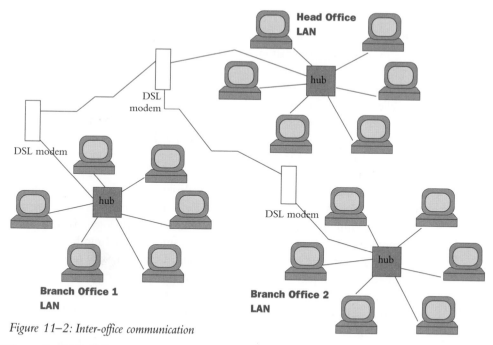

Figure 11–2: Inter-office communication

The Internet

The Internet (or simply the 'Net') is a worldwide network of computers. It is made up of many independent networks which are linked together through the telephone and satellite system. Every computer is connected, indirectly, to every other computer on the Internet via an Internet Service Provider (ISP). An ISP maintains a series of communication links for Internet data which interconnect at several points (like the local telephone exchange) and another ISP will maintain a series of links from these points. For example, assume your local ISP covers mostly Drogheda, Meath and Dublin and you want to view a website located on a server in London. Your local ISP network puts you on the quickest route to its exit point; and then you are switched to another ISP network.

Connecting to the Internet

Although you can access the Internet using a mobile phone, regular users do so via the fixed-line telephone network by subscribing to an ISP like Eircom, BT, DigiWeb, etc. The most common type of connection to the Internet is an 'Always-On' connection generally known as 'Broadband'. A 'Dial-Up' connection is also available.

In either case a modem is required. A modem is a device that connects a computer to the Internet via cable or a wireless link. The type of modem required depends on the connection type. As a modem often includes additional network functions, it may also be referred to as a 'router'.

A **Dial-Up** connection is an older technology that uses the standard telephone line and a modem which transmits data at a maximum rate of 56K (kilobits per second), which is very slow. It is known as 'Dial-up' as the ISP must be dialled via software to make a connection to the Internet, and while it is connected telephone calls cannot be made or received. The cost involved includes a monthly flat-rate fee plus a per-minute charge for the duration of time online – which can be expensive, especially if using the Internet for long periods in 'peak times'.

A **Broadband** connection is available via cable, satellite and the telephone line. A broadband connection via the telephone line is based on ADSL (Asymmetric Digital Subscriber Line) technology. Broadband is delivered through existing telephone lines using a special modem or router. Most local telephone exchanges are broadband-enabled. The term 'broad' is used because multiple types of information can travel across the line at the same time. Broadband provides faster access to the Internet and allows telephone calls to be made or received while online, unlike with a dial-up connection. Broadband speeds vary depending on the broadband category purchased. Broadband categories generally quote two speeds, eg, 'Up to 12/2Mb'. The first number refers to the 'download' speed, or how fast web pages, emails or other files can be received. The second number refers to the 'upload' speed, or how fast a computer can send information over the Internet e.g. email, images, etc. Broadband categories available are generally classified as:

◆ *Light use*: Provides speed connections of up to 1Mb/128kbps and is suitable for browsing the Web and emailing.

◆ *Average use*: Provides speed connections of either up to 12Mb/1Mb and is suitable for downloading music, playing games, watching videos or viewing websites with a high multimedia content.

◆ *Heavy use*: Provides speed connections of up to 24Mb/1Mb, and recommended for multiple very heavy users in a business.

The cost involved includes a monthly flat-rate fee, but unlike a dial-up connection you do not pay for the time spent online. However, depending on the ISP used and broadband category purchased, there may be a limit on the amount of data that can be downloaded per month, after which a charge is applied for additional downloading. The amount downloaded per month can be checked on most ISPs website by entering your telephone and account number.

The World Wide Web (WWW)

Many people mistakenly use the term 'Internet' when referring to the World Wide Web, commonly referred to as the 'Net'. However, the Internet is the communications network and the Web is one service provided over the Internet. Other services provided over the Internet are email, newsgroups, chat and file transfer.

The Web is an information-retrieval and interactive system. It consists of files referred to as websites stored on computer servers connected to the Internet. Information is available on the Web on almost any topic, ie, business, investments, computers, education, government, health, arts and entertainment.

The information for the Web is written by anybody who cares to do so, ie, an organisation or any member of the public. The information is coded with instructions, known as **XHTML** (Extensible Hypertext Mark-up Language) tags. XHTML tags instruct a Web **browser** how to display and lay out the website. Alternatively, a Web authoring application, such as Adobe Dreamweaver or Ms Frontpage, could be used to write the XHTML code automatically. The user simply creates a document with text, images, etc. similar to creating a wordprocessing document, but behind the scenes the Web authoring application is inserting the XHTML tags.

Browsing the Web

The word 'browsing' or 'surfing' simply means viewing websites. To access websites, a user must have a connection to the Internet and Web browser software such as MS Internet Explorer, Mozilla Firefox, etc.

The Web address of the site you wish to visit is entered in the 'Address Bar' of the browser window. Once a browser window is opened, more web pages or other websites can be opened within that window by using 'Tabbed' browsing as displayed in Figure 11-3. Tabbed browsing lets you open several web pages within a single browser window. Each web page is displayed in a Tab, thus freeing up space on the computer's taskbar, as a separate window is not required to display each web page.

Tabbed browsing is also particularly useful for saving the websites opened to the **Favorites** folder, thus facilitating quick access to these websites in the future. This is known as **Bookmarking**. All Tabs opened can be bookmarked at once.

Figure 11–3 – Browsing the Web

The website for Gill & Macmillan (the publisher of this book) is displayed in Figure 11–3 using the browser Firefox. The website address is www.gillmacmillan.ie, which displays the **home page** of the website. The home page provides a 'linked' list of topics covered in the site, similar to a table of contents in a book. A **link** (also known as a hyperlink) when clicked loads a specific web page into the browser window.

The **Back** button is used to go to a previously visited web page; the down arrow beside the Back button is a quick way to select a Web page just visited. Once you have gone back, you can use the **Forward** button to go forward to the pages viewed.

Purchasing On-Line

Besides information websites, e–business websites facilitate the purchase of products or services online. The customer can view an online catalogue of products or services, add items to their 'shopping basket' and review their shopping list and total bill before proceeding to pay. When the customer clicks the 'Proceed to Payment' button, a secure web page opens and offers a list of payment options.

A secure web page is identifiable by an 's' added to the http protocol and an icon of a lock is displayed on the web page. A secure web page uses the latest data encryption technology to scramble the data as it is in transit over the Internet, thus ensuring that the customer's details are kept private should they be intercepted.

Payment is usually made by a credit or debit card or through a payment provider such as PayPal. To use PayPal as a payment option, the customer opens an account with PayPal at www.paypal.com and uses the account number when making online payments. The customer can top up their PayPal account with their credit or debit card. The advantage of using a payment provider is that the customer's financial details are not revealed to the seller, and the customer doesn't have to re-enter their personal and card details every time a purchase is made. Once the payment is accepted, the products or services are delivered as per the purchase terms.

Understanding Web Addresses

Many of today's browsers assume that all web addresses begin with http:// and therefore, this is generally omitted from the web address. Web addresses generally start with a 'www.' prefix.

Every computer that connects to the Internet has a unique number called an **IP address**, which is used by the network to send data to the correct location. An IP address is a set of four numbers between 0 and 255 that are separated by full stops. An example of an IP address is: 204.130.122.232. As numbers are difficult to remember, the IP addresses are mapped to names, known as **domain names**. For example, to view a website the user would enter the domain name of the website, but the network will send the IP address of the computer being accessed.

Domain Names

Every website has a unique address, known as a domain name, usually in the format of companyname.ie or companyname.com. Domain names in Ireland generally end with the '.ie' suffix. Other suffixes you might see on websites are:

.com means a commercial site, usually based in America

.org means a non-profit organisation

.gov means a government office

.edu means an educational site

.uk means United Kingdom — some websites use the country code as their suffix.

Domain names are registered so no two websites can have the same domain name.

URLs

An **URL** (Uniform Resource Location) is the full address of a particular web page on the website, as distinct from the domain name. To go directly to a specific page on a website you need the 'full path' to the file, ie, the file name and the folder name where the file is stored.

For example, consider the web page address: *www.rte.ie/2fm/ ryanshow/education.html.* This web page address is extended beyond the domain name *rte.ie.* It is locating the Web page named *education.html,* which is stored in a folder named *ryanshow,* which is a sub-folder of *2fm.* Basically, after the domain name, the URL could be a series of folders and the last part of the address is the file name which the browser displays as the web page.

Searching the Web

A search engine is used if you don't know a web address, or if you want to search for specific information. A search engine uses software known as a 'Spider' or 'robot' that constantly searches the web, cataloguing and indexing information and maintaining a database of the web addresses and topics found. Common search engines are: Google (www.google.com), Yahoo (www.yahoo.com) and AskJeeves (www.ask.com). There is no definitive search engine for everything available on the Web, so more than one search engine may need to be used.

To search for information on the Web the search engine address (ie, www.google.ie) is entered into the 'Address Bar' of the browser window. A search window is displayed with an input box in which the user enters the search criteria, ie, keyword(s) relevant to finding the information required. The search criteria are submitted to the search engine by pressing the 'Search' button, and the search engine returns a list of topics relevant to the search criteria submitted. If the list of topics returned does not provide the user with the appropriate information required, the user will have to redefine the search criteria to make the search results more specific.

Refining the Search Criteria

If your search result yields hundreds of topics, advanced search techniques can be used to produce more relevant results:

◆ **Be as specific as possible with keywords:** ie, a search for *bicycles* is not specific; it will find web pages that have the word bicycles in them, finding hundreds of irrelevant websites.

◆ **Use only lower-case letters:** unless you want your search to be case-sensitive. Lower-case letters will find all words with varying capitalisation. For example, a search for *bicycles* will find Bicycles, BICYCLES.

◆ **Use quotation marks:** to search for a phrase, otherwise web pages with any of the words in the phrase will be found. For example, a search for *bicycle accessories*, will find web pages with the word *bicycle* in them first, then it will find web pages with the word *accessories* in them. However, enclosing the search words in quotation marks, ie, "*bicycle accessories*", will find web pages that contain those two words together.

◆ **Use a plus sign (+):** in front of a word to require that word to appear in the results. For example, *bicycles + racing* is more likely to produce useful results than a search for bicycles alone.

◆ **Use a minus sign (-):** in front of a word to exclude it from results. For example, to search for information about racing bicycles, but not accessories, news, events, try *bicycles + racing -accessories -news -events.*

◆ **Combine quotation marks with the plus sign:** for example, a search for "*raleigh bicycle*" +*gents* finds web pages that have the words *Raleigh bicycle* together, and the word *gents* somewhere on the page.

◆ **Order the keywords:** the order in which the words are placed will impact on the results. A search for *bicycles + accessories* will yield different results from a search for *accessories + bicycles.*

◆ **Use an asterisk (*) to broaden the search:** used to cater for plurals of words. For example, a search for "*Raleigh bicycle**" will find both *raleigh bicycle* and *Raleigh bicycles.* The asterisk indicates that it will find words with any letters after the initial word you typed, ie, *gent** will find gentlemen, gents, gentile, etc., so be careful about its use.

◆ **Keep in mind different spellings:** different spellings will yield different results, ie, labor/labour, color/colour.

Achieving the required results using advanced search techniques comes with practice. However, once the initial list is returned by the search engine, it becomes easier to identify the appropriate keywords and search techniques to use to obtain the required result.

Intranet and Extranet

An **intranet** is a 'private Web' implemented over a local area network (LAN), accessible by employees within an organisation and not by the general public.

The primary use of an intranet is to publish, via a web browser, internal information such as the organisation's background and policy, health and safety guidelines, Human Resources Department information, product literature, annual reports, newsletters, price lists, manuals, internal forms, current news about the business and forthcoming events – generally any information that was previously distributed via memos, leaflets or handbooks to employees.

In addition, an intranet may have a link to the organisation's database to enable employees to check names and addresses, inventory levels, status of orders, etc. An intranet generally has a connection to the Internet. Like any network, controls are put in place to allow certain groups of employees to access specific information.

An **extranet** extends an organisation's intranet to a closed community outside the organisation such as business partners, suppliers and customers with special access permissions to certain sub-sites.

Typically access may be granted to contractors or consultants who need certain business data, to suppliers who want to monitor inventory levels to plan their own production schedules and to customers who want to check on the status of pending orders. A business with access rights can log on to the organisation's website and use a password to access specific areas of the organisation's internal network as determined by the host of the extranet.

Protection against unwanted intrusion on extranets is implemented via a hardware/software system known as a 'firewall' that examines incoming and outgoing data to prevent unauthorised transmission of, or access to, information.

Short Questions

1. What is a network? List three different types of network.
2. List three benefits of a WLAN.
3. Distinguish between LAN, WLAN and WAN networks and suggest a suitable use for each type of network.
4. Compare and contrast two methods of connecting to the Internet.
5. Explain the following terms in relation to networks:
   (a) Hotspot
   (b) DSL
   (c) ISP
6. List the three categories of broadband speed available.
7. Distinguish between the Internet and the Web.
8. What language is used to write a website? List an alternative way of creating a website.
9. What is meant by the term e-business?
10. Distinguish between a domain name and a URL.
11. Explain 'tabbed' browsing and outline its advantages.
12. List four guidelines you would give users of the Internet so that their searches are more productive.
13. What precautions should purchasers take when buying online?
14. Distinguish between an intranet and an extranet.

Chapter 12 — Information Systems

Developments in information and communications technologies have increased both the quantity and quality of data generated and stored within a business. This data must be processed in order to produce meaningful information that can be used to make decisions towards enhancing the overall performance and competitiveness of the business.

An information system involves three major elements: participants, data/information and information technology, as indicated in Figure 12-1 below. Information systems are necessary to assist office administrators in their function to capture, process, store and distribute quality information to support the business operations.

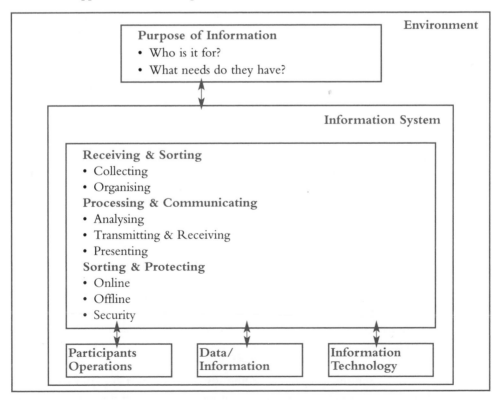

Figure 12-1 – Elements of an Information System

There may be a variety of information systems operating within the business to facilitate different levels of decision making. The information system should provide up-to-date, accurate and relevant information, usually in the form of reports. Information systems can be divided into two categories:

1. Operational Support Systems
2. Management Support Systems.

Operational Support Systems

Operational Support Systems refer to a range of information systems that capture and process data of a routine nature relating to internal activities of various departments such as sales, personnel, production, marketing and finance. Examples of Operational Support Systems are *Office Automation Systems* and *Transaction Processing Systems (TPS)*.

Office Automation Systems (OAS)

An office automation system computerises routine office tasks such as managing correspondence, scheduling activities, accounting and payroll, word processing, spreadsheets, electronic schedulers, databases and email. LANs, WANs, intranets, extranets and the Internet are integral components of an office automation system.

Transaction Processing Systems (TPS)

A transaction processing system controls and organises data involved in the daily transactions of the business. A TPS typically consists of the following elements:

◆ data entry
◆ transaction processing
◆ file and database updating
◆ document and report generation
◆ enquiry processing.

An example of a TPS is the **EPOS** system (Electronic Point of Sale) used in most retail outlets, which incorporates bar code pricing, stock controls and transaction sales data. Every product is barcoded and details such as price, product code, supplier and description are recorded on the in-store computer system. When the product is scanned at the point of sale, and the sale is complete (ie, payment is made), an itemised receipt is produced for the customer and the stock levels are reduced by the product items and the sales total increases.

The reports available from the EPOS allow managers to make quicker and more informed decisions on the stock, sales and staff performances and help management to keep tighter controls over cash and stock. For example, in a retail chain business in which all the branches are networked, sales comparisons between branches can be made more easily. Customer service is also improved as sales assistants can view stocks in other branches to see if the item required by the customer is available.

Libraries use TPS to capture and process data relating to the issuing and management of library books. When a library member borrows a book, s/he presents a library membership card, which is scanned to check the library's database for any overdue books or fines that the member may owe. The bar code on the books to be issued are also scanned, and the library database is updated automatically to show that these books are issued to that member's library card, and are unavailable until the date of return. If the borrower requests a book that is not currently available at the library, the TPS can search other network databases for the book and make a reservation.

The output information from a TPS system is used as input for other information systems such as a Management Support System.

Management Support Systems

Management Support Systems refers to systems that are designed to improve the quality of management decisions at a strategic rather than an operational level. All levels of the business from operators to senior management use information to make informed decisions that affect the efficiency levels within the business. Senior management requires information to make strategic plans for the long-term benefits of the business such as decisions regarding large-scale investment, entering new markets and planning takeovers. At middle-management level, managers develop tactical plans for the medium term, such as staffing requirements, budgets and production requirements. These plans are then implemented and monitored by the supervisory or operational management level on a day-to-day basis. The types of decision made at the different levels of management are outlined in Figure 12–2 overleaf. Examples of Management Support Systems include Management Information Systems (MIS) and Decision Support Systems (DSS).

Management Information Systems (MIS)

While operational support systems are concerned with capturing and recording data, middle and senior managers require more sophisticated reports to make tactical and strategic decisions. An MIS extrapolates and arranges the information from the operational support systems, to produce the reports necessary to make such decisions. Reports can be customised according to the type and frequency of information required, ie, scheduled reports by exception or on-demand reports. For example, branch managers may receive a *scheduled sales report* such as the total amount of sales of product X per day, and an *exception report* showing products that have not reached the minimum sales level.

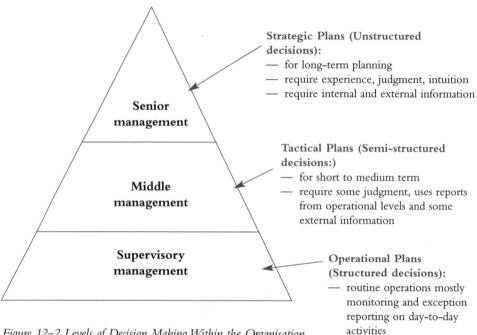

Figure 12–2 Levels of Decision Making Within the Organisation

Decision Support Systems (DSS)

Decision support systems provide the tools necessary to analyse data so that non-routine decisions can be made. Such decisions may include planning resources, determining financial budgets, etc.

A DSS incorporates analytical modelling, allowing the manager to ask *sensitivity analysis* (or 'what if?') questions. For example, 'What happens to the profit margin if the cost price increases by 10%?' The DSS will use internal information and may incorporate external information to test a variety of hypothetical situations to achieve the optimum solution to a problem.

Airlines use a variety of decision support systems for analysing seating capacity to help management maximise seat utilisation, ticket pricing, etc. Retail chains use a DSS called 'Geographical Information Systems' to help analyse the demographics of a particular region, where to locate their outlets and how to optimise distribution routes.

Designing an Information System

As Information Systems evolve constantly, office administrators have an important role in discussing the requirements regarding the design of a new system or changes to an existing system. As the administrators are the end users and are most aware of the problems within the existing system, they are key personnel when a business seeks to implement a new system. Many employees may fear that a new system will have a significant effect on their current work practices, and so may be reluctant to adopt a new system. It is therefore important that management consult end users at each step of the design process. The steps involved in the design of an Information System are outlined in Figure 12-3 below.

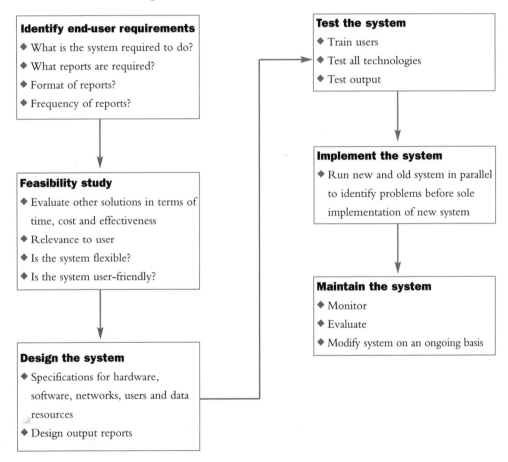

Identify end-user requirements
- What is the system required to do?
- What reports are required?
- Format of reports?
- Frequency of reports?

Feasibility study
- Evaluate other solutions in terms of time, cost and effectiveness
- Relevance to user
- Is the system flexible?
- Is the system user-friendly?

Design the system
- Specifications for hardware, software, networks, users and data resources
- Design output reports

Test the system
- Train users
- Test all technologies
- Test output

Implement the system
- Run new and old system in parallel to identify problems before sole implementation of new system

Maintain the system
- Monitor
- Evaluate
- Modify system on an ongoing basis

Figure 12–3 Stages in Designing an Information System

Short Questions

1. What is meant by the term 'information system'?
2. Outline the three components of an Information System.
3. Distinguish between an Office Automation System and a Transaction Processing System and give an example of each.
4. Briefly describe an EPOS system.
5. Briefly describe three types of decision made at the different levels of management.
6. Give an example of an Operational Support System and a Management Support System.
7. Distinguish between the type of information captured by an Operational Support System and by a Management Support System.
8. List four ways in which a Decision Support System assists management in making decisions.
9. Outline the stages involved in implementing an Information System.
10. Why is it important that management consult end users when designing or changing an Information System?

Summary

Every office uses a computer to process, store and transmit information. Purchasing a computer for either work or home use can be very challenging, due to the terminology used to outline the features of the computer. The type of computer purchased depends on its anticipated use. The purchaser should pay particular attention to processor speed, memory and hard disk capacity.

Peripheral devices such as printers, scanners and external storage media are necessary additions to a computer system. Common desktop printers are the inkjet and laser printer. Scanners vary in their versatility and the type of scanner purchased depends on the type of material to be scanned and the volume of use. External storage devices include magnetic media (ie, portable hard drives and tapes), optical media (ie, CDs, DVDs and Blu-ray) and solid-state media such as the USB drive.

A business will typically use a suite of computer applications such as word processing, spreadsheet, database and desktop publishing. Home users tend to opt for an integrated package, as it is normally installed on new computers aimed specifically at the home market.

An essential task in using a computer is to ensure that the files stored on the computer or on other storage media are protected from viruses. Antivirus software should be installed on computers and the software should be set to automatically download updates and to scan the computer for viruses on a frequent basis, ie, daily. To protect a computer from viruses, the user should never open emails or email attachments from unknown sources and should not download files from unknown websites. Files received should be scanned before opening them.

Computers in an office are generally connected to a network. Computer networks vary in size from a small local area network (LAN or WLAN, depending on technology), to a wide-area network (WAN), to a worldwide network – the Internet. Services provided over the Internet include the Web, email, newsgroups, chat and file transfer.

The Web is an information-retrieval and interactive system with information available on almost any topic. Every website has a unique address known as a 'domain name'. To find information on the Internet, the user enters keywords of the topic being sought into a search engine such as Google. Most businesses have an e-business website where consumers can purchase goods or services online. When purchasing online, consumers should ensure that they are viewing a secure web page before entering their financial details. A secure web page, identifiable by an 's' added the 'http' part of the web address, encrypts the data while it is in transit over the Internet. A business also implements Web technology using an intranet or in some cases an extranet.

Modern technology does more than just improve the normal routine functions of the office; it also enables all levels of management to make informed decisions through a variety of information systems such as Operational Support Systems (eg, TPS) and Management Support Systems (eg, MIS, DSS).

Assignments

1. Write a newspaper article entitled 'Guide to Buying a Computer'. It should be easy to understand and yet comprehensive enough to cover all the basic issues. Your final report should be typed using either a word-processing or a DTP program and should fit on a double-sided A4 page.

2. Your employer, a sole trader, has decided to upgrade two computers in the business. He has asked you to research desktop computers and to supply three specifications to include prices exclusive of VAT. His budget is €1,000 per computer. A printer is not required.

   Research the computers using at least three different suppliers. To carry out the research, gather information from computer advertisements, computer magazines, brochures, computer stores, the Web, etc.

   Provide the employer with a report outlining your research methods and recommend one of the computers as being the best value for money, justifying your answer. At the end of the report, provide a comparison sheet (similar to the one below) outlining the specification of the three computers from three different suppliers.

Comparison of Computers: Category_____			
	Company 1	**Company 2**	**Company 3**
Processor:			
Manufacturer			
Model (family name)			
Memory:			
Type			
Size			
Computer screen:			
Type			
Size			
Resolution			
Video memory			
Hard disk:			
Type			
Size			
Optical Drive:			
Reader(s) for			
Burner type(s)			
Other drives			
Sound:			
Card model			
Speakers			
Software Bundles:			
Price:			

3. Design a database to hold employee names, addresses, date of birth and gender. The relevant fields should be split up to enable the database to be searched and sorted by district, county, age and gender. Enter 10 records.
4. Write a report that compares two ISPs that provide broadband in your local area on the following issues: monthly service charge, restrictions on downloads if applicable, web space available, number of email accounts and technical support service.
5. Search the World Wide Web for the following information:
   a)   Iarnrod Éireann rail timetables
   b)   stock exchange prices for the Irish commercial banks
   c)   night courses on computer basics in Dublin.

Document the relevant findings in a report and provide the web addresses of these sites for future reference. Outline how you conducted your search and the methodology used to refine your search strategy to deliver meaningful findings.

6. Select a specific topic from your syllabus 'Information and Administration' and use the Internet to research this topic further. Note the suggestions below:

   a) Using a search engine of your choice, write down your search criteria and print the search page that resulted from your search.

   b) Refine your search criteria, documenting the reasoning behind your new search criteria based on the results of your first search. Print the search page that resulted from your second search and comment on whether it is better or worse and the action to take.

   c) Keep performing a search until the required search page is found. Write down the search criteria used each time.

   d) Once a relevant site is found, save it to disk. Extract the relevant information and prepare a two-page report on your chosen topic.

Unit 4 — Postal, Electronic and Mobile Communication

Introduction

Communication and information are the lifeblood of any business. All businesses communicate using a variety of means, such as the traditional postal system, and electronic methods such as fax, email and mobile phones. Unit 4 explores these means of communication and is divided into two chapters:

Chapter 13 — Post and Postal Services

Reviews the equipment that is typically used in the process of handling post, the general procedures for dealing with incoming and outgoing post in the office, and the wide range of services provided by An Post.

◆ Postal Equipment
◆ Dealing with Incoming Post
◆ Dealing with Outgoing Post
◆ Delivery Services Provided by An Post
◆ Other Postal Services Provided by An Post
◆ Marketing Services Provided by An Post
◆ Non-postal Services Provided by An Post

Chapter 14 — Electronic and Mobile Communication

Reviews the electronic transmission of documents such as the fax and email and other methods used to communicate and transmit information in the office, such as the pager and mobile phone.

◆ The Fax Machine and Features
◆ Compiling, Sending and Receiving Fax Messages
◆ Electronic Mail (Email)
◆ Creating and Sending Email
◆ Receiving and Managing Email
◆ Email Fraud
◆ Mobile Communication
◆ Mobile Network in Ireland

Chapter 13 — Post and Postal Services

To prevent delays in receiving or sending post, it is important to ensure that there is a proper procedure in place to deal with both incoming and outgoing post. A business that handles a large volume of post, eg, a mail-order business, may have a whole department dedicated to sorting, processing and distributing incoming and outgoing post. A medium-sized business may allocate post duties to a Post Administrator. In a small office, the receptionist or office junior may take responsibility for dealing with the post.

Postal Equipment

The volume of post flowing through the business determines what type of equipment will be used in the post room. For example, a small business may not require a franking machine and may operate a manual weigh scales and a manual letter opener. A business with large volumes of post generally operates sophisticated postal equipment.

Incoming Postal Equipment

Typical equipment for dealing with incoming post includes the following:

Mail Scanner

Mail scanners use x-ray technology to scan the contents of a package for dangerous items such as bombs or contagious substances, and are generally used to search incoming post in high-risk areas such as government buildings and Garda stations. Most mail scanners have a built-in video screen that displays the image of the package.

Mail Scanner

Letter Openers

A **paper knife** is used to open sealed letters manually.

An **automatic letter-opening machine** is used to open a large volume of letters. Envelopes are fed automatically through an envelope feeder and a minute strip is cut from the

Automatic letter opening machine

envelope by a blade. The width of the cut can be adjusted to open larger envelopes. Some models have a built-in envelope-counter and waste bin to collect the cuts from the envelopes. High-end models can extract the contents from the envelope, print the date and time on the contents, place the contents on a separate tray and the 'empty envelope detection facility' checks that all contents of the envelope are removed.

Date/Time Stamping

A date/time stamp machine is used to mark all incoming post as evidence of receipt of the post on a particular date and at a particular time. Once the operator sets up the correct date and time on an electric date/time machine, the date and time advances automatically each day. If a manual date/time stamp is used, the controls need to be changed manually each day.

Date/Time Stamping machine

Postal Rates Guide

Every office should have a copy of An Post's *Postal Rates* guide so that the correct value of postage is attached to outgoing letters or parcels. Rates of postage vary according to the size and weight of the envelope or parcel, the destination of the item and the customer's preference for standard or express delivery.

If the stamp or franking value is under the postal value, the addressee is charged with the difference in postage

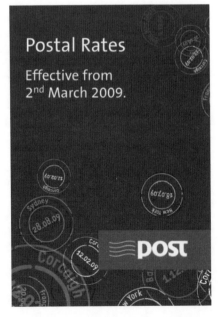

Postal Rates

Effective from
2nd March 2009.

POST

An Post's Postal Rates *guide*

and a small fee. If the addressee refuses to pay the charge, the sender is obliged to pay.

Outgoing Postal Equipment

Typical equipment for dealing with outgoing post includes the following:

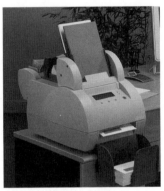

Folder and Inserter Machine

A folder and inserter machine is used to automatically fold and insert documents into envelopes. Depending on the model, the number of feeder trays determines the number of documents that can be folded and inserted into appropriately sized envelopes. Some machines will also seal the envelopes.

Folder and Inserter machine

Document Sealer

A document sealer is used for sealing one page documents such as payslips, P60 forms, etc. The document is fed from a top feeder and the machine folds and seals the document and sends it automatically to a collection tray. The feeder can be adjusted to accommodate different document sizes.

Document Sealer machine

Addressing Machine

An addressing machine is connected to a computer and can accommodate envelopes of different sizes.

The names and addresses held on a computer database are printed on to the envelopes as they are fed through the addressing machine. The addressing machine eliminates the need to attach printed labels onto envelopes manually.

Addressing machine

Postal Scales

A postal scales is used to weigh non-standard letters and parcels so that the correct postage value is placed on the post.

Advanced postal scales can be programmed to calculate the correct postal charges and can be interfaced with a franking machine to print the appropriate frank value.

Postal scales

Franking Machine

A franking machine places an impression of the postage value (a 'frank') on envelopes or parcels which are accepted by the postal system as stamped post.

Franking machine

The envelopes are stacked on a feeder tray, and the required settings, ie, date, envelope width, weight and frank value are set. As the envelope passes through the machine, the stamp value and date of postage are imprinted (franked) on the envelope. Some businesses place an advertising slogan on their frank. Gummed postage stamps can be printed individually for large parcels or bulky envelopes that cannot be fed through the machine. Sophisticated franking machines have an electronic postal scale that weighs and displays the correct postage value before applying the frank to the post.

The business can purchase or lease the franking machine from the manufacturer, but must obtain a licence and a franking card with franking units (similar to a telephone call card) from An Post. A meter displays the franking units remaining. Training should be provided in the use of the franking machine to avoid wasting franking units.

Dealing with Incoming Post

The following procedure is generally implemented when dealing with incoming post to the office:

◆ Sign for registered post.

◆ Sort the post according to: general, private, confidential, personal and urgent.

◆ Open general post.

◆ Do *not* open:

1. Post addressed to individuals as private, confidential or personal unless authorised to do so. These items should be distributed unopened to the addressees.

2. Post that is incorrectly addressed to the business, eg, Allied Irish Finance, 12 Drury Street, Carlow, receives a letter addressed to Allied Irish Banks Ltd, 10 Main Street, Carlow. This letter should be marked 'Return to Sender' and placed in a post box.

◆ Check envelopes for enclosures. Secure enclosures with a paper clip or staple. Record missing enclosures as 'enc omitted' on documentation received.

◆ Date/time stamp the post.

◆ Record remittances (ie, monies received) in the remittance book.

◆ Distribute post to individual trays, pigeon-holes, or department post trays.

Remittance Book

A remittance book is maintained by an administrator to record remittances received. The remittance book logs the date the post is received, who the remittance is from, the type and amount of remittance and is signed by the person opening the post.

Remittance Book				
Date	**Addressee**	**Remittance Type**	**Amount**	**Signed**
July 7 2010	Star Ltd	Postal Order	€35.00	M Murphy
July 7 2010	Cambridge	Cheque	€64.00	M Murphy
July 7 2010	Calcus Ltd	Bank Draft	€13.00	M Murphy

Dealing with Outgoing Post

Administration staff will usually have 'in/out trays' for receiving and dispatching post. The post will be collected from the out trays at specified times during the day. The following procedure is generally implemented when dealing with outgoing post:

Letters

- Ensure all letters are signed.
- Check all enclosures (eg, cheques, documentation) are attached.
- Check the address on the letter matches the address on the envelope.
- Fold letters and any attachments neatly and place in an appropriately sized envelope. Particular attention should be paid when inserting letters into window envelopes. Ensure address is visible and confidential information (eg, amount due on account) is not in view.
- Seal envelopes.
- Prepare post for franking, batching similarly sized envelopes together.
- Place appropriate postal labels on post requiring special attention, eg, registered post, express post, etc.
- Weigh non-standard items individually to determine the correct postage value. (Use An Post's *Postal Rates* guide.)
- Frank post.
- Dispatch post to the Post Office and obtain receipts as proof of postage and to track items through An Post's website, www.anpost.ie.

Example — Preparing Post for Dispatch

A heavy envelope arrives at the post room from Purchasing, to be dispatched to the UK. Outline procedure for dispatch.

1. Check envelope is sealed and addressed properly.
2. Weigh the envelope and note weight (assume weight of 236 g).
3. Check *Postal Rates* guide for charges to UK for post weighing not more than 250 g. (Current charge is €9.60 for express posting.)
4. Adjust franking machine to emit a stamp to the value of €9.60.
5. Place franking machine stamp on the envelope and dispatch.

Parcels and Packing

To ensure a safe delivery the following guidelines may be adopted when packing parcels for dispatch:

1. Pack the items tightly together to prevent movement. Aerofoam or bubble wrap is often used.
2. Wrap the outer parcel with plain paper or place in a cardboard box.

3. Ensure that the name and address of the recipient is clearly labelled on the front of the parcel.

4. Ensure that the sender's name and address is clearly labelled on the back of the parcel. Mark with the words 'SENDER'S ADDRESS' clearly to avoid confusion.

5. Place any postal labels, eg, registered or express labels, etc., on the left-hand side of the front of the parcel.

Delivery Services Provided by An Post

An Post is Ireland's national postal service provider. An Post provides many different delivery services which vary according to cost and speed of delivery. The cost of postage depends on the size, weight, destination of the item and the type of delivery required.

Most of An Post's delivery services provide the sender with a tracking service. When posting an item, the sender is issued with a receipt with a unique reference number. This reference number is used to track the progress of the delivery through the An Post website, www.anpost.ie. The receipt is also the sender's Proof of Postage.

National and International post that contains valuable items or important documents should be registered at the Post Office to ensure secure delivery. Registered post receives secure, priority handling by An Post. Items are insured to the value declared on the registered label to a maximum of €320.

To register post, the sender completes a registered label, stating a description and value of the contents and the recipient and senders' name and address. The sender attaches the label to the item and pays the correct postage

Registered Post label

charge. For international delivery, a Customs Declaration Form may need to be completed.

Other delivery services explained below relate to letters, packets and light parcels not weighing more than 20 kg:

♦ **Standard Post** is the cheapest method for both national and international post, but delivery times are not guaranteed. However, 90% of national standard post is delivered within 24 hours.

◆ **Express Post** is used when the sender requires an item to be delivered nationally with a guaranteed delivery time. Express Post guarantees delivery by the next working day. The sender attaches an 'Express Post' label (available from the Post Office) to the item and

Express Post label

pays the appropriate postage rate. If the sender requires a signature from the recipient when the post is delivered, an Express Post (with Signature and Insurance) label must be used. There is extra fee for this service of €2 and the item is insured up to a value of €350.

◆ **Express Post International** is used only to send letters and light parcels up to a limited weight of 2kg abroad. Delivery times are only estimated. At present, this service is limited to 15 countries. The sender attaches an Express Post International label to the item and pays the appropriate postage. A signature from the recipient is not available with this service.

Express International Post label

◆ **Priority Parcel International** is used when posting parcels weighing up to a maximum of 20kg to the UK, certain European destinations and the USA. Delivery times are not guaranteed. The sender attaches a Priority Parcel International label to the item and pays the appropriate postage. The service includes

Priority Parcel Post label

transit insurance up to a value of €150. A customs declaration form must be completed by the sender for all international parcels.

◆ **Courier Post** is used when the sender requires items to be delivered nationally or worldwide with a guaranteed delivery date. Courier Post guarantees delivery the next working day before 12 noon in major urban centres in Ireland, and day-certain deliveries to more than 200 countries worldwide. The sender brings the item to be delivered to the Post Office. If the item is to be delivered abroad, the item should be brought unsealed to the Post Office and the sender must complete a Customs Declaration Form. The sender attaches the Courier Post label to the item and pays the appropriate postage fee. Insurance is included in the cost of postage to a maximum value of €350.

Courier Post label

The table below outlines the postal costs for various delivery services for items weighing less than 100g within Ireland and Europe. An Post provides full details of postal costs according to weight, destination, delivery service required etc. in their *Postal Rates* guide and on the An Post website – www.anpost.ie.

Postal Costs and Delivery Service for items sent within Ireland & Europe weighing less than 100g						
Delivery Service	**Cost**		**Delivery Time/ Day Guaranteed**		**Tracking**	
	Ireland	Europe	Ireland	Europe	Ireland	Europe
Standard Post	€0.55	€0.82	No	No	Parcels only	Yes
Express Post	€5.50	N/A	Yes	N/A	Yes	N/A
Express Post International	N/A	€8.70	N/A	Estimated only	N/A	Yes
Courier Post	€15.95	€28.00	Yes	Yes	Yes	Yes
Priority Parcel International	N/A	€26.15	N/A	Estimated only	N/A	Yes

Other Postal Services Provided by An Post

Redirection

This service redirects post to an address nominated by the customer for a period of time. The service is very convenient for people moving house or who spend periods of time working abroad. Booking forms for this service are available at the Post Office.

Mail Minder

An Post will retain post at the Post Office for up to 12 weeks while the customer is away from their usual address. Booking forms for this service are available at the Post Office, on which the customer enters the date when normal delivery is to recommence.

Poste Restante

Poste Restante or post 'to be called for' is a facility offered by An Post for those who do not have a known address, eg, people travelling. Post can be addressed to the recipient in the care of a specified Post Office. The post is held at the Post Office for three months.

Private Post Box

An Post operates a private post box facility for customers who do not have a regular address or who do not wish correspondents to know their address. The customer/business is allocated a private box number where post can be addressed and delivered. Private box numbers are common where employers have a job vacancy but do not wish to declare the location of the vacancy to the public. Respondents are given a box number to apply to and the employer collects the replies from the private post box.

Passport Express

Passport application forms are available at the Post Office. The customer places the completed form in a special passport express envelope and returns it to the Post Office clerk with the appropriate fee, ie, the passport fee plus the cost of the service. The passport is delivered to the customer within 10 working days.

Sending Money Through An Post

It is not advisable to send cash through the post. An Post provides a range of services for transferring money nationally and internationally through the postal system. In all cases a receipt is given as proof of purchase.

1. **Postal Money Order:** Used to send money within Ireland, replacing the traditional postal order and money order. A Postal Money Order can be purchased for any amount up to a maximum of €650. A fee is charged depending on the value of the Order, ranging from 80c for an Order up to a value of €15 to €3.75 for an Order up to the maximum value of €650. The recipient can cash the Postal Money Order at any Post Office or can lodge it in their bank account. Proof of identity is required to cash the Postal Money Order.

2. **Sterling Draft:** Used to send money worldwide. A sterling draft can be purchased to a maximum of £2,000 sterling. The sterling draft must be lodged in the recipient's bank account, so it is a safe means of sending money through the post.

3. **Eurogiro:** Used to transfer money electronically in the currency of the receiving European country up to a maximum of €1904.61. Eurogiro can be used in the following countries: Ireland, Belgium, France, Germany, Great Britain, Italy, Luxembourg, Spain and Switzerland. The money can be lodged directly into a bank account, or collected at a nominated post office abroad by the recipient. It generally takes up to four working days for the funds to be transferred.

4. **Western Union Money Transfer:** Used to transfer money electronically both nationally and worldwide, available only at selected Post Offices. Unlike Eurogiro, the transfer takes places within a matter of minutes and is used for urgent transactions. The recipient can collect the money in local currency at a designated Western Union agency and is not required to have a bank account, but proof of identity is required. The fee for the service varies depending on the amount of money that is transferred.

Marketing Services Provided by An Post

Data Ireland, a subsidiary of An Post, offers services to businesses such as compiling databases, preparing business listings, geographical customer targeting, business analysis and business surveying. Services provided by Data Ireland and distributed by An Post are:

Business Response Services

An Post provides businesses with opportunities to use the postal system to allow customers to reply to their business free of charge using **business reply** and **freepost** services. To avail of these two services, a business response licence is obtained from the Post Office and the business pays the postage charge plus a handling fee for every item that is received using these services.

Business reply service

The business reply service consists of special pre-printed envelopes or cards with the business licence number, name and address, followed by the words 'Business Reply' and the post district. No postage is paid by the recipient and the business pays only for the replies it receives.

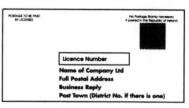

Business reply envelope

Freepost

A business using the Freepost service *does not* have to enclose a pre-printed envelope or card. The customer replying to the business can use their own stationery and will address the envelope with the business Freepost address as agreed with the Post Office.

A Freepost address is used by a business that advertises in media such as newspapers, radio or TV where the inclusion of a pre-printed card or envelope is not possible.

Direct Marketing Services

Postaim

Postaim is a service that allows a business to distribute mailshots, product samples, leaflets, brochures or other promotional material through the normal postal system to a specific target market – for example, people on a mailing list with a specific interest. The material to be delivered is addressed by the business, and delivered with the normal post. The fee charged depends on the number and weight of the items to be distributed. This service is used to distribute 2,000 or more items with a maximum individual weight of 1 kg.

Publicity post

Publicity post is similar to Postaim, but it does not require names and addresses on the items to be delivered. It is therefore suitable for general promotions to a non-specific target market. The promotional material is delivered to every address in a postal district. The fee charged depends on the number of leaflets dropped, the district covered and the weight of each item (maximum 100g).

Non-postal Services Provided by An Post

An Post operates many other services for the general public through the Post Office network. Such services include:

◆ social welfare payments
◆ deposit and savings accounts
◆ prize bonds
◆ bill pay (eg, telephone, gas, electricity)
◆ licences (TV and dog licences)
◆ insurance (via An Post's subsidiary insurance company, One Direct)
◆ retail services (such as gift vouchers, National Lottery tickets, mobile phone top-ups, stationery, and developing of photographs via the Photoexpress service).

Most Post Offices offer savings, investments, current accounts and other banking facilities.

Short Questions

1. Outline a procedure for dealing with incoming post.
2. Outline a procedure for dealing with outgoing letters and parcels.
3. What is a franking machine and briefly describe four features?
4. Briefly describe three items of equipment used for handling incoming post and three items of equipment for dealing with outgoing post in a large mail-order business.
5. What mail should an administrator not open?
6. Give an example of when the following items would be used:
   a) remittance book
   b) Eurogiro
   c) An Post's *Postal Rates* guide
7. Outline the difference between the following postal services:
   a) Standard Post
   b) Express Post
   c) Courier Post
   d) Priority Parcel
8. Outline how An Post's tracking system operates.
9. Outline a procedure to follow for receiving registered post.
10. Distinguish between the following postal services:
    a) *Poste Restante*
    b) private post box
    c) Mail Minder

11. Give an example of when it is more appropriate to send money through the post using:
    a) Postal money order
    b) Sterling draft
    c) Eurogiro
    d) Western Union money transfer.
12. Which is the fastest way to send €250 to the UK through the Post Office?
13. Give an example of why a business might offer a Freepost address as distinct from a Business Reply service.
14. Distinguish between the following direct marketing facilities: Postaim and Publicity post.
15. List four non–postal services offered by An Post.

Chapter 14 — Electronic and Mobile Communication

Electronic and mobile communication devices enable one to stay in touch with the office while on the move. Such devices allow users to send, receive or access information through computer and mobile phone networks.

Today, information can be transmitted directly from one electronic device to almost any other electronic device: for example, an email or fax can be transmitted from a computer to a mobile phone or vice versa. This interconnection between devices greatly facilitates communication by employees on the move and has resulted in the so-called 'mobile office'.

The Fax Machine and Features

The Fax Machine

A fax machine transmits an image of a page over a telephone line. While email has largely taken over from the fax, a fax machine is the easiest way to transmit a printed or hand-written document to another fax device. Generally, a fax machine is assigned its own telephone line and fax number. It is possible to share the telephone line between the telephone and fax, but this is only suitable for low-volume fax use.

A fax can be sent and received from any fax-capable device such as a multifunctional printer (MFP), which combines four technologies into one machine, incorporating a scanner, fax, photocopier and printer. MFPs are used in offices where the volume of faxes sent or received is low. Other technologies include computer software to send/receive faxes and websites that offer a fax service, where a fax can be sent to an email account.

Features of a dedicated fax machine

◆ **Automatic Document Feeder (ADF):** a tray that automatically transmits sequential pages of an outgoing document, eliminating the need for the sender to send each page manually.

◆ **LCD (Liquid Crystal Display):** a panel which displays the fax number dialled and status of transmission, ie, 'dialling', 'sending', etc.

◆ **Fax/Tel Auto Switch:** allows a fax machine to double as a telephone. The fax machine can automatically distinguish between voice and fax calls when the telephone line is shared.

◆ **Autodial:** a function similar to 'Contacts', with which frequently used fax numbers are programmed into the memory by contact name. To dial a fax number, the contact's name is selected, which reduces the risk of misdialling a fax number.

◆ **Automatic Redial:** automatically redials a fax number repeatedly when a busy signal is received, eliminating the need to manually redial an engaged fax number.

◆ **Activity Report:** a record can be provided of all incoming and outgoing faxes.

◆ **Transmission Report:** a record which is printed each time an outgoing fax is transmitted. The report that gives details of the date and time of transmission, the receiving fax machine's number, the number of pages sent and whether the transmission was successful or not.

◆ **Dual Access:** a facility which allows faxes to be sent and received simultaneously. The fax machine stores incoming faxes in its memory while transmitting an outgoing fax, or an outgoing fax can be scanned into memory while receiving a fax. The fax transmission is completed when the machine is free.

◆ **Out of Paper Reception:** a facility that allows the machine to hold incoming faxes in the memory if the fax machine runs out of paper. The fax is printed when the paper is reloaded.

◆ **Delayed Transmission:** outgoing faxes can be stored in memory and transmitted at a scheduled time to avail of off-peak telephone rates.

◆ **Confidential Faxing:** incoming faxes are not printed, but are stored in the memory and accessed with a PIN number.

◆ **Retrieval/Forwarding**: faxes stored in memory can be picked up at another fax machine by dialling the fax number and entering a PIN number, similar to accessing voicemail messages. This is useful if the recipient is not in the office.

◆ **Broadcasting/Group Dialling**: the same fax can be sent to multiple destinations. The fax is scanned once and the recipient's group is selected. A transmission report informs the sender of successful and unsuccessful transmissions.

◆ **PC–based Faxing:** the ability to fax to a computer with fax software installed. The fax is received as an email attachment.

Compiling, Sending and Receiving Fax Messages

Compiling Fax Messages

A business generally prepares its own fax coversheet using the templates available with word processing software. A fax coversheet generally contains the following information on the business letterhead: attention of; from; date; number of pages including this coversheet.

SHARPMAN
Fax Message

Computer Books and Software
11 Northgate Street   Tel No: 0902 342675
Athlone   Fax: 0902 342677
Co. Westmeath   www.cbs.ie
                              info@cbs.ie

Attention of: _____   Dept: _____

From: _____   Date: _____

Number of Pages including Coversheet: [   ]

Sending Fax Messages (via a dedicated fax machine)

1. Place the original(s) in the input tray.
2. Enter the fax number or use the 'autodial' facility. If the message is to be transmitted at a later time (ie, after office hours) the 'delayed transmission' facility is used.
3. Press the 'start' button to dial the number.
4. When the receiving fax machine answers, the page(s) are scanned through the transmitting fax machine. The mode and speed of communication depend on the capabilities of both machines and the quality of the telephone line.
5. At the end of the transmission, the transmitting fax machine prints a transmission report which should be attached to the fax as proof that the fax was sent.

Receiving Fax Messages (via a dedicated fax machine)

1. Set the fax machine to ON.
2. Ensure sufficient paper is loaded to print incoming messages, unless the 'out of paper reception' facility is available.
3. Check the fax to ensure that the number of pages received is correct, as indicated on the fax coversheet.
4. Distribute the fax to the appropriate person(s).

Electronic Mail (Email)

Electronic Mail or email refers to the exchange of digital messages via a computer or mobile phone. An email message is created, sent and received using email software over an Internet connection. Email systems range from basic to advanced, ie, from web-based systems that offer free email accounts (eg, Google, Yahoo, etc.) to business email systems (eg, Ms Outlook 2007) that can integrate with other software on the business network.

The main advantages of email over the postal system ('snail mail') are that messages are delivered to anywhere in the world almost immediately, and digital documents or images can be attached with the email.

Setting up an Email Account

An email address is necessary to send and receive email. An email address typically takes the form of 'username@domainname.country', and is obtained by setting up an email account through a service provider's website. The procedure is:

1. Log on to a preferred service provider's website, eg, www.digiweb.ie, www.iol.ie, www.yahoo.com, www.google.com, etc.
2. Select option 'Create New Email Account' and provide the following details:
   - personal information, ie: name, address and phone number
   - the 'username' to be used in the email address. 'Username' refers to the recipient's mailbox name
   - a password to access the email
3. Submit the details.

The service provider appends their 'domainname', (ie, the registered name of their mail server, eg, .iol.ie, .gmail.com etc.) to the username and checks if the username is available to use. If the username is already taken, the service provider returns a message requesting a different username. The username selected must be unique. This is achieved by adding the initial of a second name or by using a number, eg, nlhegarty@iol.ie or n2hegarty@iol.ie.

Creating and Sending Email

Using Ms Outlook 2007 as the email program, an email message is created by selecting the **New** button from the Tool Bar. A message window is divided into a **header** and a **message** section as displayed in Figure 14.1.

1. When creating a business email message, use the **addressing fields** correctly, ie, 'To', 'Cc', or 'Bcc' to distinguish who is responsible for replying to the email and to protect the identity of email addresses:

   To: Anyone listed in the 'To:' field is responsible for replying to the email. The email addresses are entered manually or selected from the 'Contacts' list created by the user by clicking on the To: field.

   Cc: 'Cc' means carbon copy. Anyone listed here receives a copy of the email for information purposes. All email addresses on the Cc list are forwarded to each recipient. The Cc field is generally used for internal communication.

   Bcc: 'Bcc' means 'blind carbon copy'. The Bcc field is generally used to send emails to an external mailing list (ie, a subscription list or marketing list). A recipient listed in the Bcc field of the email will only see their own email address.

— Header Section

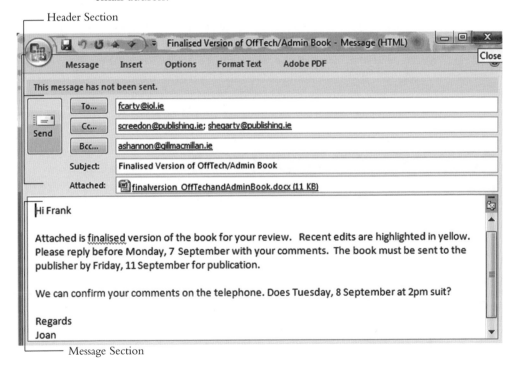

— Message Section

Figure 14–1   Ms Outlook 2007 – displaying components of an email message

2. In the **Subject** field, enter a heading to indicate the contents of the message. This is used by the recipient to scan incoming messages for priority reading. Messages with no subject line are often considered to be junk email or 'spam' by business email systems.

3. In the **Attach** field, attach any document or images to be sent with the email. Files are selected from a storage device, ie, hard drive, USB drive, etc.

4. In the **Message** section, type the email message. Adopt a professional tone and appropriate language, avoiding 'texting' language or slang. Remember, an email represents the business to the recipient and should reflect the business's image.

5. Check the email for spelling and grammar using the tools available in the email program.

6. Attach your **signature** to the email, although this can be set up to automatically appear at the end of a new message. (A signature is prepared text that generally includes: a person's name, job title, business name and contact details.)

7. Use other options available on email systems appropriately, ie, do not:
   ◆ mark an email as 'high priority' or 'urgent' if it is not. This will annoy the receiver.
   ◆ request a 'delivery notification' or a 'read notification' if not necessary, as this will increase the amount of emails received and reduce the amount of space available in the mailbox.

8. To send the message, the **Send** button on the email message screen is selected. If you are unsure about the content of the message, or if you are in a hurry, do not send the message straight away. Once the message is sent, it cannot be retrieved. The message should be saved to 'Drafts' so that it can be reviewed and amended before it is sent.

Receiving and Managing Emails

Email addressed to a recipient is stored in a 'mailbox' on the service provider's server. Figure 14–2 displays the opening screen of Ms Outlook 2007. The opening screen of Ms Outlook 2007 is divided into panes: the **navigation pane** on the left and the **reading pane** on the right.

Navigation Pane

The navigation pane contains folders to manage incoming and outgoing mail:
◆ **Inbox:** received emails are automatically stored in the 'Inbox' folder.
◆ **Sent Items:** sent emails are automatically stored in the Sent Items folder.

◆ **Junk E-mail:** junk emails received (also known as 'spam') are automatically stored in the Junk E-mail folder. A filter can be set to classify incoming mail as junk depending on email addresses, subject, etc.

◆ **Drafts:** unfinished emails are automatically saved to the Drafts folder.

◆ **Outbox:** emails which are assigned a future date or time to be sent are stored in the Outbox. A future date and time is generally used on email systems that use a dial-up connection to avail of off-peak telephone rates.

◆ **Deleted Items:** deleted emails are placed in the Deleted Items folder.

◆ **RSS Feeds:** RSS feeds (Really Simple Syndication) automatically notifies subscribers to an RSS feed on a website that new content has been added. Subscribers to RSS feeds will receive emails with a summary and a link to the new content on a website. These emails are automatically stored in the RSS Feeds folder.

Paper clip symbol indicates that this email has a file attached

Selected email is displayed in Reading Pane or in a new email depending on view set-up

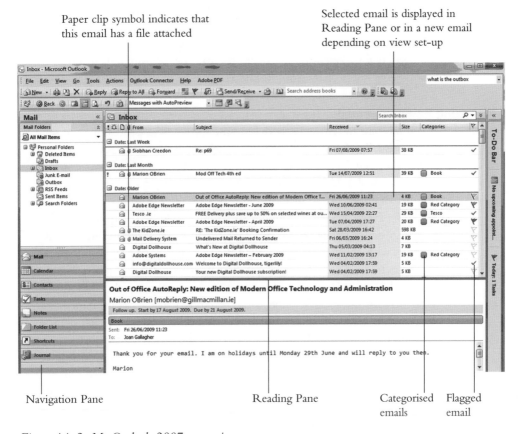

Navigation Pane   Reading Pane   Categorised emails   Flagged email

Figure 14–2: Ms Outlook 2007 – opening screen

Reading Pane

The reading pane displays all messages in a selected folder. In Figure 14–2, the inbox is selected and the reading pane displays all incoming messages. Messages are arranged in chronological order of receipt and display the sender, subject heading and size of the email. The paper clip symbol next to a message indicates that this email has a file attached.

Receiving Email

Incoming emails are stored in the service provider's mailbox. To retrieve emails, the user logs on to the email system. Received emails are downloaded automatically from the service provider's server, or the recipient may have to check for new emails, depending on the connection. In either case, new messages are downloaded to the recipient's **Inbox** folder.

To be read, a message is selected and either appears in a new window, or at the bottom of the reading pane, depending on how the 'view' is set up.

To read an attachment, it is advisable to save it and scan with anti-virus software before opening it as viruses can be transmitted through email attachments – especially from unknown sources.

Managing Received Email

It is important to set up a scheduled time for reading, processing and sending emails, usually two periods per day, once in the morning, and once in the afternoon. Regular checking of email is non-productive and time consuming.

Email should be managed properly; it is easy to let an overwhelming number of emails accumulate in the Inbox. Some tips to manage emails are:

◆ *Set up folders for emails*: A folder structure should be set up for specific categories of emails. For example, let's assume that the business regularly deals with another business called 'Perfect Insurance Ltd' about specific topics like fire insurance and public liability insurance. An email folder called 'Perfect Insurance' should be set up, and within this folder, sub-folders for the specific subjects of correspondence – fire insurance, etc.

◆ *Categorise emails*: Regular emails received on a particular topic, or from a particular person or business, should be categorised. A category is a word or phrase that can be added to an email to facilitate finding, sorting or grouping emails across multiple folders. In Figure 14–2, three categories are used with two of the categories renamed. To set a category, right-click on the email under the Category column and select a colour from the drop down menu.

◆ *Flag emails*: Flagging is helpful towards prioritising emails that need to be followed up. Flags have different colours to represent when the message needs to be followed up, be it today, tomorrow, this week, or a custom start date, due date and a reminder can be set. In Figure 14–2, three emails are flagged. To set a flag, right-click on the email under the Flag column and select 'Follow-up' from the drop down menu. An entry is automatically placed on the to-do-list for flagged emails, so, for example, emails flagged to be completed today will be placed on today's to-do-list.

◆ *Filter email*: The filter can be set to automatically file emails (sent or received) to an appropriate folder based on the email address.

◆ *Junk email*: Review junk email to ensure that emails have not automatically ended up in the junk folder in error. Move non-junk email to the inbox and delete all other junk emails.

◆ *Delete email*: Delete unwanted email. Deleted email is placed in the Deleted Items folder, but is not yet permanently deleted, and so the folder should be emptied on a regular basis.

Replying to Email

In general there are two ways to reply to an email:

1. *Reply by sending the message received with your reply:* Select the message you want to reply to in the reading pane. Click the **Reply** icon on the Toolbar or in the opened message window. The original message will be displayed preceded by an underline with space above it for typing the reply. This type of reply is not really suitable for ongoing correspondence, as the email message will become very long. This option has the following advantages:

   a) the recipient's email address and the subject heading are completed automatically

   b) the sender can send a short reply as there is no need to remind the recipient of the content of the original email

   The Reply icon sends the reply to the sender only; the **Reply to All** icon sends the reply to the sender and to all addresses listed in both the To: field and the Cc: field.

2. *Reply by creating a new message:* The received message is not sent. A new message is created and the recipient's email address and a subject heading is entered, along with the contents of the reply.

Forwarding Email

Email can be forwarded directly to others by clicking the forward icon and entering the email addresses of those who are to receive the message or by selecting email addresses from the contacts.

To forward email internally within the business, a private email system must be in place, ie, a network configured to manage email.

Email Fraud

Email Fraud – Phishing

Phishing (pronounced 'fishing') is an online fraud technique used by criminals to lure users into disclosing personal information over email. A common phishing practice uses spoofed emails that are disguised to look like they are from a well-known business with links to a spoofed website that imitates the image of legitimate websites, for example, a particular bank, credit card company, charity, etc.

The purpose of these spoofed messages is to trick the user into providing personal information such as bank account number, PIN number, debit/credit card number, PPS (Personal Public Service) number, etc. This information is used in many ways by criminals for financial gain. For example, a common practice is identity theft, whereby the thief steals your personal information, and takes on your identity to empty your bank account and charge expenses to the limit of your credit card.

How to protect yourself from a Phishing Scheme

1. **Never reply to an email that requests your personal information.** Be very suspicious of any email message from a business or individual asking for your personal information, or one that sends you personal information and asks you to update or confirm it. Instead, use the phone number printed on earlier correspondence from the business or individual to call to confirm that the email is legitimate. Do not call a number listed in the email message. Similarly, never volunteer any personal information to someone who places an unsolicited call to you.

2. **Don't click a link in a suspicious email.** A link in a suspicious email might not be trustworthy. Instead, visit websites by typing their URL into your browser or by using your Favourites link. Do not copy and paste links from email messages into your browser.

3. **Study links in a suspicious email.** Some of the techniques that criminals have used to forge links are as follows:
   - *Link masks*: 'Masked' means that the link that you see does not take you to that address but to an imitated website. In the example

   https://www.woodgrovebank.com/loginscript/user2.jsp

   http://192.168.255.205/wood/index.htm

   here, resting the cursor over the link in an email reveals a numeric Internet address. This should make you suspicious.

- *Web Addresses that include the @ sign in its URL:* Never click a website that includes the @ sign in its URL because browsers ignore anything before the @ sign in the URL. For example, the Web address https://www.woodgrovebank.com@nl.tv/secure_verification.aspx would take you to the location that comes after the @ sign, not to Wood Grove Bank. The real location, nl.tv/secure_verification.aspx, could be an unsafe site.
- *Homographs:* A homograph is a word with the same spelling as another word but with a different meaning. In sophisticated homograph attacks, the Web address looks exactly like that of a legitimate website. For example, the Web address www.gillmacmillan.ie looks legitimate, but what you can't see is that the 'i' is a Cyrillic character from the Russian alphabet, and the address could take you to a different site entirely.

4. **Never open attachments in emails from unknown senders.** Many phishing schemes ask you to open attachments which generally have 'spyware' included. If the attachment is opened, spyware is downloaded to your computer which can record the keystrokes that you use to log into your personal online accounts. Any attachment that you want to view should be saved first, and then scanned with up-to-date anti-virus software and anti-spyware software.

5. **Make sure websites are secure on web pages where a transaction is being completed.** The Web address should be preceded by https:// instead of the usual http:// in the browser's address bar and contain the lock icon 🔒. Clicking the lock icon displays the digital certificate for the site. The name that follows 'Issued to' in the certificate should match the site that you think you are on. If you suspect that a website is not what it should be, leave the site immediately and report it. Don't follow any of the instructions that it presents.

6. **Protect your PC.** Ensure that up-to-date anti-virus software and anti-spyware software is installed on your computer.

7. **Monitor your transactions.** Review your credit card and bank statements to make sure that you are charged only for transactions that you made. Report any irregularities in your accounts immediately by dialling the number shown on your statement.

Mobile Communication

Mobile communication technology has become an essential part of business as it enables employees to work off-site and communicate from a location remote to the office. Examples of mobile communication include pagers and mobile phones.

Pagers operate within a limited radius of a telephone network and are therefore best suited to in-house mobile communication, eg, within hospitals, factories, etc. The pager however, is facing strong competition from the mobile phone.

Mobile phones operate over cellular networks which facilitate worldwide communication, so employees are not restricted by distance and can use their mobile phones abroad. There are many models of business mobile phones on the market which can be classified as Smartphones.

Smartphones

A Smartphone combines the functions of a traditional mobile phone and a handheld computer (PDA) in a single device. It differs from a traditional mobile phone in that it has an operating system, increased processing power and storage capacity. Besides making/receiving phone calls and texts, a user can fax, email, browse the Web, take photographs, record and edit video, use software applications and maintain and synchronise their Smartphone with their office computer. Examples of popular Smartphones are the Blackberry, Nokia N97 or iPhone 3GS. A Smartphone gives users the best of both worlds, as they combine mobility and connectivity. They are replacing the traditional mobile phone and PDA and also reduce reliance on laptops for access to email, the Internet and computer applications. As with laptops and other computers, data transmitted through mobile phones is prone to viruses as with data transmitted over a computer network.

Features of a Smartphone

The features available on a fixed-line telephone are available with Smartphones, such as call display, speed dialling, last-number redial, clear last digit, hold, call forwarding, call waiting and call barring. Additional features include:

◆ **SMS (Short Messaging Service) – 'Texting'** is an inexpensive and quick method of communicating via a short text message to another mobile or fixed-line phone. All phones have 'predictive text' also known as 'T9' (Text on 9 keys) input technology. As combinations of letters are entered, the phone 'predicts' the word intended by searching a dictionary.

◆ **MMS (Multimedia Message Service)** is used to send messages containing audio, pictures and video to other compatible mobile phones. MP3 players, FM radio and digital imaging (eg, photography and video) are standard on most mobile phones, but Smartphones allow the user to edit the video clip.

◆ **Voice Mail** allows messages to be left on the mobile provider's answering service. Messages are retrieved by dialling the mobile provider's voicemail retrieval number.

◆ **Voice Calling** is built-in voice-recognition software that enables a voice command to call a number from the contacts list, allowing hands-free calling. Conference calling may also be possible.

◆ **Voice Memo** allows voice recordings of notes, reminders, ideas, etc., which can be inserted into the memo or calendar function of the phone.

◆ **Internet** access is available on Smartphones which can display websites as they would appear on a computer screen. This is distinct from earlier WAP sites designed for less advanced mobile phones.

◆ **Fax and Email** can be sent to and received from other compatible devices such as computers, PDA and other mobile phones.

◆ **Roaming** is a facility which automatically switches the user to a new cell network when the mobile phone is used abroad. Higher per-minute rates are charged for international calls, and both the caller and the receiver are charged.

◆ **WiFi** allows a mobile phone user to connect to the Internet and communicate with other WiFi-enabled devices when they are in a WiFi hotspot.

◆ **Bluetooth and Infrared** are wireless technologies used to transfer and synchronise data between a mobile phone and compatible devices such as computers or PDAs. This enables the transfer of updated information between compatible devices. Both Bluetooth and Infrared communicate to devices within a limited range of approximately 10 meters. Bluetooth technology is also used to make and receive calls using a headset, facilitating hands-free calls.

◆ **Satellite Navigation (Sat Nav)** uses a built-in Global Positioning System (GPS) and/or the Internet to direct users to required locations or to locate facilities in an unfamiliar area.

◆ **Input Methods** for Smartphones include touch screens or a full QWERTY keyboard to enter text more quickly when creating emails or using applications.

Mobile Network in Ireland

The mobile network in Ireland is operated by five providers: O_2, Vodafone, Meteor, 3 and Tesco mobile. All mobile providers offer the following types of subscription connection to their networks:

◆ **Fixed contract:** A contract is entered into for a fixed term, generally one year. With a contract there is a range of payment options to choose from, depending on your usage of the phone. Each payment option has a different monthly fee, which will include a bundle of free 'call minutes' and free SMS texts. In addition, there is a greater selection of mobile phones to choose from and the cost of the mobile phone is subsidised by the mobile provider's network. However, if the phone is not used, or you switch to another network, the monthly subscription must be paid to the end of the contract.

◆ **Prepaid package:** The prepaid package is known by different names according to the network, ie, 'Ready-to-Go' with Vodafone, 'Speakeasy' with O2, etc.

With this option, there is no contract, monthly fee or phone bills. However, the choice of mobile phones and rate options is limited. A prepaid phone is purchased which includes an amount of 'free call credit'. When the phone is running low on call credit, a message is sent to the phone. Call credit can be topped up by purchasing 'top-up' vouchers at various retail outlets, through an ATM, online, etc.

Guide to Connection Option

When deciding which type of connection to choose (ie, contract or prepaid) consider how many calls you would typically make (peak/off peak) per month. If the total cost is greater than the 'basic' monthly contract fee, a contract should be considered, as this has built-in free calls and texts and the phone can be upgraded for a nominal fee at the end of the contract. The prepaid packages are suitable for low-volume or controlled usage.

If the decision is to go for a contract package, the first step is to compare the various payment options across networks (ie, the monthly fee, free call credit and text credit).

The next step is to compare the cost of the following services outside the free call/text limit, during peak and off-peak rates:
◆ call from a mobile network to a fixed-line phone
◆ call to the same mobile network
◆ call to another mobile network
◆ check voicemail
◆ access the Internet and email.

Roaming, MMS texting and data transfer (by fax, email or on the Internet) are not usually covered by a 'bundle' package, so the user should pay particular attention to the cost of these services. The website www.comreg.ie should be used to assist in selecting a mobile provider suitable to a person's phone usage.

Having done the analysis, choose the network provider that offers best value for your needs. Your needs could be just simply calls to all mobile networks, SMS and MMS, mostly during off-peak times.

Short Questions

1. Define electronic and mobile communication.
2. Describe the following features of a fax machine:
   a) group dialling
   b) dual access
   c) confidential faxing
   d) transmission report.
3. Describe the following features of a fax machine:
   a) retrieval/forwarding
   b) delayed transmission
   c) PC-based faxing
   d) fax/tel autoswitch.
4. What information should be included on a fax coversheet?
5. Define the term 'email'.
6. Explain the format of an email address.
7. What details should be included in the following fields of an email message?
   a) To:
   b) Cc:
   c) Bcc:
   d) Subject:

8. Distinguish between the following features of email:
   a) forward
   b) reply
   c) reply to all.
9. Describe how emails are received by a recipient.
10. List and briefly describe four ways to manage email.
11. Explain the following terms in relation to email fraud:
    (a) phishing
    (b) masking links
    (c) homographs
12. Identify four ways to protect yourself or your business from a phishing scheme.
13. Distinguish between the following features of a mobile phone:
    a) MMS and SMS
    b) voicemail and voice calling
    c) roaming and Bluetooth
14. What is a Smartphone? Describe three advanced features of a Smartphone.
15. List four factors you would consider when deciding between a prepaid phone and a contract-based connection to a mobile network.

Summary

In a small business, the office administrator(s) may be responsible for processing and distributing incoming post. Outgoing letters and parcels are packaged and franked, ready for dispatch to the Post Office or for collection by a courier. The administrator franking the post will use the *Postal Rate* guide to ensure that the correct postage value is applied to items.

Some postal items may need to be registered, or a certificate of postage may be required. Most postal items can be tracked online through An Post's tracking system on www.anpost.ie. Beside postal services, An Post provides a range of other services such as marketing (Postaim), and banking and retail services which include insurance, social welfare payments, prize bonds, lotto, photo express, mobile phone top-ups, etc.

Large businesses that rely heavily on the postal system, eg, a mail-order business, will have a separate mail department and will use elaborate equipment for dealing with both incoming and outgoing post.

In addition to handling the regular post, the office processes electronic data received in faxes, emails and messages received on mobile phones. The office administrator needs to be alert to phishing schemes and never open emails or email attachments from a suspicious source, as spyware could be downloaded.

Developments in mobile communication technology, such as Smartphones, have enabled employees to operate more effectively while off-site. Access to emails, planning and scheduling tools, software applications on the mobile phone enables employees to conduct their business as if they were at the office.

Assignments

1. You have just been appointed Post Clerk for a new mail-order magazine company and are responsible for developing a procedure for handling the post. Write a report outlining, step by step, the procedure you intend to implement. Recommend the equipment you will need to accomplish the handling of incoming and outgoing post.

2. Your business needs a franking machine to deal with the increased volume of outgoing post. Examine three models of franking machine available and associated prices. Which machine would you recommend?

3. Use the current An Post *Postal Rate* guide to cost the following:
   a) parcel to France weighing 1kg
   b) parcel to Zambia weighing 4kg
   c) parcel to Roscommon weighing 2kg 159g.
   For each of the above, recommend a postal service that will ensure that these parcels arrive by the fastest method.

4. Compare and contrast three types of fax machine available on the market today and write a report recommending one to the manager.

5. Mobile phone operators in Ireland offer different packages which generally include free-call and text value and different peak rates depending on the monthly subscription fee paid. Compare three operators on the assumption that your boss uses the phone approximately 500 minutes per month with approximately 60% of these calls being made before 6pm weekdays. He also sends approximately 80 texts per month. Recommend the best option, justifying your answer.

6. Most businesses communicate to a large extent by email. Prepare a presentation explaining how to send an email with an attachment, how to reply to an email and how best to organise incoming email.

7. Learn how to use the email system at your college. Briefly describe how you perform each of the following tasks:
   a) compose and send a message
   b) reply to a message you received
   c) delete a message you received
   d) forward a message you received to someone other than the person who sent the message

e)   send a carbon copy of the message
f)   send a message to a mailing list.

8. You have been given the task of purchasing four mobile phones for the sales team. Each salesperson will need a phone that can access the Internet, email and can enter data into the ordering system. Research three types of Smartphones and prepare a report for your office manager recommending the best phone in terms of price, memory, processing power and functionality.

Unit 5 — Storing and Retrieving Information

Introduction

As businesses are constantly generating a great deal of correspondence through various media (post, fax, telephone, email etc.), a business needs a system to store and protect all records, active and non-active, for current and future reference. Files are stored using a combination of manual and computerised filing systems. Unit 5 is divided into two chapters:

Chapter 15 — Manual Filing System

Reviews the essential elements to consider when designing a filing system, the equipment necessary for filing and rules and procedures for a manual filing system.
- ◆ Elements of a Manual Filing System
- ◆ Categorising and Sorting Information
- ◆ Rules for Alphabetical Filing
- ◆ Filing Equipment
- ◆ Filing Procedure
- ◆ Cross-referencing and Indexing

Chapter 16 — Electronic Document Management (EDM)

Reviews electronic filing systems where all files, including paper files, are stored either on microform or computer media.
- ◆ Microform Filing System
- ◆ Electronic Document Management System

Chapter 15 — Manual Filing System

Filing is a methodical way of storing information so that the file can be located when required. A manual filing system is where files are stored in paper format in appropriately sized filing cabinets or folders. The basic principle of any filing system is that the required documents should be accessible as quickly as possible. The filing system should also allow users to replace the documents in the correct location for future access easily. An efficient filing system will ensure files:

a) are not lost or misplaced

b) are up to date and complete

c) are accurate (avoid duplication)

d) can be retrieved quickly

e) are secure and kept confidential.

Elements of a Manual Filing System

When a manual filing system is being devised, the following factors are taken into account:

a) location of the files (centralised or decentralised)

b) categories of information to be set up (eg, customers, suppliers, products)

c) methods of sorting within chosen categories (eg, alphabetical, numerical)

d) equipment to be used

e) procedure for filing and retrieving documents

f) retention and back-up policy

g) procedure for confidential files

h) security and access rights.

Location of Filing System

The physical location where files are stored depends on the volume of records to be maintained, the number of users accessing the files, the frequency of access and the confidentiality of the information. When files are used by several users, it is not advisable to allow each user to maintain private copies of files, as amendments to one private copy may lead to different versions of the file being created, which would cause confusion. The management of the filing system is vital. The filing system operated may be:

a) **centralised filing:** where all the files for the whole business are stored in one central location;

b) **decentralised filing:** where all the files for a department are stored centrally within that department;

c) **individual filing:** where individuals store their own files;

d) **a combination of the above:** For example, centralised filing could be implemented in respect of files which are not in constant use and those which are not specific to any one department. Decentralised filing could be used for files that are specific to a department, while files that are specific to an individual's work may be stored by that individual.

The decision as to where files are located is a management decision. The advantages and disadvantages of centralised and decentralised filing systems are outlined below:

Centralised Filing	
Advantages	**Disadvantages**
1. The staff involved will be trained in the filing system. 2. Safety of records is guaranteed because strict procedures will be devised regarding the retrieval of files. 3. Related matters from all departments will be filed together or appropriately cross-referenced, thus ensuring files are accurate. 4. Less equipment is required as centralisation ensures better utilisation of equipment, thus saving space and costs.	1. There may be a delay in obtaining files due to the location of the Filing Department and/or the file requested may be with another user. 2. The classification system chosen may not suit the needs of all departments, yet they have to conform to the standardised system.

Decentralised Filing	
Advantages	**Disadvantages**
1. Information relating to a particular department is stored within that department thus reducing delays in obtaining files. 2. The department can implement a classification system suitable for its needs.	1. More filing equipment is required as full utilisation of equipment is not possible, thus increasing the space required and costs involved.

Categorising and Sorting Information

Information is held about several aspects of a business's life such as staff, stock, customers, suppliers, legal documents, financial documents, etc. When deciding how to organise information, broad **categories** of information must be determined. For example, customers could be one broad category, equipment could be another.

When the information has been categorised, the next decision is how to sort the information within each category. For example, using the customer category, are customers filed alphabetically by surname or is each customer allocated a number and filed in numerical order?

Files can be sorted in the following orders:

a) alphabetical

b) numerical

c) chronological

d) subject

e) geographical.

The method chosen depends on many factors, including:

◆ category of information (eg, customers, products)

◆ volume of information (implications for expansion)

◆ frequency of use (time factor in locating information, ie, direct versus indirect system)

◆ whether related information is to be filed together, ie, all details relating to a certain region (geographical) or all expenses for a business (subject) or all related books (Dewey system).

Alphabetical Order

The alphabetical order is a widely used method for filing correspondence. The files are sorted in alphabetical order of the category. For example, if the category is customers, the files will be sorted alphabetically by surname. Alphabetical filing systems are also known as **direct filing systems**, as there is no need to look up an index to find a file.

The filing cabinet will have labels on the drawer to indicate the contents, eg, Customers A–F, etc. Inside the drawers, **guide cards** are inserted to divide the alphabet, which makes locating a group of files easier. The customers' files whose surnames begin with the letter on the guide card are located behind the guide card.

Each file is labelled with the customer's name and filed alphabetically by surname. For example, in the following diagram, customers Leech, Doyle & Co. and Mr Harry Louth are filed alphabetically after the guide card 'L'.

There may also be a file for **miscellaneous information** which is used for storing infrequent correspondence. For example, there could be other customers whose surname begins with 'L' but with whom the volume of correspondence is minor and infrequent. A separate file will not be opened for each of these customers; they are placed in a file called 'Miscellaneous L'. If the correspondence increases for any of the miscellaneous 'L' customers, a new file is opened for that customer and the details transferred from the miscellaneous file to the new file.

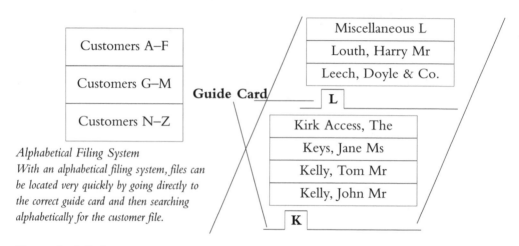

Alphabetical Filing System
With an alphabetical filing system, files can be located very quickly by going directly to the correct guide card and then searching alphabetically for the customer file.

Numerical Order

The files are allocated a number and a new file is simply given the next consecutive number. A **separate alphabetical index** will be kept to 'cross-reference' the file number.

Numerical filing is an **indirect system**, as you cannot go directly to the filing cabinet and locate the file. For example, if you do not know a customer's number, you would have to: (a) look up an alphabetical index of customers' surnames, (b) read the number associated with that customer and (c) go to the filing cabinet and search numerically to locate the file.

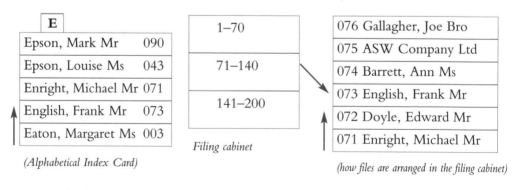

Numerical Filing System
To locate a file in a numerical system, an alphabetical index of customers' names is first referenced for the file number. The file is then located by going to the filing cabinet and searching numerically for the correct customer file.

Other Numerical Systems

There are other numerical systems used for more complex filing. These include:

Alphanumeric system

An alphanumeric system allocates a letter and a number to a document. For example, a document relating to a business called Office Supplies could be filed under OS/3. The letters 'OS' refer to the file called Office Supplies, and the number is the position of the document within the file. An alphabetical index of the files would be maintained.

Dewey decimal system

The Dewey decimal system is used for filing books in a library. It consists of three pairs of digits. The first pair refers to the **subject**, the middle pair refers to the **topic** within that subject, and the last pair refers to the particular **book**. For example, the following numbers could be allocated to subjects:

Business Studies 10

Accounting 20

Law 30

The **topics** within a subject are allocated the *second pair of digits* in sequence. For example, the subject Law 30 could be divided into:

Business Law 30.01

Company Law 30.02

Land Law 30.03

The books within each topic are allocated the *third pair of digits* in sequence. For example, using the topics Business Law and Company Law, you could have the following books:

30.01.01 *Business Law in Ireland*

30.01.02 *Business Law Simplified*

30.01.03 *A Guide to Business Law*

30.02.01 *Companies Act 1963*

Using this system, when a new book is added to the system it is placed with the correct subject and topic, simply by giving it the next number within the subject and topic classification. For example, if the library purchased another business law book, it would get the number 30.01.04 and would be placed on the shelf beside the other business law books.

An alphabetic index is also maintained listing the books in alphabetical order of subject.

The Dewey decimal system could also be used in business. For example, in a college the following system could be used:

FULL-TIME COURSES	20		
Secretarial		20.01	
Certificate in Secretarial Studies			20.01.01
Diploma in Secretarial Studies			20.01.02
Business Studies		20.02	
PART-TIME COURSES	30		
Computers		30.01	
Spreadsheets			30.01.01
Database			30.01.02
Word Processing			30.01.03
EXAMINATION RESULTS	40		
Certificate in Business Studies		40.01	
Sept 2007			40.01.01
Sept 2008			40.01.02
Sept 2009			40.01.03

Terminal digit system

This is a numerical system which consists of three pairs of digits read from right to left. The last pair refers to a drawer, the middle pair refers to the position of the file within that drawer, and the first pair refers to a document within that file. For example, the number 20.02.04 refers to drawer 4, file number 2, document number 20 within that file. Every document will be numbered and placed in the correct position within the filing cabinet. An alphabetical index has to be maintained.

Other Classifications

Chronological order

Chronological means sorting by date order. Documents are filed according to the date, with the most recent date first. Chronological filing is not generally used as a core system, but it is the typical method of filing within files, ie, the most recent correspondence received will be placed on the top of the appropriate file.

It is used as a core classification method only where the date would have meaning; for example, in a school when files are archived (put away permanently) it is appropriate to file by academic year. You could have an 'examination results' file for 2009/10 and the results within that file sorted in alphabetical order by classes or subjects.

Subject order

There are certain categories of information where subject filing is appropriate. For example, in relation to insurances for a business, it may be more appropriate to have a file labelled insurance rather than filing under the individual insurance brokers' names. In this way, all information concerning insurance will be in the same place rather than split between the individual brokers.

The subject insurance may be subdivided into categories like fire insurance, public liability insurance, etc., where the volume of data in relation to each type of insurance justifies it. The subjects are filed in alphabetical order. Where subjects are subdivided into topics, the topics are also filed alphabetically within the subject.

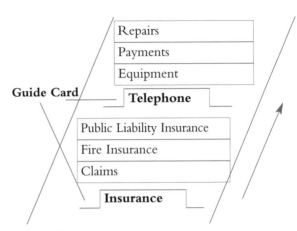

Subject Filing
The files are organised according to subject topic. Within each subject topic files are stored alphabetically.

Other examples where subject filing is appropriate are expenses, training, products, repairs, etc. Subject filing is used by students; their lever arch file is divided into sections such as office procedures, bookkeeping and communications.

Geographical order

Geographical classification is suitable for businesses with a high level of sales, mail order, imports, exports, etc. The organisation divides its business into regions. For example, a business with many sales outlets in Ireland would divide the filing system up into counties; the sales force in each county would then be filed in either

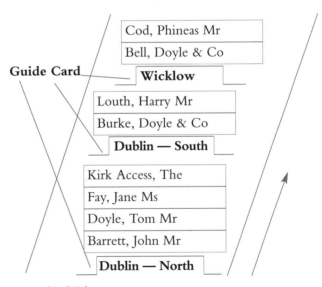

Geographical Filing
To locate a file in a geographical system, an alphabetical index of customers is first referenced for the geographical region. The file is then located by going alphabetically to the correct region and searching alphabetically for the correct customer file.

alphabetical or numerical order. An index is required to link a person to a county. The index stores the names in alphabetical order and states under which county that person is filed. It is an indirect system like the numerical system.

Colour-coding system

Where the filing system is used to store different categories of information a colour-coding system may be used. The files are subdivided into their categories, and different-coloured 'name' tabs or folders are used for each category. This prevents someone placing a document in the correct name file but in the wrong file.

For example, if the filing system contains customers, suppliers and employees, blue-coloured name tabs may be used for customers, red for suppliers and yellow for employees. The files will be arranged in alphabetical order of category, ie, customers followed by employees then suppliers. The files within each category will also be arranged in alphabetical order.

Colour-coding systems could also be used in a subject or geographical system; for example, in a geographical system counties could be colour-divided by regional area.

Comparison of Various Sorting Methods		
Sort Method	**Advantages**	**Disadvantages**
Alphabetical	• Easy to understand and operate • A direct system – no need to consult an index • Miscellaneous files can be set up	• The system is not easily expanded; considerable reshuffling of files may be necessary • Where surnames are the same, there is a danger of misfiling a document
Numerical	• System is easily expanded • No need to pre-allocate space in the filing cabinet • The file number can be used as a reference • The index provides useful information in its own right	• An indirect system – an index must be consulted • Files could be mis-filed if the number was read incorrectly

Comparison of Various Sorting Methods *(continued)*		
Sort Method	**Advantages**	**Disadvantages**
Other numerical systems	• Each document can be given a unique number • Efficient in large filing systems • Unlimited expansion • High level of accuracy is possible • Dewey system is particularly suitable for libraries	• Intricate to learn and operate • Requires indexing
Chronological	• The most recent correspondence is first in the file • Simple to accomplish	• For some applications, it can be difficult over time to locate specific documents, ie, you may forget the time period when a particular transaction occurred • Not a common core filing system
Subject	• Similar to the alphabetical system – direct • Related information is filed together	• The system is not easily expanded • Subject areas may overlap, therefore cross-referencing may be necessary
Geographical	• A convenient way of subdividing customers or sales representatives • Colour coding can be used to speed up location of files	• An indirect system – an index must be consulted • A good knowledge of the geographical region is required

Rules for Alphabetical Filing

1. The surname is placed before the first name and if the surnames are the same, the first name decides the position. Titles are placed after the first name, eg:

Before Filing	**After Filing**
Prof John Keyes	Brady, Alice (Ms)
Ms Jane Keyes	Keyes, Jane (Ms)
Ms Alice Brady	Keyes, John (Prof)
Mrs Lucy Power	Power, Lucy (Mrs)

2. If no first name is given, the surname comes first. Nothing comes before something, eg:

Before Filing	After Filing
Mr John Smith	Smith
Fr J Smith	Smith, J (Fr)
Smith	Smith, John (Mr)

3. If the business name has a personal name, the surname is written first, followed by the first name and the remainder of the name, eg:

Before Filing	After Filing
Sharon Smith & Co	Black, Peter & Co
Peter Black & Co	Smith, Sharon & Co

4. If a business has several names, the first name is taken as the surname and filed accordingly, eg:

Before Filing	After Filing
Messrs Hegarty, Gallagher & Coghlan	Hegarty, Gallagher & Coghlan, Messrs

5. When 'The' is the first word of the name, it is placed at the end of the name, eg:

Before Filing	After Filing
The Open University	Open University, The

6. Prefixes such as De, La, etc. are included as part of the name and filed accordingly. However, names beginning with Mac, Mc, M' are treated as if they were all spelt Mac and names beginning St and Saint are treated as if they were all fully spelt. However, the original spelling is kept, eg:

Before Filing	After Filing
Gerry Devries	De Vries, Ciaran
Jane De Vries	Devries, Gerry
Ciaran De Vries	De Vries, Jane
La Stampa Restaurant	La Stampa Restaurant
Patricia M'Sparran	McCarthy, John
Gerald MacDonagh & Sons	MacDonagh, Gerald & Sons
Ciara MacSweeney	M'Sparran, Patricia
John McCarthy	MacSweeney, Ciara
Saint Michael's Church	St Brendan's College
St Brendan's College	Saint Michael's Church

7. The apostrophe is ignored. The word is treated as one, but the original spelling is kept, eg:

Before Filing	After Filing
Brian D'arcy	Darcy, Brendan
Brendan Darcy	D'arcy, Brian
ORM Sales Agents	O'Riordan's Pharmacy
O'Riordan's Pharmacy	Orlagh Park House
Orlagh Park House	ORM Sales Agents

8. Treat numbers as if they were spelt out in words but keep the original name, eg:

Before Filing	After Filing
400 Supercal Co.	500 ABC Ltd (filed under 'F')
500 ABC Ltd	400 Supercal Co. (filed under 'F')
60 Calls Ltd	700 Cab Call Ltd (filed under 'S')
700 Cab Call Ltd	60 Calls Ltd (filed under 'S')

9. Departments are filed by keyword of department, eg:

Before Filing	After Filing
Department of Foreign Affairs	Business Studies, Department
Department of Social Welfare	Foreign Affairs, Department of
Business Studies Department	Social Welfare, Department of

10. Treat known abbreviated names as being spelt out in full and file them under their full name (see cross-reference), eg:

Before Filing	After Filing
VHI	Educational Building Society
ESB	Electricity Supply Board
EBS	Voluntary Health Insurance

11. Leave made-up abbreviations in their abbreviated form, but file the same abbreviations in a group according to the word that follows the abbreviated name.

Before Filing	After Filing
ABC Computer Training Ltd	ABBA Taxis
ABC Services	Abbey Leisure
Abbey Leisure	ABC Computer Training Ltd
ABBA Taxis	ABC Services
Abco Interior Design	Abco Interior Design

Filing Equipment

Filing equipment used to store files manually ranges from folders to expansive filing cabinets.

Box file

- ◆ **Box file:** A box has a strong spring clip inside the box to hold the items inserted. It is used to hold miscellaneous items such as leaflets, catalogues or information which is not referenced frequently. The information is generally filed in chronological order, ie, date order, where the most recent item is placed on top of the pile.

- ◆ **Ring binder:** A ring binder is a folder with two or more rings used for filing frequently referenced information, such as price lists, lists of spare parts, etc. The document is punched with holes (generally two) so that it can be placed into the rings of the binder. Dividers which are pre-punched with holes are used to separate the information in the folder. The ring binder is opened by pulling the rings apart.

Lever arch binder

- ◆ **Lever arch binder:** This is similar to a ring binder except that there is a lever for opening and closing the rings. A lever arch binder has greater capacity than a ring binder.

- ◆ **Concertina folder:** A folder that consists of a succession of pockets which open out; each pocket can be labelled by subject order or date order depending on its use. It is generally used for storing items which have yet to be processed.

Concertina folder

- ◆ **Filing cabinets:** A wide range of different filing cabinets is available on the market. The models differ in size and in the way files are arranged in the filing cabinet.

Storage Arrangement of Files

How files are arranged and the type of cabinets used depends on the amount of space available, access requirements, cost of the equipment and its suitability for the intended purpose. There are four main storage arrangements:

1. **Vertical storage:** Files are stored upright one behind the other. A vertical filing cabinet is fitted with frames which are positioned on either side of the drawer. Suspension folders, which are fitted with hooks, rest on the frames one behind the other. Name tags are placed on the top of each suspension folder to indicate the name or number of the file. To subdivide the information which is held in a suspension folder, manila folders are used. The drawers of the filing cabinet are also labelled for ease of reference.

Vertical filing system

2. **Lateral storage:** Files are stored **side by side** using suspension folders like books on a shelf. Name tabs are placed on the **side** of each suspension folder which indicate the name or number of the file. Lateral storage is a suitable arrangement for a large filing system. The filing equipment selected

Lateral filing system   *suspension folder*

may be closed (ie, with doors or sliding shutters), open, or a computerised rotating filing cabinet in which the shelves rotate on a tracking system and a light indicates the location of the required file.

3. **Horizontal storage:** Files are stored flat, one on top of the other. This method is suitable for small-volume temporary storage (ie, in/out trays) or to store large documents unfolded, such as plans and drawings.

4. **Combination of the above:**
Filing cabinets can be purchased which accommodate a variety of storage arrangements, ie, vertical, lateral and horizontal. These filing cabinets are suitable for a small office which requires a versatile arrangement, ie, to store books, lever arch files, box files, large documents unfolded and suspension folders, etc.

Combination filing system

Storage Arrangement — Advantages/Disadvantages		
	Advantages	**Disadvantages**
Vertical	1. All files in a drawer can be seen at a glance. 2. Files are stored at a height which is accessible. 3. Files are protected from dust by being enclosed in the cabinet. 4. Files can be made secure by locking the cabinet.	1. Utilises a large amount of floor space as extra space is required for opening the drawers. 2. Wasted storage space. There is a limit to the height of the cabinets for safety reasons. 3. Two drawers cannot be opened at the same time for safety reasons, (ie, weight would be unevenly distributed), therefore staff have to wait their turn to use the system.
Lateral	1. Less storage space is required for filing cabinets which are open or which have sliding shutters, as no space is required to open drawers. 2. Lateral filing cabinets can be built higher than vertical cabinets. 3. More files can be seen at the same time. 4. More than one person can access the files at the same time.	1. Difficult to read file titles, especially files placed at a height. 2. Difficult to access files stored higher up and lower down. 3. With an open shelf arrangement less protection is given to the files.
Horizontal	1. Simple equipment. 2. Cheap. 3. Can hold large documents flat. 4. Suitable for temporary storage or large documents.	1. Difficult and time-consuming to locate specific files. 2. Can become unmanageable. 3. Files are subject to wear and tear. 4. Can be difficult to replace file in correct position.

Filing Procedure

To ensure an efficient filing system the following should be in place:
1. a clear cross-reference system
2. procedures for borrowing files
3. a 'follow-up' system
4. a policy relating to the retention of files
5. a policy relating to confidential files and security measures.

Filing should be carried out on a regular basis to avoid pile-ups and disorganisation. Whether you have dealt with the correspondence received, or intend to deal with it at a later date, it should be filed. A typical procedure for filing would be:
1. Documents are sorted into related batches
2. Sort the documents in each batch into chronological order.
3. Insert documents in the appropriate file on top of the previous correspondence. In this way, the most recent documents are placed first.
4. If no file exists for the document, a new file is opened. In a centralised filing system this will involve getting authorisation to open a new file to avoid duplication of files and misfiling.
5. Opening a file means getting the appropriate folder and writing up the name tag with the correct classification, in the correct format. For example, in an alphabetical system write 'Hegarty, Siobhan', not 'Siobhan Hegarty'. The folder is inserted in the correct position of the filing cabinet. In an indirect system, eg, numerical, the index will also be updated with the appropriate details of the new file.
6. Where a file cannot hold any more documents a continuation file is necessary. The original file is closed and labelled with a date. The continuation file is placed behind it.

Cross-referencing and Indexing

Cross-referencing

A cross-reference is used to relate one file to another. Examples of uses are:
1. **to locate information in an indirect filing system.** For example, in a numerical system when a file is requested and the file number is unknown, the alphabetical index is referenced to get the file number.
2. **where a file could be filed under two names.** For example, confusion sometimes arises as to where to locate a file. A file on VHI could be filed under VHI or Voluntary Health Insurance. There are rules for filing, but sometimes an organisation adapts the rules to suit its particular needs. To

avoid confusion it may be best to set up two files for that particular organisation; one file named VHI and the other named Voluntary Health Insurance. All the information would be stored in one file, say the Voluntary Health Insurance file, and the other file, the VHI file, would be empty with a reference saying 'see Voluntary Health Insurance'.

A cross-reference card is set up and placed in the alternative location (in this case in the VHI file) so that staff are directed to the correct location.

Cross-reference card inserted in file

3. **to refer a person to a related file.** When a business changes its name, a cross-reference card is placed in the old file directing users to the new file. The old file is closed and the date noted. A card is also placed in the new file so that users can reference past data.

4. **where files are related or linked.** For example, where do we file documents relating to the maintenance of an item of equipment? Is it in the servicer's file or in the equipment file? The answer to these questions may seem simple enough, but what if the servicer also services other equipment and/or the equipment is serviced by more than one person? Here we need separate files for each item of equipment and for each of the servicers. The servicer's file would contain correspondence and the equipment files would contain a service history. A cross-reference card is placed with each servicer's file, linking that person to all the equipment s/he services. A cross-reference card is also placed with each equipment file linking those files to the servicer's file.

This problem can also be overcome by putting a copy of the linked information in the appropriate files. For example, if Mr X services the photocopier, then the details can be placed in both the Mr X file and the photocopier file. Where the information is duplicated, a cross-reference is not necessary. However, this is not recommended, as the files become bulky. There is also the danger of the information being omitted from one file, leading to inaccurate records.

Indexing

An index is used with the numerical and geographical filing systems to locate files. The index is arranged in alphabetical order of file names and is referenced to find the particular file number.

An index will also contain some other information, which may be enough to eliminate the need for further reference. For instance, if a request is for a customer's phone number, the index may provide this information.

An index can be used to highlight or signal particular items of information by using a colour-coded index method. For example, a red index card may signal an overdue account.

An index should be kept up to date; for example, when a file is added to a numeric filing system an entry should be made in the index.

Indexing equipment

Various types of indexing equipment are used to record information like the page index, card index and strip index.

Vertical Card Index: Cards, A6 or A7 in size are stored upright in a filing box. Alphabetical guide cards are used to separate. Coloured cards are available for classification purposes. With this system it is easy to add or remove cards as required, as the alphabetical order will not be affected.

Vertical card index

Visible Card Index: Cards overlap each other but the first line of each card is visible. The essential details are recorded on the first line to enable the card to be located.

Rotary Card Index: Cards overlap each other but are separated by alphabetical guide cards. The wheel is turned to get the required card section.

Rotary card index

Strip Index: Consists of strips of cards which are inserted into plastic frames of a folder. The pages of the folder are arranged alphabetically. These systems are available in folder format or free-standing desk units. They are used for simple data which can be held on one or two lines, eg, telephone numbers, product prices, etc.

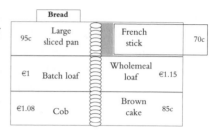

Strip index

The choice of indexing system will depend on:

◆ how much information needs to be recorded (strip versus card)
◆ space required for the system (visible card index versus vertical card index)
◆ maintenance of the system, ie, easy removal or addition of information
◆ how frequently the information will be accessed (system needs to be close at hand).

Procedure for Borrowing Files

When a file is borrowed, a record must be kept of the date the file was borrowed, the file name/number, and the borrower's name and department. These details are recorded chronologically in a log book or on a **file outcard** which is inserted in place of the file borrowed and remains in the filing system until the file is returned. When the file is returned, the date of return is recorded on the outcard and the outcard is removed from the system. The card can be used again when another file is borrowed.

Recording files borrowed in a logbook is suitable only for small systems, as the whole book may have to be searched to discover where the file is.

File Outcard				
Date Taken	**File Identification**	**By**	**Dept**	**Date Returned**
7/6/10	File B009	JH	Marketing	

A file outcard

In a large filing system a combination of a logbook and an outcard may be used. For example, to keep track of which files are out, the logbook will be checked; or when a file is requested, you know immediately who has the file by the details recorded on the outcard.

If more than one person needs to use a file, it may be passed from person to person without being returned to the filing department. However, in order to keep track of where the file is, a **file-passing slip** is filled in, detailing the file name, who passed the file, the new holder of the file and the date. The file-passing slip is returned to the filing administrator, so that the outcard can be updated.

Follow-up System

A follow-up system (also known as a 'bring-forward' system or 'tickler' system) is a filing procedure implemented to enable documents to be filed until required. A reminder of the activity that needs to be attended to on a specific date is recorded so that the appropriate file can then be retrieved.

A follow-up system can be implemented in many ways:

◆ A note is put into a diary indicating when the file is required again.

◆ A 'date file' is set up. This may take the form of a concertina folder with a pocket of the folder used for each day of the month and one pocket for the coming months. A note is placed in the appropriate pocket detailing the name of the file to be retrieved. Each day the appropriate pocket is checked – the notes act as a reminder to retrieve the appropriate file(s).

◆ When documents are sent to a centralised filing department, a pre-printed 'follow-up slip' is completed and attached to the document. The filing administrator detaches the follow-up slip and places it in the appropriate pocket of the follow-up system and the documents are filed away. The slips for each day are checked by the filing administrator. The files are then sent to the appropriate person with the follow-up slip attached to the file. Details of the file sent are recorded on an outcard and the logbook.

◆ If files are stored on a computer, the user can signal when the file is required again by placing an entry in a diary or more appropriately in an electronic diary.

Retention of Files

Documentation relating to the business may be used on a regular basis for a particular period of time and then may be referenced only on an occasional basis.

Retention periods vary for documentation. For example, some documents must be kept for ever, (ie, documents relating to the set-up of the business, financial accounts); other documents need to be kept legally for a stated period, usually six years (ie, tax records, business transaction records); while other documents like correspondence, minutes of meetings, memoranda, etc. are kept at the organisation's discretion.

The current filing system should not be clogged with information which is not accessed on a regular basis. The business should have a file-retention policy in relation to the classification of files. Files can be classified as:

◆ **Active files** are files in current use and generally span one year. These files are stored in the current filing system.

◆ **Semi-active files** are files not referenced on a daily basis but which may be referenced from time to time. These files are stored separately from the current filing system, ie, in a separate filing cabinet.

◆ **Non-active files** are files that are not referenced but must be kept until their retention period expires. These files are taken from the semi-active files and archived, ie, either stored elsewhere or converted into digital format and stored in an electronic document management system (EDM); the paper-based information can then be destroyed.

◆ **Dead files** are non-active files where the retention period has expired. Dead files are destroyed. Confidential information should be put through a shredder which reduces the information to strips of paper. The output from the shredder can be used as packing material or recycled.

If you are responsible for your own filing system, the decision to discard documents should be taken with great care.

Confidential Files

Strict procedures should be laid down for confidential files. These include a list of authorised people who can access the files, and which files cannot be copied or removed from the filing department. Files should be kept under lock and key. Valuable files should be stored in a fireproof cabinet, safe or at another location.

Short Questions

1. List four essential elements of an efficient filing system.
2. List three factors to consider when deciding whether to work with a centralised or decentralised filing system for the business.
3. Give two advantages and two disadvantages of centralised and decentralised filing.
4. Distinguish between a direct and an indirect filing system.
5. Place the following in alphabetical order:
   The Gainsborough Hotel
   Green & Patterson
   Department of Education and Science
   St George's House
   Saint Vincent's
   Sally Sainte
   Patterson and Brown

Mr Tony MacDonnell

Ms Jane M'Donnell

5-Star Services.

6. Distinguish between the following numerical filing methods:
   a) alphanumeric
   b) Dewey
   c) terminal digit.

7. List four factors you would consider when deciding on a method of sorting files.

8. List one advantage, one disadvantage and a typical use of the following sorting methods:
   a) alphabetical
   b) numerical
   c) geographical.

9. Name three items of equipment necessary for a manual filing system.

10. What type of correspondence could be filed in the following:
    a) box file
    b) lever arch file
    c) concertina folder?

11. List and briefly describe the three main storage arrangements of files.

12. Give two advantages and two disadvantages of the three main storage arrangements of files.

13. List and briefly describe five main sorting methods that can be used in a filing system.

14. Give four examples of where it is appropriate to use a cross-reference.

15. When would a colour-coding system be used?

16. Outline the difference between the following indexing systems and give one appropriate use for each:
    a) vertical card index
    b) visual card index
    c) strip index.

17. Distinguish between a file outcard and a file-passing slip.

18. How are files generally classified under a retention policy?

19. What is a shredder used for?

20. Briefly describe what a follow-up system is and how it is used.

21. List four points for managing confidential files.

Chapter 16 — Electronic Document Management (EDM)

While the information age promised a paperless office, the reality is that it created a significant increase in the amount of paper that needs to be sorted, filed and stored. One explanation for this is: the electronic *production* of documents was not matched with an equivalent system for the electronic *capture, storage* and *distribution* of these documents. For example, a business letter, while it is created electronically, is generally printed and distributed manually, ie, by post. Invariably, this electronically produced document must then be filed.

Paper-based filing has many problems, such as the cost of paper, filing equipment and space. Other problems include filing errors, which can result in the business spending considerable time trying to locate misfiled documents.

Many businesses operate a complete electronic document management system (EDM) as a means to enhance their paper storage and retrieval system. With the advances in hardware and software EDM is now an affordable technology, which can be done in-house or outsourced to an EDM agency.

An EDM System is in effect a large-scale, computerised filing system where all files, including paper files and microform, are stored digitally, on computer media and distributed electronically via email, an intranet, an extranet or the Internet.

Before discussing an EDM system, it is necessary to review traditional document-management systems, ie, microform and how microform is integrated into an EDM system.

Microform Filing System

Microform Filing System

A microform filing system stores files in film format (like negatives of a photograph) and was/is used mainly to store archived paper files. It reduces the space required to store files, as many pages can be stored on a single film.

The word 'microform' is the generic term used to describe the format of the film used, ie, a film strip or a microfiche (a 4″ × 6″ sheet of film about the size of a postcard).

In the past, microform was the storage media used by businesses with significant volumes of printed material, eg, the newspaper industry, libraries and the banks. With the development of advanced digital technologies for scanning, storing and distributing information electronically, businesses that have extensively used microform are continuing with a hybrid approach, ie, a combination of microform and digitisation.

With the hybrid approach, the archives are first transferred to microform and then the microform is scanned into digital format using a special scanner. Using this approach the microform is used for long-term storage, and the digital files allow direct access to the information. The rationale behind this hybrid approach is from a risk-management perspective; microform was developed in the 1940s and is proven and well supported, whereas with digital technology the storage media devices continually change and the fear is of being unable to access digital files in years to come, unless the files are continually migrated to current storage media.

Producing Microform

Microform can be produced in two ways:

1. *For paper documents*: A microform camera is used to photograph original documents. The camera is built into a unit that holds the documents, which are fed automatically to the camera like a photocopier.
2. *For computer documents*: A special printer, known as a **microform printer**, and software are used to print computer files directly onto microform, thereby avoiding the steps of printing and photographing. This process is known as COM (Computer Output Microform).

Reading Microform

Microform cannot be read by the naked eye. A microform reader/printer is used to display the image in an enlarged format on the screen which can then be printed if required. A search facility allows the required information to be brought into view.

A microform duplicator is used to make working copies of the microform (film or fiche). Microform is duplicated for distribution purposes.

Microform reader/printer

Storing Microform

Microform should be stored in special sealed containers in a controlled environment, preferably in an air-conditioned room. Extremes of temperature or humidity should be avoided, as well as direct exposure to sunlight. Microform storage equipment is similar to general indexing equipment, except that special plastic is used to protect the sensitive microform. Storage equipment includes:

Microfiche index box: Similar to a card index box but consists of plastic jackets to hold the microfiche. Each jacket has a tab for indexing.

Microfiche visible panel index: A ring binder consisting of panels in which to insert the microfiche. The top line of each microfiche is displayed, showing the details of the microfiche.

Microfilm jacket-strip index: A ring binder consisting of transparent jackets in which to insert a strip of film.

Various microfiche storage systems

Electronic Document Management System

EDM combines different technologies to scan, index and store paper-based documents in electronic format. Once information is in electronic format it can be retrieved, searched, distributed electronically and shared with others across a network.

EDM systems are available at different levels of complexity to cater for the level of computerised filing required in a business. This includes converting paper-based information (ie, documents, books, catalogues, manuals, photographs, etc.) and microform to digital format, and converting analogue VHS tapes to DVD, etc.

Before discussing the implementation and benefits of an EDM system, an explanation of how files should be organised on a computer to accomplish an efficient digital filing system is required.

Organising and Storing Files on a Computer

A folder structure is created on storage media, eg, the network drive, to provide a location for storing files. Folders may be divided into sub-folders.

For example, consider a filing system for an auctioneering business. A subset of the work involved in an auctioneering business is the sale of houses. This part of the filing system could be organised as follows:

In the example shown in Figure 16–1, the main folder, **sales,** is subdivided into sub-folders for the different areas where the auctioneer has houses for sale. These are: Dublin City, North Dublin, South Dublin and Other Areas (the software arranges the folders in alphabetical order).

An auctioneering business may also categorise the houses within each area according to a price range. In Figure 16–1 each area folder has further sub-folders to categorise the houses in price ranges of 'Under €300k', '€300k to €500k' and 'Over €500k'. Again, the software arranges the folders in alphabetical order.

Within each price range, the houses may be further categorised according to their condition. For example, excellent, good and repairs.

Using this filing system, the required file(s) can be located easily. For example, if information was requested on houses for sale in the Dublin City area which were under €300k and in excellent condition, the user of the system would go to the folder called 'Dublin City', select the sub-folder 'Under €300k' and in this folder select the sub-folder called 'Excellent'.

The 'Excellent' folder contains the relevant files for the information requested, ie, houses in Dublin City under €300k and in excellent condition.

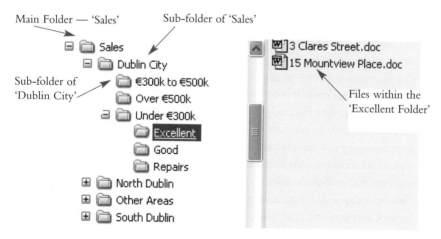

Figure 16–1 Layout of folders on a disk
The plus sign (+) beside each folder means that the folder is not opened. They are called expandable folders. If it were opened, a breakdown similar to the 'Dublin City' folder would be displayed.

Implementing an EDM System

To allow sharing of files among many users, a network of computers must be set up. Files which are shared by individuals are stored centrally on the 'file server' and can be accessed by authorised users from their own computer.

To input paper-based information into the system, the information is generally batched, scanned and indexed.

1. *Batch Preparation:* Typically pages are sorted into batches of similar documents (ie, orders, invoices, etc.) and then scanned.

2. *Scanning:* A scanner takes an image of the page (as a photocopier does) and inputs it into the computer. Document scanning falls into two categories:

    a) **Digital permanent image** such as signed contracts, handwritten text, legal documents, etc. Such documents must be saved with the entire look and content of the original.

    b) **Digital editable image** such as typed documents where edits to the content of the documents may be required. This is achieved by opening the scanned document with Optical Character Recognition (OCR) software, which converts the scanned image into text that can be edited.

3. *Indexing:* Indexing is the most critical and time-consuming step in the capture process. To assist with the retrieval of files, keywords are defined for each document. The keywords would include common things such as the customer's name and file reference, as well as words that would be appropriate for searches in the future.

4. *Storing:* Where the files are stored depends on whether the files are active or should be archived. If the files are active, they are generally stored on the file server to be available to network users. If the files should be archived, a decision has to be made as to whether these files should be stored on-line or off-line.

    If the decision is taken to store archived files on-line they are generally stored on optical media, ie, CD/DVD. A jukebox (capable of holding many CDs/DVDs) can be added to the network so that the network users can access the files on-line.

    If the decision is taken to store archived files off-line, then depending on budget and personal preferences, the files can be archived onto magnetic tape, microform and optical recordable media. However, the CD/DVDs would not be available on the network, ie, they would be stored off-line in an appropriate holder.

Benefits of an EDM System

1. Saves storage space and eliminates the need for filing cabinets.
2. The cost associated with storing paper documents, printing and publishing internal information (ie, safety manuals, company policies manuals) is eliminated, as this information can now be published on the intranet for employees to view.
3. Files exist on the file server and can be viewed simultaneously by authorised users across a network.
4. No duplicate files exist, which means that all files are current. For example, there is no danger of recording a person's change of address in one department and not in another department.
5. Electronic files can be linked with existing applications. For example, in a customer database, a 'field' could contain a link to all correspondence relating to a particular customer.
6. No time is wasted searching or waiting for files. The search facility allows network users to find specific information in multiple electronic documents.
7. Software tools can be used to emphasise or clarify information in a document: for example, information can be highlighted, notes can be added using electronic 'sticky notes' and vocal comments can be recorded with a document.
8. It is easy to transfer non-active files to off-line storage.
9. Strict control procedures can be implemented using software. Certain users can be locked out of the system by means of passwords and access rights can be set up to control what individuals can do within the system, ie, which files they can view, update, etc. Documents can be password-protected to prevent an unauthorised person viewing the document.
10. Retention and deletion procedures can be enforced, by the system administrator in charge of the file server.

Short Questions

1. What is an EDM system?
2. Describe a microform filing system and give one example of its use.
3. Distinguish between a microfiche and microfilm.
4. Briefly describe two ways of outputting documents to microform.
5. How is microform read and stored?
6. List the steps to prepare paper documents for entry into an EDM system.
7. Briefly describe two requirements of document scanning in an EDM system.

8. Compare and contrast the choices available for storing files on-line and off-line in an EDM system.
9. State five benefits of an EDM system.

Summary

Every business must maintain an efficient filing system, be it a manual system or an EDM system or a combination of both. In a manual system files are categorised according to the information to be filed, eg, customers, suppliers etc., and are then sorted either alphabetically, numerically or chronologically. Manual systems have many disadvantages such as the cost of storage space, misfiled documents and time involved in locating documents.

Electronic document management (EDM) has become essential in businesses owing to the volumes of information generated today. EDM combines different technologies to scan, index and store paper-based documents and microform in electronic format and facilitates the distribution of documents across a network. With advances in digital technology, microform has been repositioned to a backstage role, owing to the capacity and active retrieval capabilities of digital media.

Regardless of the filing system, all files must be carefully maintained and procedures must be in place to prevent unauthorised access to files.

In a manual system, this can be achieved by locking filing cabinets and implementing a centralised filing system for which a filing administrator will operate a strict retrieval policy for employees who wish to access the files. In an EDM system, authorised access is ensured by using passwords and firewall software. Part of the management of any filing system is ensuring that files are purged regularly and 'dead' and 'inactive' files are removed from the current files and archived. This can be done by transferring files to microform format, optical storage media, or to an off-site location.

Assignments

1. You are employed as an administrator and your office manager wants to improve the operation of its centralised manual filing system and requests that you:
   a) write a report detailing a procedure to follow in relation to:
      (i)   borrowing files
      (ii) retention of files
      (iii) confidential files and security arrangements;

b) write guidelines to be followed by all staff in relation to the filing of documents alphabetically. Examples should be given where necessary.

2. Place the examples below in alphabetical order – then combine the three examples and place them in alphabetical order.

Example 1	Example 2	Example 3
Fred B. Walsh	Dr Tom Healy	Dr J.P. O'Sullivan
Walsh Family Foods Ltd	John Healy and Associates Ltd	Department of Education
The Highway Lounge	Ms Marie Collins	The Business Studies Department
Gerry McGovern	Collins Conor	O'Meara (Auctioneer) Ltd
Hugh McGovern	Arthur Gibney and Partners	Pro William O'Meara
Tom MacGovern	The Kerry Company Ltd	Finlay's Lounge
Oasis Design Ltd	William Farrell Ltd	Fr F. Carthy
O B Marine Ltd	Saint Clare's Nursery	The Two Sisters
Frank O'Brien	St Theresa's Swimming Pool	2's Company (Artists)
Star Society	Colm De Buitlear	David Twohig
The Three Bears Ltd	John Deasy	1-Hour Repairs
1st Cleaning Services	One Hour Photo	One-to-One Swap Shop

3. You have been asked to devise a computerised folder structure for storing exam results at a college based on the information given below, and to indicate where the files should be stored.

The main folders should be organised by *course category* (ie, Business and Computing) with sub-folders for the *course names*. Within each *course name* folder there will be further sub-folders for *exam years*. The *exam results* files are stored in the appropriate *exam year* folder. You should use appropriate abbreviated course names and file names.

Course Names: Business Studies, Multimedia Computing, Computer Programming, Marketing, Secretarial, Business Administration, Computer Applications, Banking and Auctioneering

Exam Years: 2006–7, 2007–8, 2008–9

File Names: Class A (Business Studies for year 2007–8)
Class B (Business Studies for year 2007–8)
Class A (Multimedia Computing for years 2006–7 and 2007–8)

4. You are employed as the office manager of an existing business. However, your manager is very reluctant to change from the manual filing system. While there is a computer network in place, staff print off emails, and file them.

   You have spoken to your manager on numerous occasions about the benefits of transferring over to an EDM system, but he is not convinced. Use the Golden Pages or other relevant sources to search for businesses that sell EDM systems. Write a report detailing the benefits of an EDM system and construct a table comparing the systems available from three different sources.

Leabharlanna Fhine Gall

Appendix — Blank Documents for Business Transactions

Purchase Requisition Form

Purchase Requisition		Ref. No: _____

Department: _____

Supplier's Name: _____

Supplier's Address: _____

Qty	Details	Cat. No.	Unit Price €
Signature		Date	

Order Form

Order No: _____

VAT No: 284 3455 89

Tel. No: _____

Fax No: _____

Quotation No: _____

Date: _____

Please supply the following:

Qty	Description	Cat. No.	Unit Price €	Total Price €

Terms of Sale

Delivery Note

Delivery Note No: _____

VAT No: 284 3455 89

Tel. No: _____

Fax No: _____

Quotation No: _____

Date: _____

Qty	Description	Cat. No.

Delivery:

Received by:

Goods Received Note

Goods Received Note No:

Supplier: _____

Date Received: _____

Delivery/Advice Note No: _____

Order No.	Description	Qty Received

Received by:	Date:	Entered in stock by:	Date:

Inspected by:	Date:

Shortages:

Damage Recorded:

Invoice

Invoice No: _____			VAT No:_____	

VAT No:_____

Date: _____

Tel. No: _____

Fax No: _____

Delivery Note No: _____

Order No: _____

Qty	Description	Cat. No.	Unit Price €	Total Cost €

Credit Note

Credit Note No: _____

VAT No: _____

Date: _____

Tel. No: _____

Fax No: _____

Delivery Note No: _____

Order No: _____

Qty	Description	Cat. No.	Unit Price €	Total Cost €

Debit Note

Debit Note No: _____

VAT No:_____

Date: _____

Tel. No: _____

Fax No: _____

Delivery Note No: _____

Order No: _____

Ref.	Description	Cat. No.	Unit Price €	Total Cost €

Statement

Statement					
VAT No: _____					
Date: _____					
Tel. No: _____					
Fax No: _____					

Date	Ref. No.	Details	Debits €	Credits €	Balance €